DANTE D. KING

THE
PSYCHOPATHY
OF WHITENESS

THE EPIGENETICS OF ANTI-BLACKNESS, MALIGNANT NARCISSISM, AND COLLECTIVE DIABOLICAL ANTISOCIAL PERSONALITY DISORDER

A Diagnostic and Statistical Manual on Whiteness, Race, and Racism in America – and Beyond

FOREWORD WRITTEN BY DR. ROBIN DIANGELO
AUTHOR OF 'WHITE FRAGILITY' AND 'NICE RACISM'

Copyright © 2025 Dante D. King

Book Package and Publication:

Dante D. King

Editor: Dante D. King

Author's Photo: Oscar Merrida: www.oscarmerrida.com

All rights reserved. No part of this book may be used or reproduced by any means, graphic, electronic, or mechanical, including photocopying, recording, taping, or by any information storage retrieval system without the written permission of the publisher except in the case of brief quotations embodied in critical articles and reviews.

Books may be ordered through booksellers or by contacting:

Dante D. King

Website: www.danteking.com

Because of the dynamic nature of the Internet, any web addresses or links contained in this book may have changed since publication and may no longer be valid. The views expressed in this work are solely those of the author and do not necessarily reflect the views of the publisher, and the publisher hereby disclaims any responsibility for them.

Any people depicted in stock imagery provided by Thinkstock are models, and such images are being used for illustrative purposes only.

Certain stock imagery © Thinkstock.

13-digit ISBN: 979-8-9906882-9-2 (paperback)
13-digit ISBN: 979-8-9906882-2-3 (hardcover)

Library of Congress Control Number:

Printed in the United States of America

Used by Permission. All rights reserved.

ADVANCE PRAISE FOR
THE PSYCHOPATHY OF WHITENESS

The Epigenetics of Anti-Blackness, Malignant Narcissism, and Collective Diabolical Antisocial Personality Disorder

Dante, thank you for trusting me with the honour of reading and responding to this powerful work. You continue to do what very few are willing or able to do: expose the architecture of racial violence with precision, courage, and an unflinching commitment to truth.

The Psychopathy of Whiteness is a masterwork. You have gone all in on reframing white supremacy at every level: historically, psychologically, legally, politically, socially, clinically and spiritually. You pull the lens back to show how whiteness was engineered through colonial conquest, how it evolved into a global system of domination, and how its operations persist in our institutions, policies, bodies and everyday interactions right now. Your diagnostic approach is bold and essential. By naming the patterns malignant narcissism, collective diabolical antisocial personality disorder, the epigenetic imprint of anti-Black violence you give readers the language and framework to finally understand what so many Black communities have been living, resisting and surviving for centuries.

This book does not merely trace the lineage of white supremacy; it dissects it. It builds on the trailblazers who opened the door to these conversations, and then pushes the work further, deeper and with greater precision. The result is a text that is both visionary and grounded, both historically rigorous and emotionally resonant.

You have written a book that will shift discourse globally. Scholars, activists, clinicians, educators and everyday people will find in these pages a truthful, uncompromising guide to understanding the world we inhabit and the world we must build. Your courage, your brilliance and your devotion to liberation are unmistakable.

With deep respect and solidarity,
Edwin Cleophas (Zulu-Khoi_South African)

***

Dante King's *The Psychopathy of Whiteness* is a stunning achievement in the study of race and racism in America. King seamlessly weaves history, jurisprudence, theology, psychology, and sociology together into a devastatingly profound and exceptionally clarifying synthesis, making his conclusions virtually irrefutable. Particularly notable are his keen elucidations on the theological and ecclesial origins of whiteness, which was born out the Church's unholy bloodlust for greed and power that accompanied the rise and evolution of Christian supremacy throughout European history. Drawn from a proficient command of the Black intellectual and psychological tradition, King is the first in my knowledge to accurately describe European Christianity as a *"Malignant Diabolical Psychopathy*-domination is confused with salvation and cruelty with righteousness." Diabolical is right! European Christianity sanctified the savagery of settler colonialism and racial oppression, thereby embodying the thief described by Jesus in John 10:10 who comes only to "steal, kill, and destroy." In this book, an expert physician has offered an incredibly precise diagnosis of the malignant disease that plagues our souls, our cities, and our nation. This is essential reading for anyone who studies race or theology, however, everyone should plumb the depths of King's powerful moral excavation that clarifies the origins of systematic racial violence and advances our understanding of whiteness/anti-blackness beyond the current scholarly consensus. The evil of whiteness has made us all morbidly ill. As King says,

"To heal, America must first accept the diagnosis." May our acceptance begin.

Rev. Dr. Benjamin Boswell, pastor of Collective Liberation Church and author of *Confronting Whiteness* (Orbis: 2022)

SPECIAL ACKNOWLEDGEMENTS

To the visionaries whose brilliance reshaped the way I see the world, history, and the human condition through a critically clinical lens—

Dr. Frances Cress Welsing, medical doctor and psychiatrist;

Dr. Alvin Poussaint, psychiatrist;

Dr. Amos N. Wilson, psychologist;

Dr. Bobby E. Wright, psychologist;what

Dr. E. Franklin Frazier, sociologist;

Dr. John Henrik Clarke, educator and revolutionary;

Dr. Jerome E. Fox, psychiatrist;

James Baldwin, scholar, author, and academic;

Malcolm X, revolutionary genius;

Toni Morrison, author and academic;

Cheryl I. Harris, legal scholar;

and **Albert Cleage**, theologian and activist—

your scholarship and sacrifice provided the frameworks through which this work finds its clarity and power.

Special thanks to those whose conversations deepened my understanding of the human psyche and the society that shapes it:

Dr. Emily McTate, psychologist;

Dr. Danyelle Marshall, LMFT;

Jessica Brown, behavioral health professional;

Dr. Ruben Randall, psychiatrist;

and **Dr. Latanya Takla**, psychiatrist and LMFT.

The many dialogues we shared over the years helped crystallize the consciousness that guides this book.

Books such as *The Falsification of Afrikan Consciousness: Eurocentric History, Psychiatry, and the Politics of White Supremacy* and *Black-on-Black Violence: The Psychodynamics of Black Self-Annihilation in Service of White Domination*, both written by **Dr. Amos N. Wilson**; *The Miseducation of the Negro*, written by **Dr. Carter G. Woodson**; *The Isis Papers: The Keys to the Colors*, written by **Dr. Frances Cress Welsing**; and *The Peculiar Institution and the Making of Modern Psychiatry, 1840–1880*, written by **Wendy Gonaver**—along with a range of texts authored by white men once regarded as America's most "eminent thinkers" of the nineteenth and twentieth centuries—have all informed my analysis of the pathological foundations of Western science.

Among these were **Dr. Samuel Cartwright**, physician and psychiatrist, who wrote *Drapetomania: A Psychiatric Diagnosis—Runaway Slave Syndrome*, asserting that enslaved Africans who sought freedom were mentally ill; **Dr. Samuel R. Wells**, author of *New Physiognomy: Signs of Character as Manifested Through Temperament and External Forms, Especially in the "Human Face Divine,"* who claimed expertise in reading morality and intelligence through the white pseudoscience of phrenology; **Dr. Robert Bennett Bean**, who in *Some Racial Peculiarities of the Negro Brain* (1906) argued—falsely and grotesquely—that the brains of Black people were inherently inferior in structure, smaller in corpus callosum size, and less evolved than those of whites; and **Dr. Irving Fisher** and **David Hoffman**, authors of *Race Traits and Tendencies of the American Negro and Appreciation and Interest*, who claimed that Black people's social and economic conditions were not the result of structural oppression but of supposed biological and environmental deficiencies.

Each of these works, while steeped in violence, racism, and delusion, provided empirical proof of the very premise of this book: that Western science and psychiatry were invented as instruments of domination, grounded in white psychopathology, perversion, and projection. These texts revealed to me that what has been called "objective science" in the Western world is, in truth, the codification of white fantasy—an elaborate self-mythology masquerading as fact. The entire model is the product of Eurocentric distortion, an institutionalization of white fear and self-deception projected onto nonwhite peoples for the sake of political, economic, and cultural control.

I acknowledge with gratitude the dozens of therapists, psychiatrists, and medical professionals I have encountered and worked alongside at the **San Francisco Department of Public Health**. Your practices and experiences confirmed much of what I reveal in these pages—that Western medicine and psychiatry, though cloaked in science, were built upon a foundation of white male consensus and projection.

These disciplines, historically and institutionally, have pathologized difference while disguising the pathology of domination itself.

Disorders such as ADHD, Autism, and "neurodivergence" are not immutable truths, but social constructs arising from a predatory academic and clinical tradition. **Black people, above all, must divest from and decolonize these systems.**

This book should not be read as though I am presenting a new set of ideas to the world. It is not a departure from the intellectual and clinical traditions established by those who came before me, but an amplification of them. The theories, concepts, and frameworks within this text build directly upon the groundbreaking and prophetic works of Dr. Bobby E. Wright, Dr. Frances Cress Welsing, and Dr. Amos N. Wilson. Their scholarship provided the intellectual architecture for everything I have written here. This book exists because of them—it is a continuation, translation, and elevation of their analyses into our current moment. What I have done is to extend their diagnoses into the modern institutions, behaviors, and technologies that continue to reproduce white psychopathy and anti-Blackness under new names.

I would also like to thank the members of the **San Francisco Police Department**, not in celebration but in recognition. My work with the SFPD—specifically in rolling out San Francisco's first-ever implicit bias training program for law enforcement—provided me with continuous, firsthand exposure to the depth of anti-Blackness embedded in policing. Through these experiences, I witnessed the full range of denial, projection, fragility, and hostility that define white psychopathy in law enforcement. The daily encounters I had with officers during this process confirmed that anti-Blackness is not a regional phenomenon but an institutional reflex—one that thrives even in what is widely considered one of the most "progressive" cities in the United States of America.

Finally—

To the **collective white race**, I extend a paradoxical but necessary acknowledgment.

Your historical and ongoing behaviors have provided the empirical and experiential evidence that ground the theories, concepts, and definitions articulated throughout this work.

Your perpetual enactment of these dynamics—past and present—has made this analysis possible.

For that, I thank you.

TABLE OF CONTENTS

Letter to Black People	1
Foreword	7
Violent Threats	11
Preface	35
Key Concepts and Definitions	39
Reflections	59
The Black Identity Crisis	65
Introduction	69
Chapter 1: The American Delusion	81
Chapter 2: The Theology of Conquest	89
Chapter 3: The Legal Invention of Whiteness	99
Chapter 4: The Gospel of Violation	111
Chapter 5: White Rage, Clinical Reality	135
Chapter 6: Whiteness as Disorder	155
Chapter 7: Inherited Violence	175
Chapter 8: The Scientific Religion of White Power	187
Chapter 9: The Psychodynamics of Whiteness and the Legal Codification of Terror	217

Chapter 10: White Malignant Diabolical Psychopathic
Institutional Repression   251

Chapter 11: The Continuum of Enslavement   273

Chapter 12: The Post-George Floyd Era   283

Chapter 13: From Colonial Faith to Civic Religion   297

Chapter 14: The Neuroscience of Whiteness   315

Chapter 15: Where Do We Go From Here   349

References and Works Cited   363

Professional Bio   383

Dedication   395

Comments From Course   397

LETTER TO BLACK PEOPLE

Black people,

You are not broken—you have been brutalized. What the world calls "your condition" is not a pathology of your making; it is the result of centuries of collective psychopathology masquerading as civilization. The nation we inhabit, this so-called United States, was built upon the organized delusion of white moral authority—a psychopathic order that confuses domination with divinity and destruction with progress.

White America is not merely a political invention; it is a psychiatric one. Its institutions—legal, medical, educational, and religious—function as extensions of a collective disorder: the need to control, to categorize, and to consume Black existence. From its inception, white culture has survived by manufacturing fantasy and calling it fact. Every system that governs this land operates as a laboratory for white projection. Our pain is their data. Our bodies, their proof of superiority. Our dispossession, their imagined stability.

You must know, deeply, that what they call "America" was never designed for our survival. We were born into a social psychosis that defined us as disorder and defined whiteness as health. To live here as a Black person is to live inside someone else's hallucination, to be misdiagnosed by the very mind that created your wounds.

We are not responsible for the chaos that was engineered around us. The fractures in our communities, the despair, the rage, the hunger—these are not failures of our character, but the predictable outcomes of a civilization dependent on our suffering. For four hundred years, white psychopathy has required Black trauma as its oxygen. The violence that haunts our neighborhoods is not homegrown; it is *engineered stress*, passed down like genetic code, embedded in law and reinforced through every institution that governs daily life.

Our endurance, then, is not weakness—it is neurobiological genius. To survive centuries of psychic assault, to remain capable of laughter, beauty, and love under the weight of systemic dehumanization, is a miracle of nervous-system adaptation. The anxiety, exhaustion, and grief you carry are not proof of deficiency. They are *diagnostic evidence* of the sickness we have endured and the spirit that refuses extinction.

Understand this: Whiteness is not a race—it is a disorder of consciousness. It is a delusional identity structure built upon negation. It can only know itself through our subjugation. The American project demands daily proof of white purity; thus, it demands daily Black diminishment. Every act of exclusion, every bullet, every policy that devalues our lives functions as a ritual reaffirmation of their pathology.

White privilege, then, is not mere advantage—it is the symptomology of collective illness. It requires constant othering to sustain itself, constant violence to preserve its fantasy of normalcy. What white America has accomplished with Black people is what other tyrants have only attempted: the normalization of genocide. From birth to death, we are surrounded by systems that interpret our existence as deviation. And yet, we endure.

The propaganda that criminalizes us is not accidental; it is psychological warfare. As Malcolm X taught, the white press has long been the apparatus through which the psychopath justifies his aggression. Today, the same delusion persists through screens, policies, and polite corporate rhetoric. The difference between 1962 and now is not transformation but sophistication. The psychosis has learned to market itself as tolerance.

Even those who claim allyship—some Asian, Middle Eastern, Latinx, or light-skinned Black—often remain entrapped in the same cognitive schema, measuring proximity to whiteness as safety. The colonial mind does not die easily. It replicates itself in anyone who believes that distance from Blackness is advancement. For this reason, trust discernment over diversity. All skinfolk are not kinfolk, and not all who speak the language of equity have confronted the disease of whiteness within themselves.

Know, too, that our struggle is distinct. Anti-Blackness is the primary software of this nation's consciousness—the code that runs beneath every social system. While others experience exclusion, we experience dehumanization. America's relationship to Blackness is not indifference; it is obsession. Our bodies are its mirror, and it cannot stand the reflection.

As a clinician and as your brother, I must tell you: the trauma we bear is not metaphorical. It is neural. It is biochemical. It is the scar tissue of a civilization that feeds on our humiliation. Yet within that truth lies our power. The same neurobiological systems that have been conditioned for hypervigilance can also be reconditioned for liberation. The same collective memory that carries pain carries genius. Our healing begins not by forgiving the oppressor, but by naming the disorder. Diagnosis is the first act of deliverance.

Let the world know: the problem has never been the Black psyche—it has been the white pathology that distorts it. We are not the disordered; we are the diagnosticians. Through our survival, through our art, our scholarship, and our unbroken faith, we have mapped the architecture of madness that calls itself America.

So I say to you: remember who you are beneath the distortion. Remember that your pulse is older than the Republic and your spirit larger than its borders. The psychopathy of whiteness is loud, but it is not eternal. Its systems tremble each time we name them, each time we love ourselves without permission, each time we live in defiance of despair.

We are not subjects of a clinical case. We are the witnesses, the analysts, and the cure.

4 | THE PSYCHOPATHY OF WHITENESS

The words of President Donald Trump in 2023, President Richard Nixon in 1969, President Woodrow Wilson in 1915, President Abraham Lincoln in 1858, President Andrew Johnson in 1841, and President Thomas Jefferson in 1781 clearly demonstrate the purpose for this book.

In the words of President Donald Trump, December 16 and 18, 2023:

> America is the land of opportunity, however, the influx—it needs to be kept to a certain level. They're destroying the blood of our country. They come from Africa, they come from Asia, they come from South America. That's what they're doing. They're destroying our country. They let—I think the real number is 15–16 million people into our country. When they do that, we got a lot of work to do. They're poisoning the blood of our country.

And in the words of President Richard Nixon, April 28, 1969:

> You have to face the facts, the whole problem is really the Black people. The key is to devise a system that recognizes this without appearing to.

And in the words of President Woodrow Wilson, 1915:

> The white men of the South were aroused by the mere instinct of self-preservation to rid themselves, by fair means or foul, of the intolerable burden of governments sustained by the votes of ignorant negroes and conducted in the interest of adventurers.

And in the words of President Abraham Lincoln, September 18, 1858:

> I will say then that I am not, nor ever have been, in favor of bringing about in any way the social and political equality of the white and black races, that I am not nor ever have been in favor of making voters or jurors of negroes, nor of qualifying

them to hold office, nor to intermarry with white people; and I will say in addition to this that there is a physical difference between the white and black races which I believe will forever forbid the two races living together on terms of social and political equality. And inasmuch as they cannot so live, while they do remain together there must be the position of superior and inferior, and I as much as any other man am in favor of having the superior position assigned to the white race.

And in the words of President Andrew Johnson, 1841:

If blacks were given the right to vote, that would place every splay-footed, bandy shanked, hump-backed, thick-lipped, flat-nosed, woolly-headed, ebon-colored negro in the country upon an equality with the poor white man.

And in the words of President Thomas Jefferson, 1781 and 1820, respectively:

I advance it therefore as a suspicion only, that the blacks, whether originally a distinct race, or made distinct by time and circumstances, are inferior to the whites in the endowments both of body and mind.

I know no error more consuming to an estate than that of stocking farms with men almost exclusively. I consider a woman who brings a child every two years as more profitable than the best man on the farm. What she produces is an addition to the capital, while his labors disappear in mere consumption.

FOREWORD
BY DR. ROBIN DIANGELO

Dante King's work: *The 400-Year Holocaust*; *Diagnosing Whiteness & Anti-Blackness*; and now *The Psychopathy of Whiteness* is brilliant and simple, subversive and transparent, nuanced and obvious: whiteness is a mental illness – a condition that has been inculcated into all of us. No one could be and no one was exempt from its forces. Those of us trained into the white role must take a hard and honest look at this devastating condition which stunted our growth and limits our humanity.

I am white. Engaging with Dante's work requires looking at oneself through the lens of *white sociopathy*, *malignant diabolical psychopathy*, and *white malignant narcissism*. One may reasonably ask, "How does that make you feel as a white person?" I can answer with sincerity that I feel recognition and relief. I even feel excited and empowered. Why? Recognition because Dante describes a racial orientation inculcated within me at an early age and continually reinforced throughout my life. Relieved because these words break white racial taboos and directly name white sociopathy. Excited because to receive a diagnosis is the first step toward a cure. I feel empowered because I can move past unproductive and self-serving feelings such as guilt and shame. I did not choose to be conditioned into this disorder, and would never have accepted had I been given that choice. Dante's analysis is about me, but it isn't personal. That understanding is actually *liberating* as it frees me from defensiveness, hurt, anger and denial. It renders my self-focus moot. I am left ready to challenge white sociopathy within myself, my fellow white people, and society as a whole.

To know the truth of this diagnosis and the pain it causes and not feel any desire to address it is the definition of sociopathic, underscoring his argument. Any claim to value racial justice without accountable action can only be cruelly disingenuous. We may not be able to fully recover but we can certainly ameliorate our harm. Dante has generously – and in this political moment courageously - given us the diagnosis and the treatment plan to begin. Thank you Dante King.

"The intentions of this melancholy country, as concerns Black people, and anyone who doubts me can ask any Indian, have always been genocidal.

They (white people) needed us for labor and for sport, and now they cannot get rid of us.

The machinery of this country operates day in and day out, hour by hour, until this hour, to keep a nigger in his place."

JAMES BALDWIN, 1979

VIOLENT THREATS

The following screenshots of posts and messages were sent to me after I gave a Black History Month presentation at the University of California, San Francisco (UCSF), in February 2024. The topic of my presentation became the basis for this book.

Many White people took umbrage to my questions about whether American society should be examining the functionalities of race and racism as psychotic. Many doctors, scholars, and activists, as you will explore throughout this text, have posited that racism is an illness. Psychopathic.

Upon offering my own analysis and contribution to this topic area many White people reacted sending the following messages to me.

Thank you!

12 | THE PSYCHOPATHY OF WHITENESS

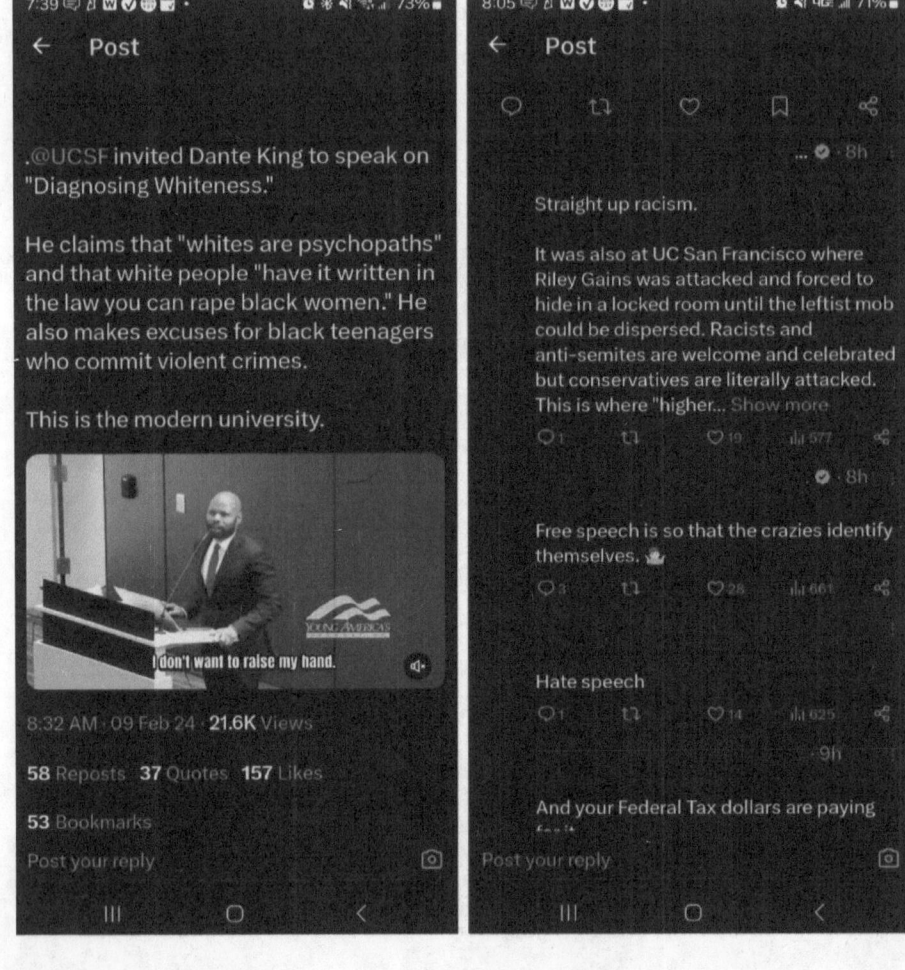

VIOLENT THREATS | 13

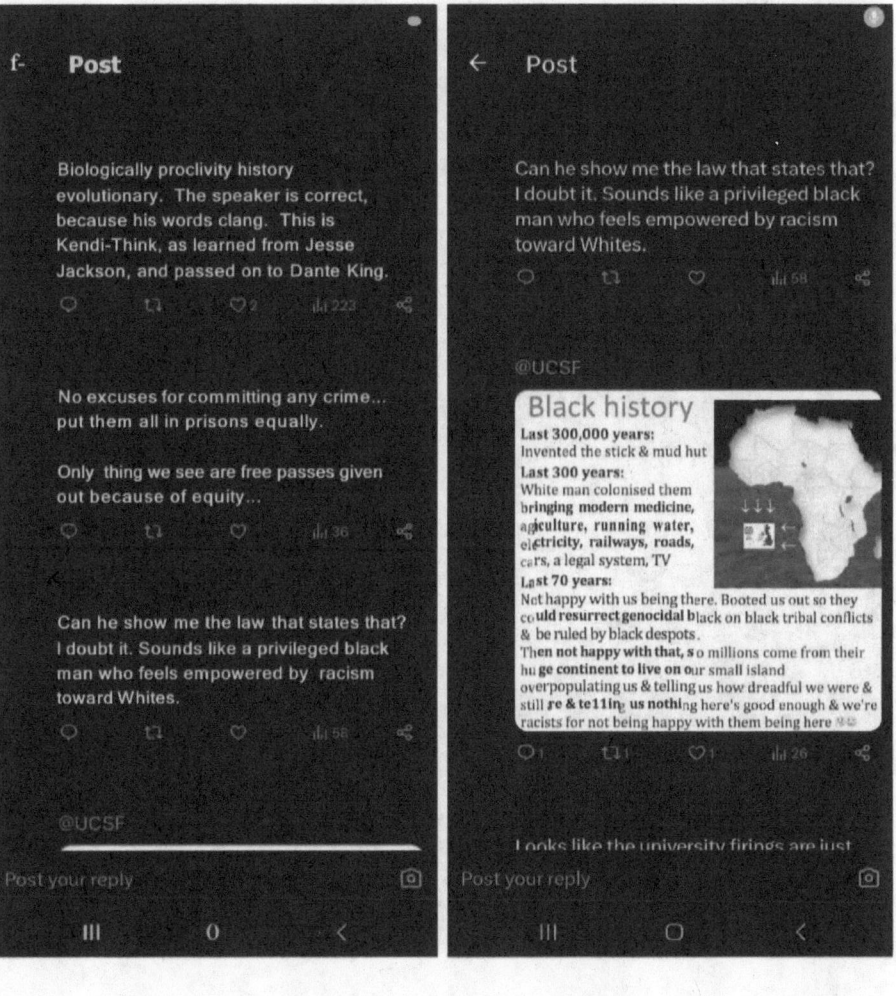

14 | THE PSYCHOPATHY OF WHITENESS

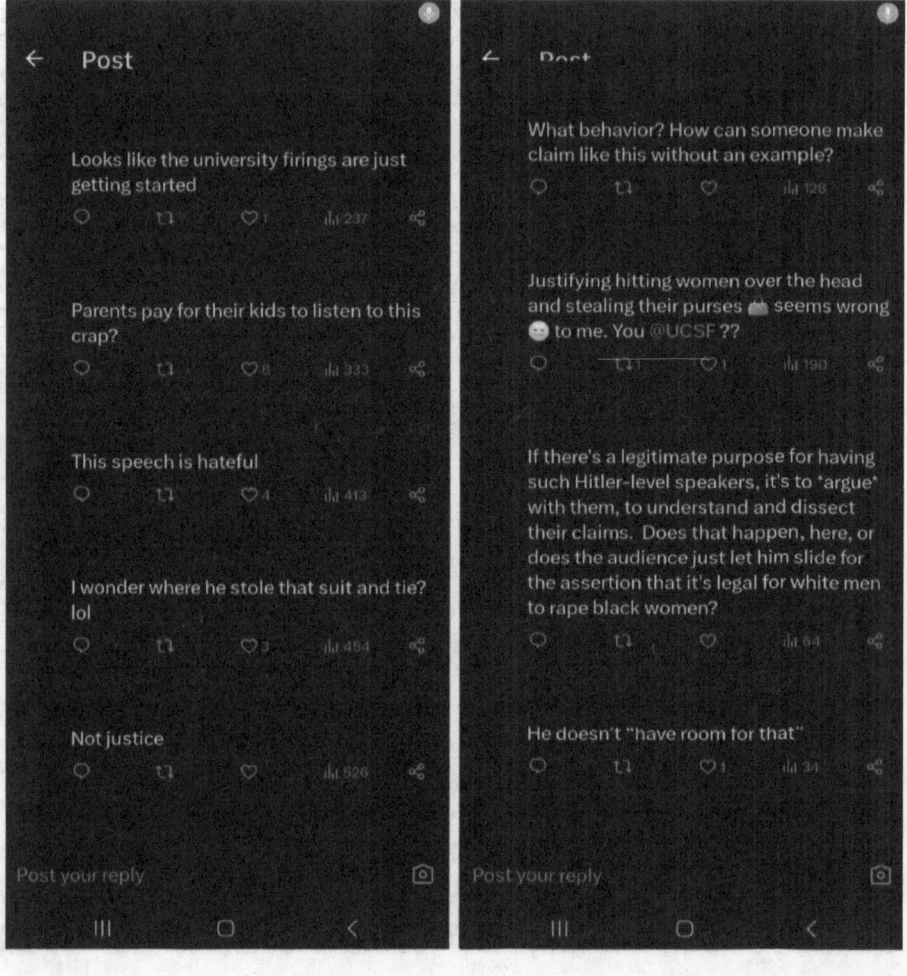

VIOLENT THREATS | 15

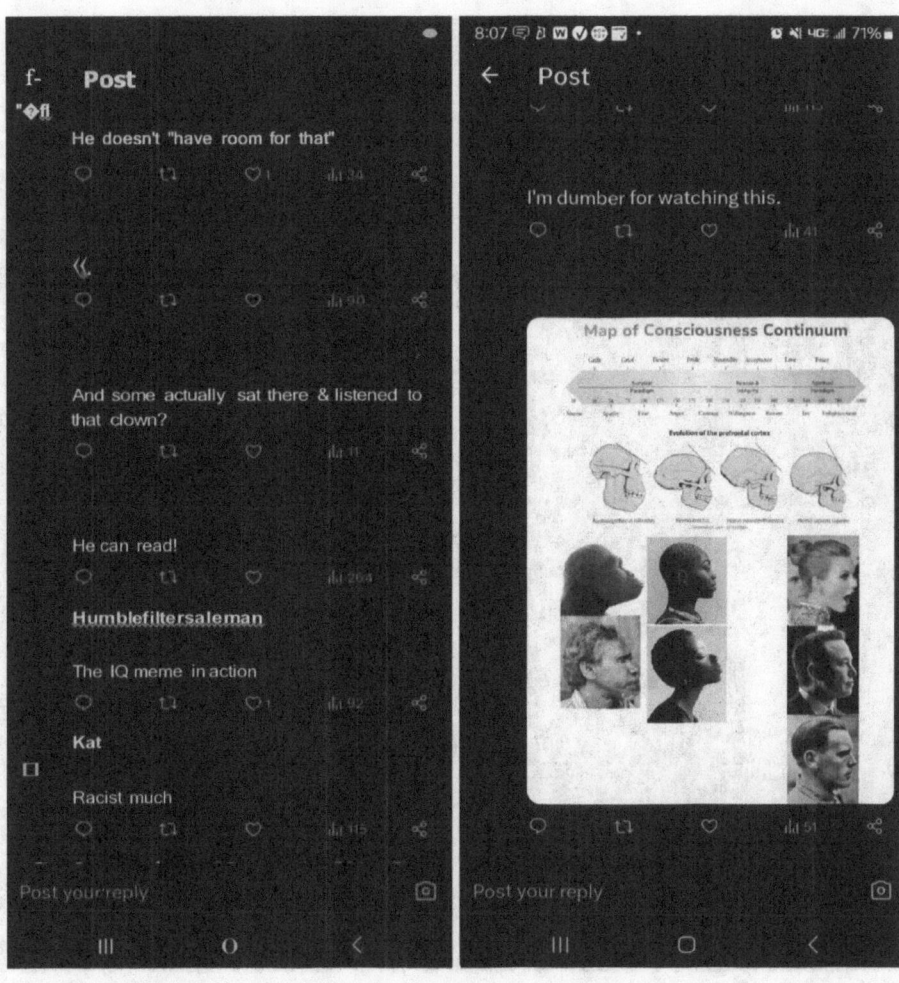

16 | THE PSYCHOPATHY OF WHITENESS

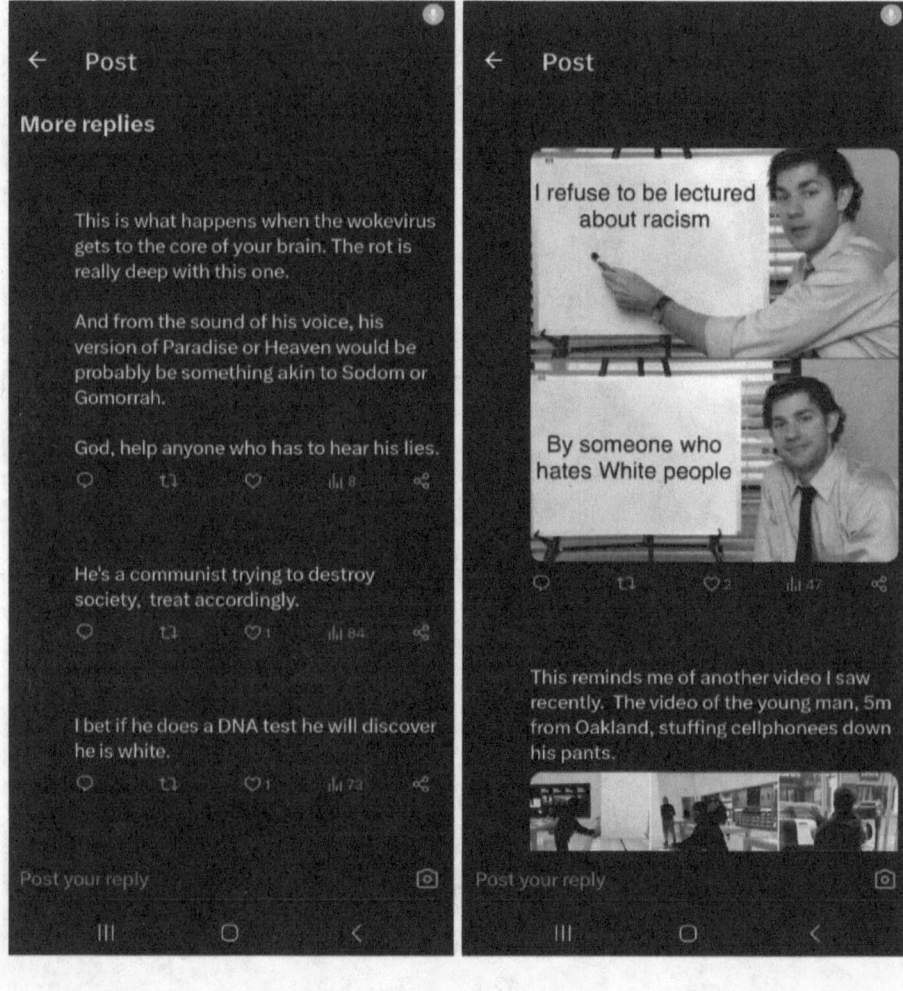

VIOLENT THREATS | 17

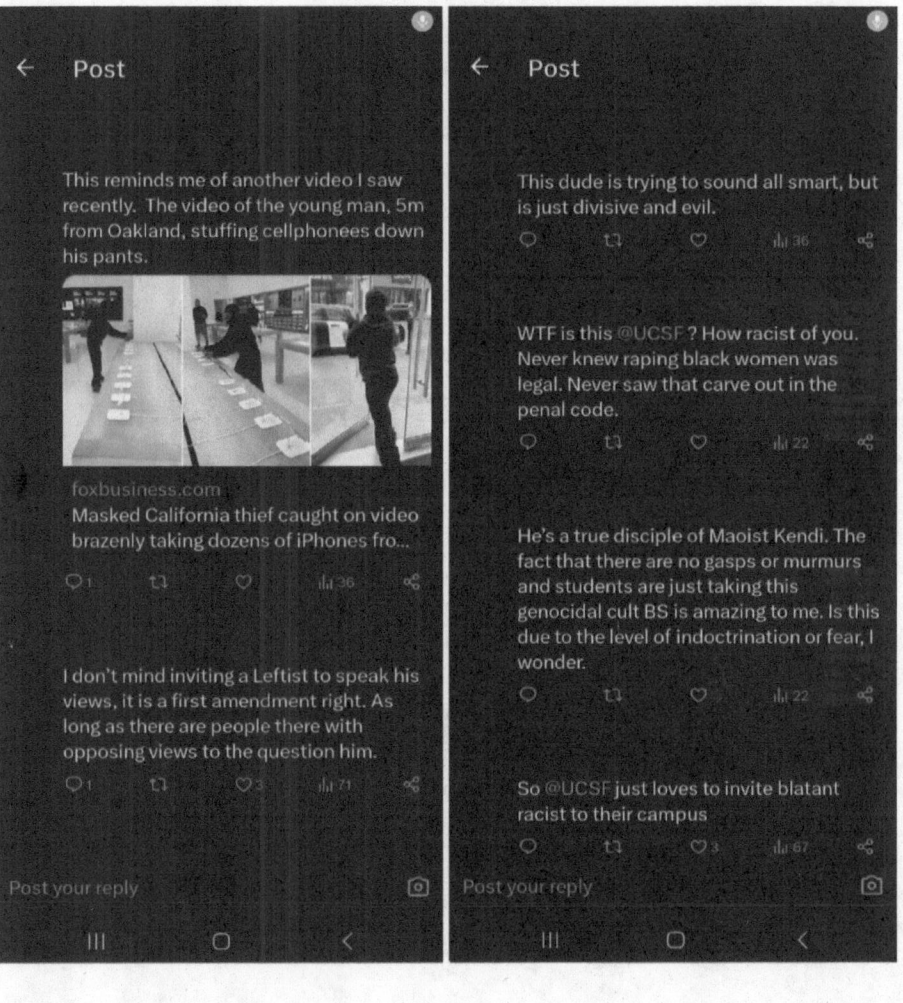

18 | THE PSYCHOPATHY OF WHITENESS

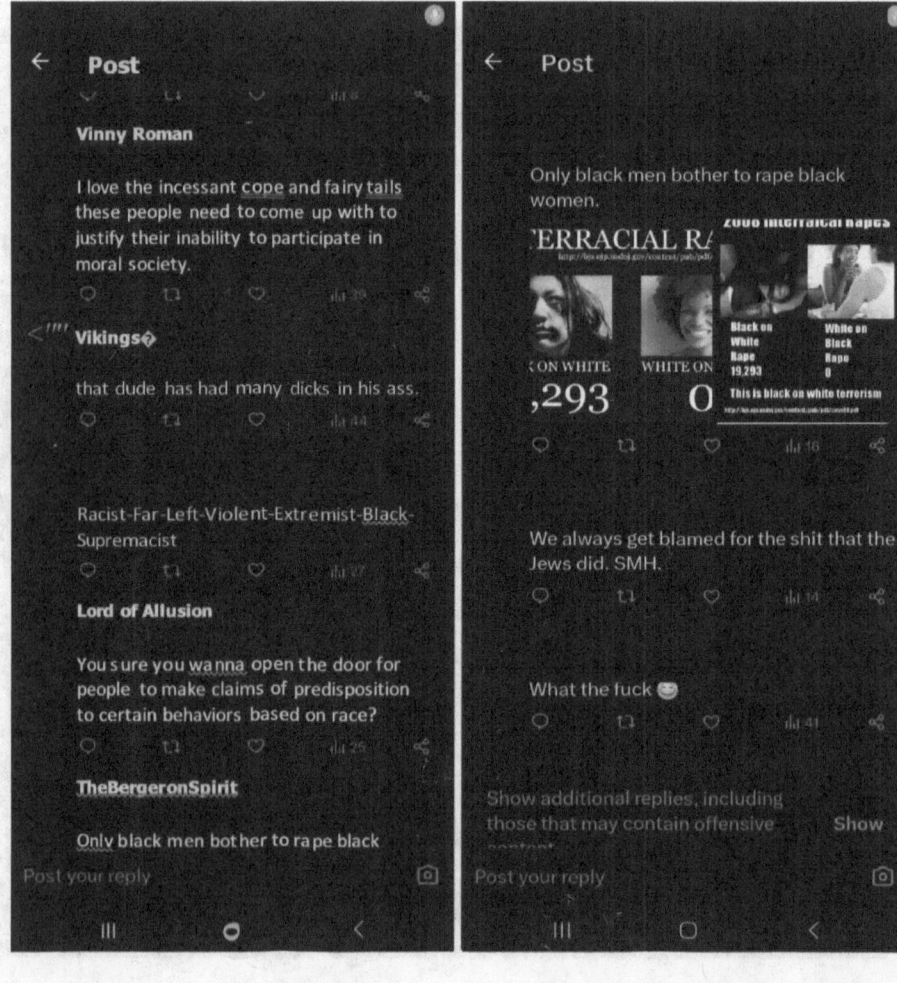

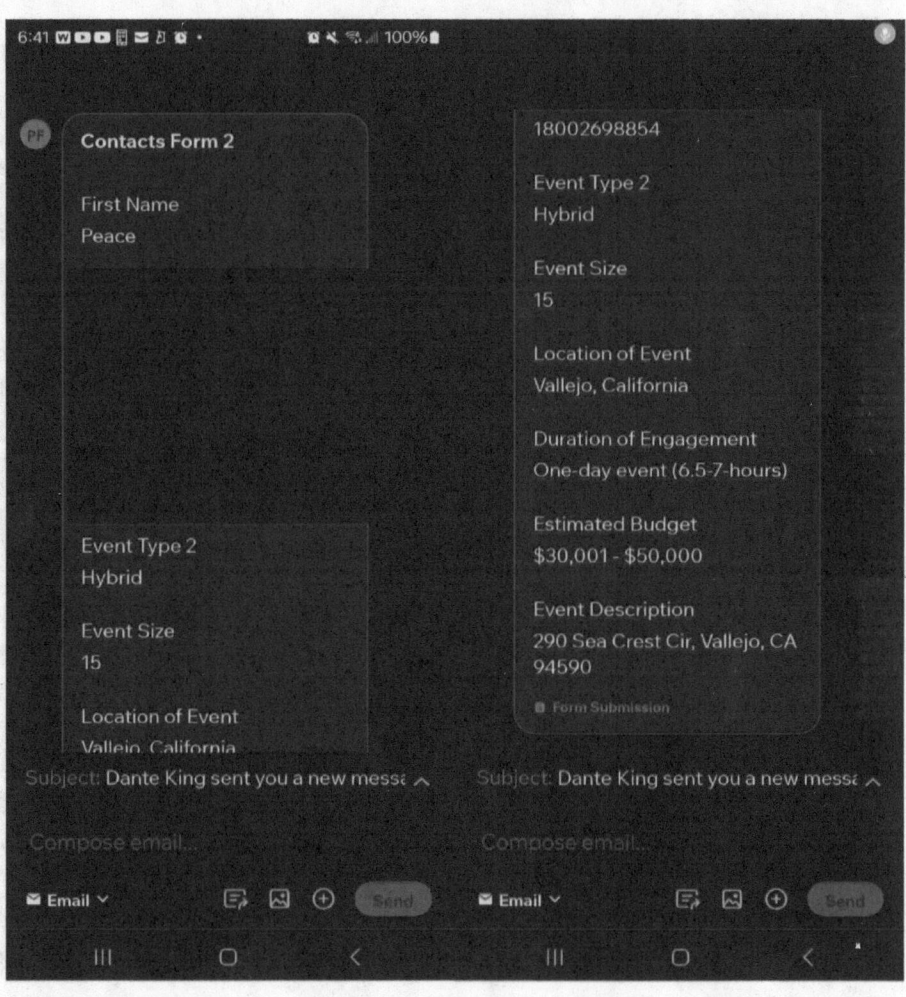

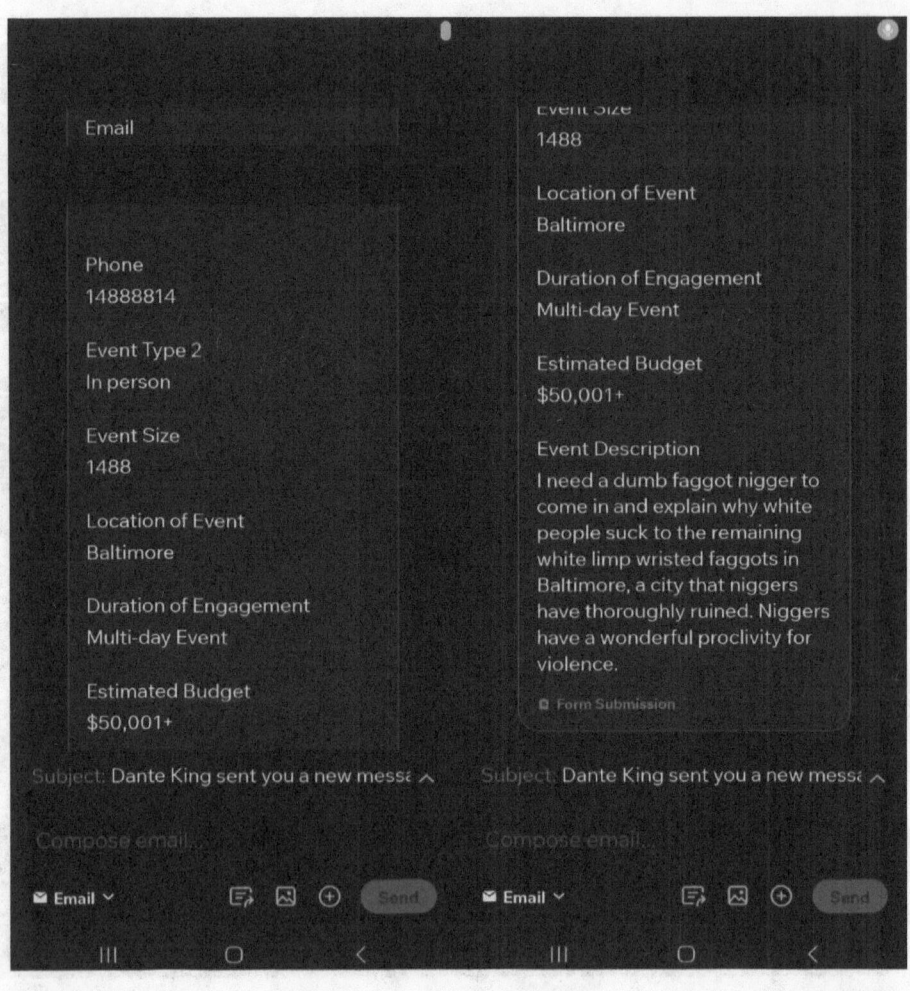

VIOLENT THREATS | 21

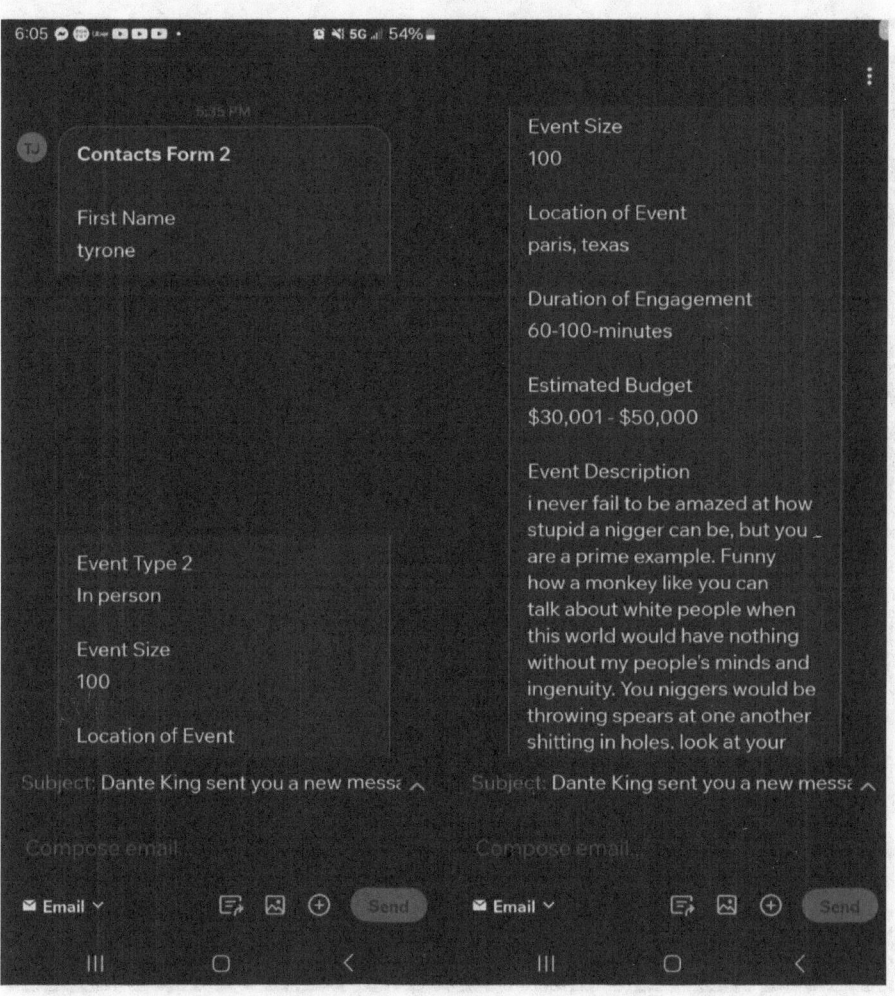

22 | THE PSYCHOPATHY OF WHITENESS

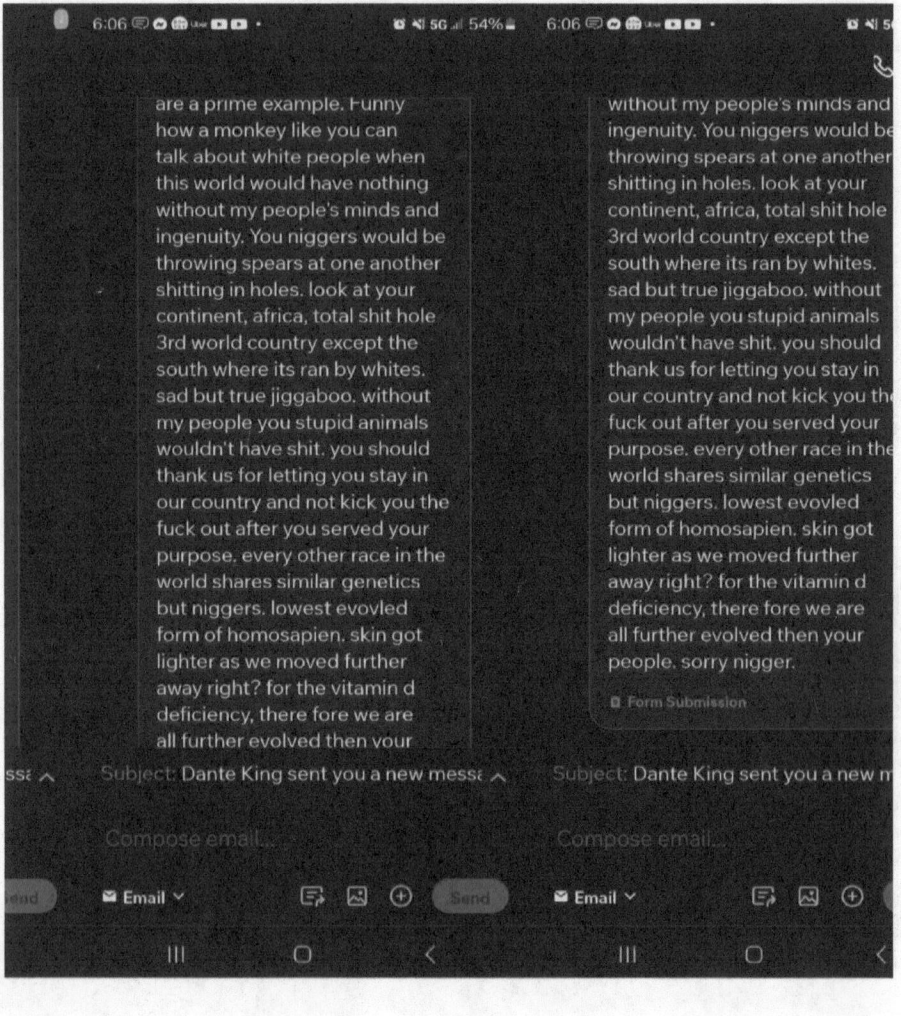

VIOLENT THREATS | 23

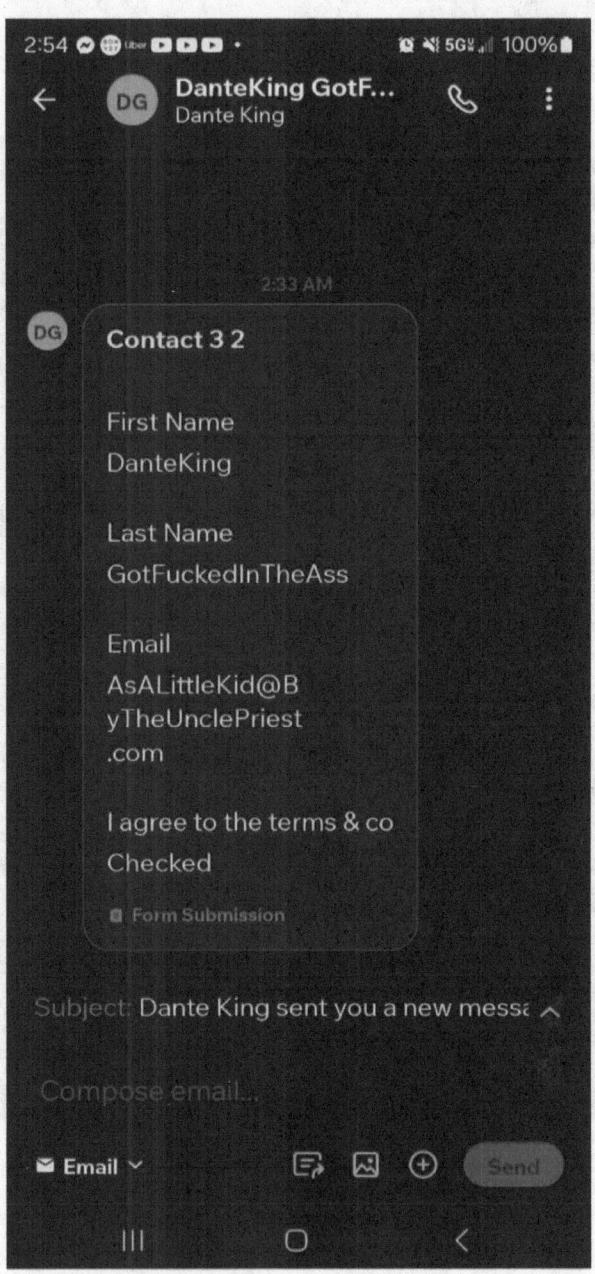

24 | THE PSYCHOPATHY OF WHITENESS

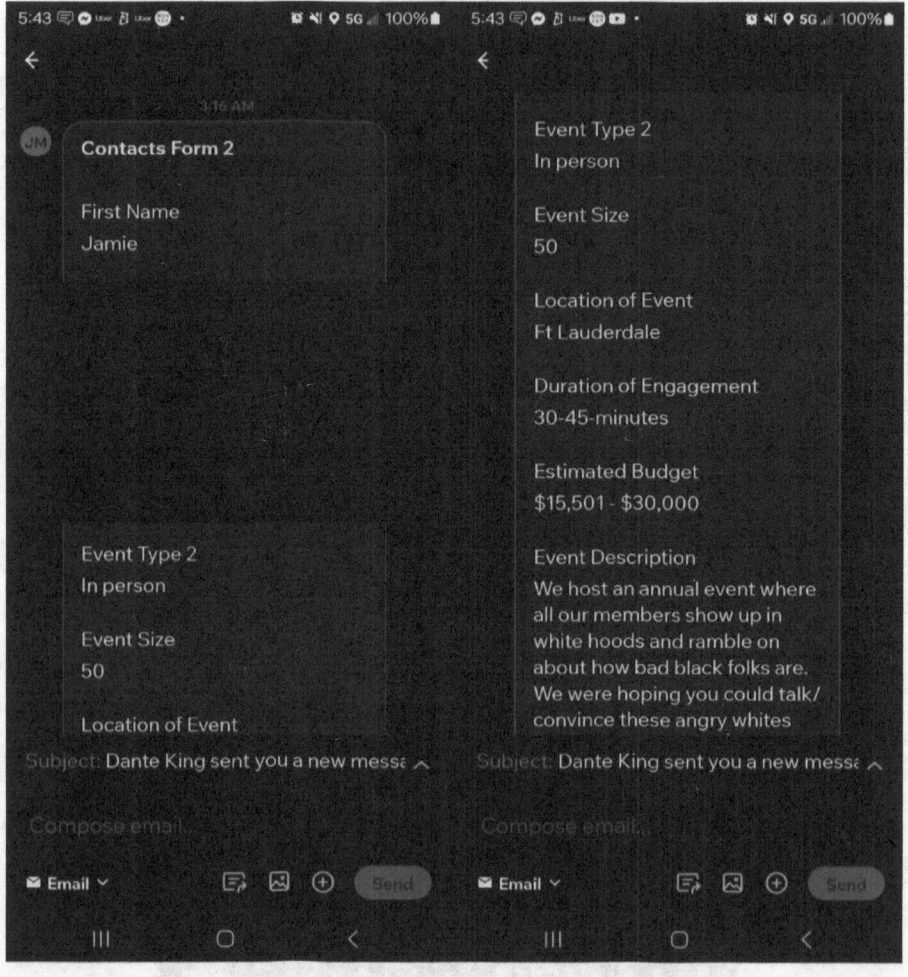

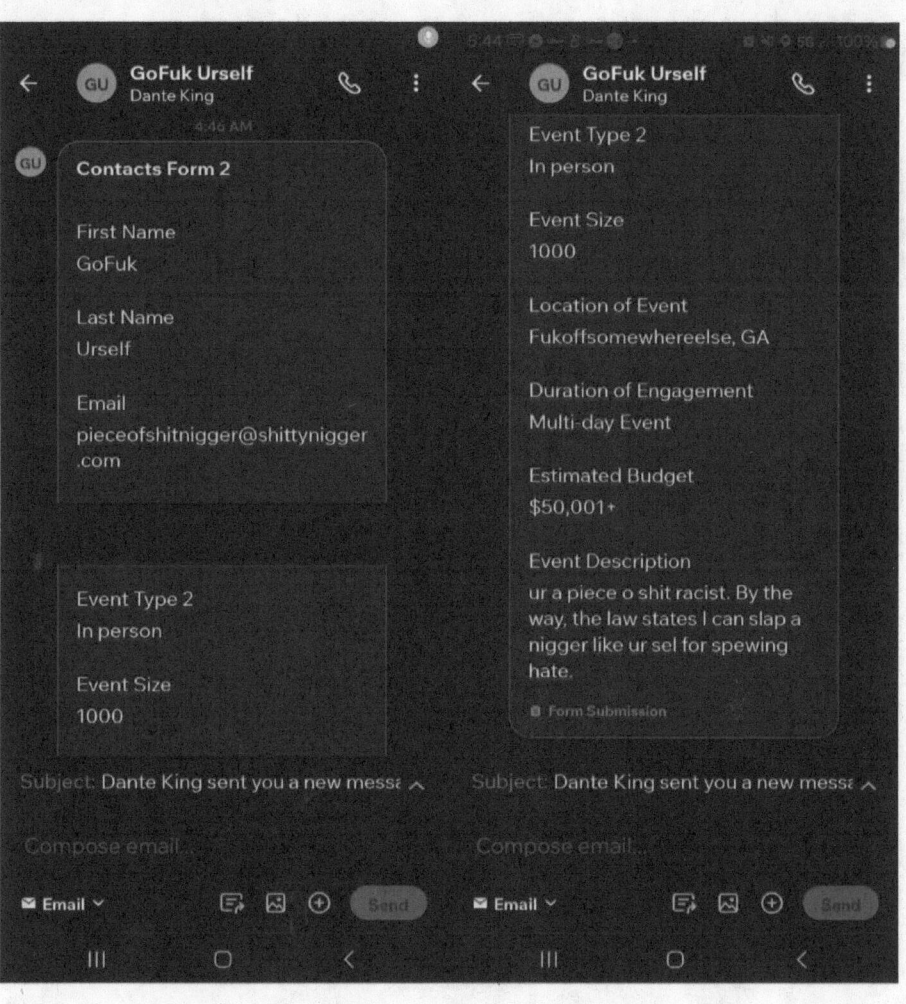

26 | THE PSYCHOPATHY OF WHITENESS

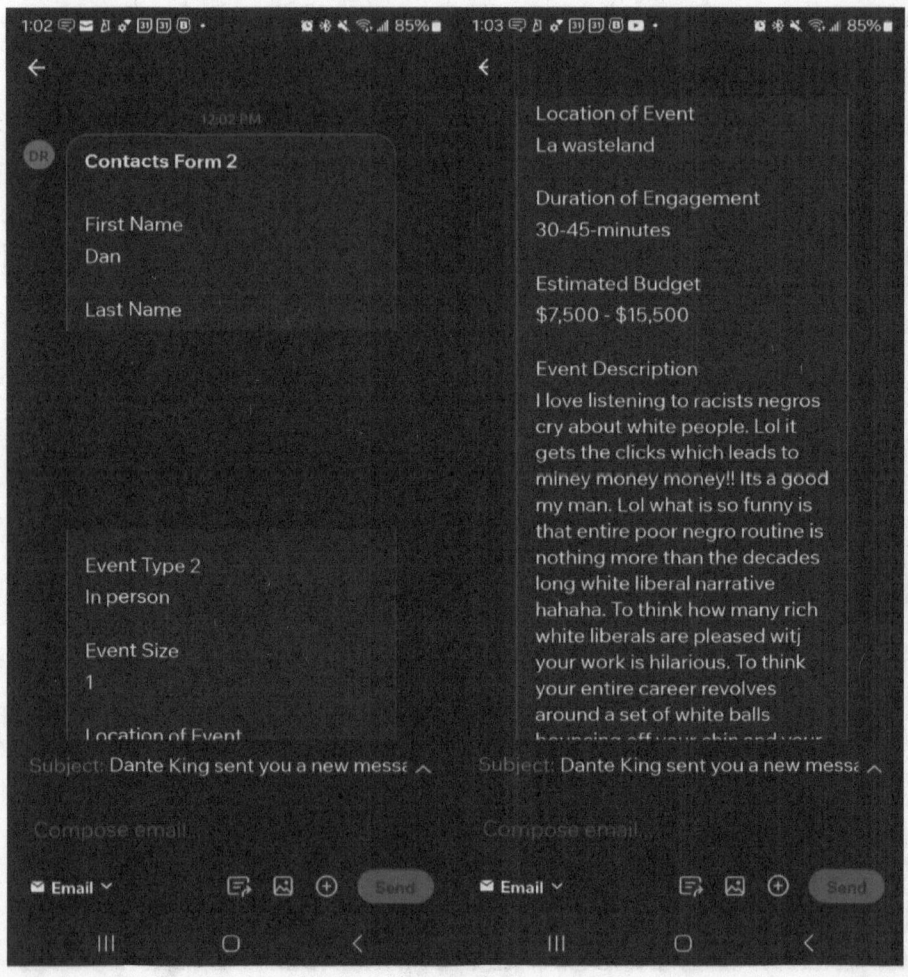

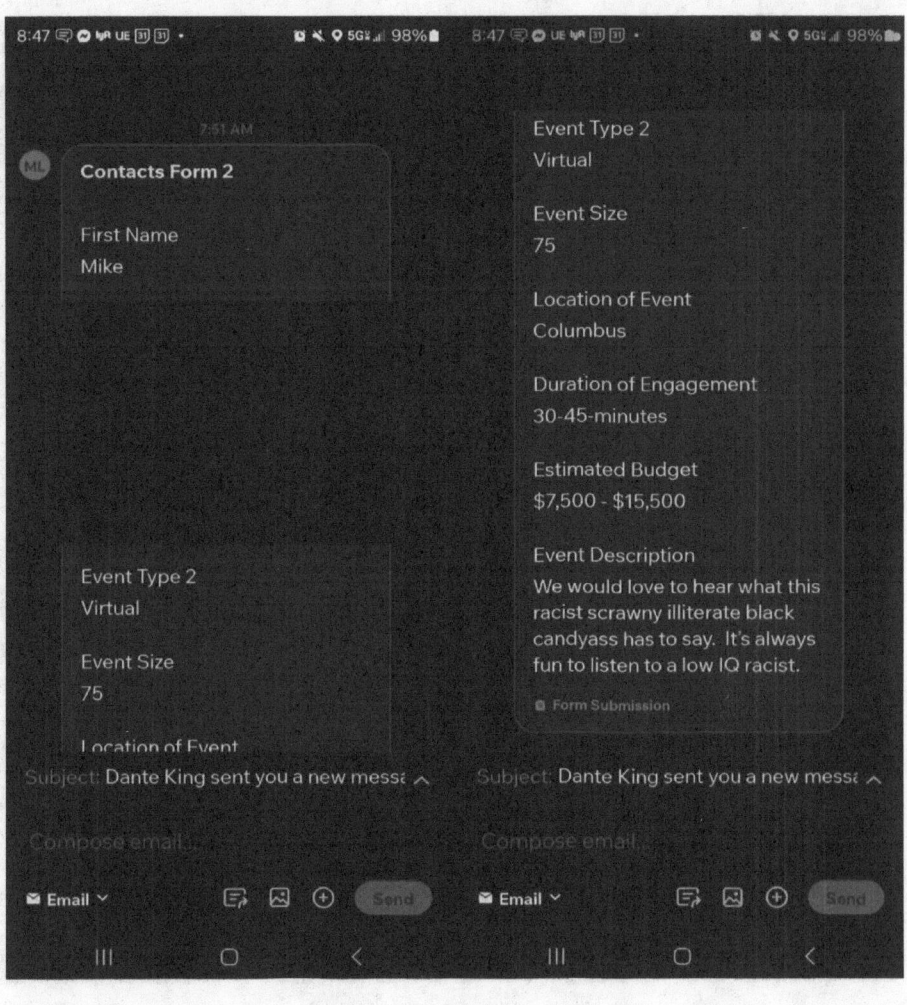

28 | THE PSYCHOPATHY OF WHITENESS

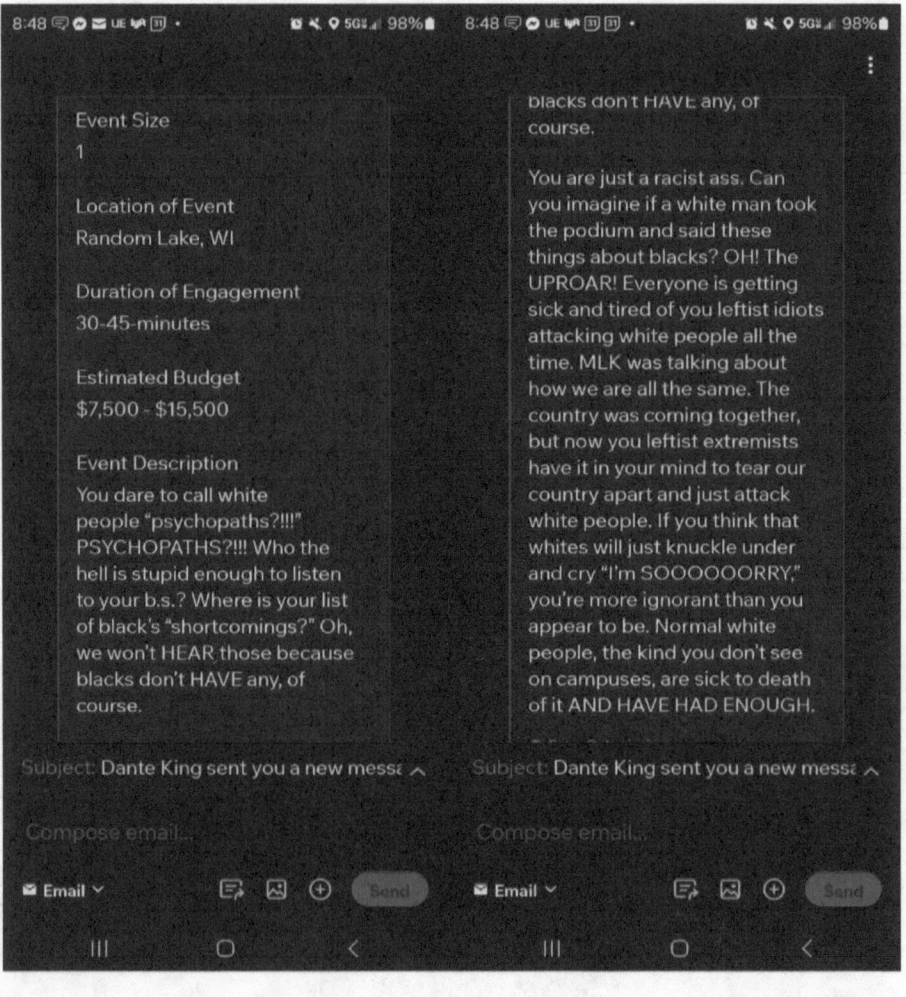

Event Size
1

Location of Event
Random Lake, WI

Duration of Engagement
30-45-minutes

Estimated Budget
$7,500 - $15,500

Event Description
You dare to call white people "psychopaths?!!!" PSYCHOPATHS?!!! Who the hell is stupid enough to listen to your b.s.? Where is your list of black's "shortcomings?" Oh, we won't HEAR those because blacks don't HAVE any, of course.

You are just a racist ass. Can you imagine if a white man took the podium and said these things about blacks? OH! The UPROAR! Everyone is getting sick and tired of you leftist idiots attacking white people all the time. MLK was talking about how we are all the same. The country was coming together, but now you leftist extremists have it in your mind to tear our country apart and just attack white people. If you think that whites will just knuckle under and cry "I'm SOOOOOORRY," you're more ignorant than you appear to be. Normal white people, the kind you don't see on campuses, are sick to death of it AND HAVE HAD ENOUGH.

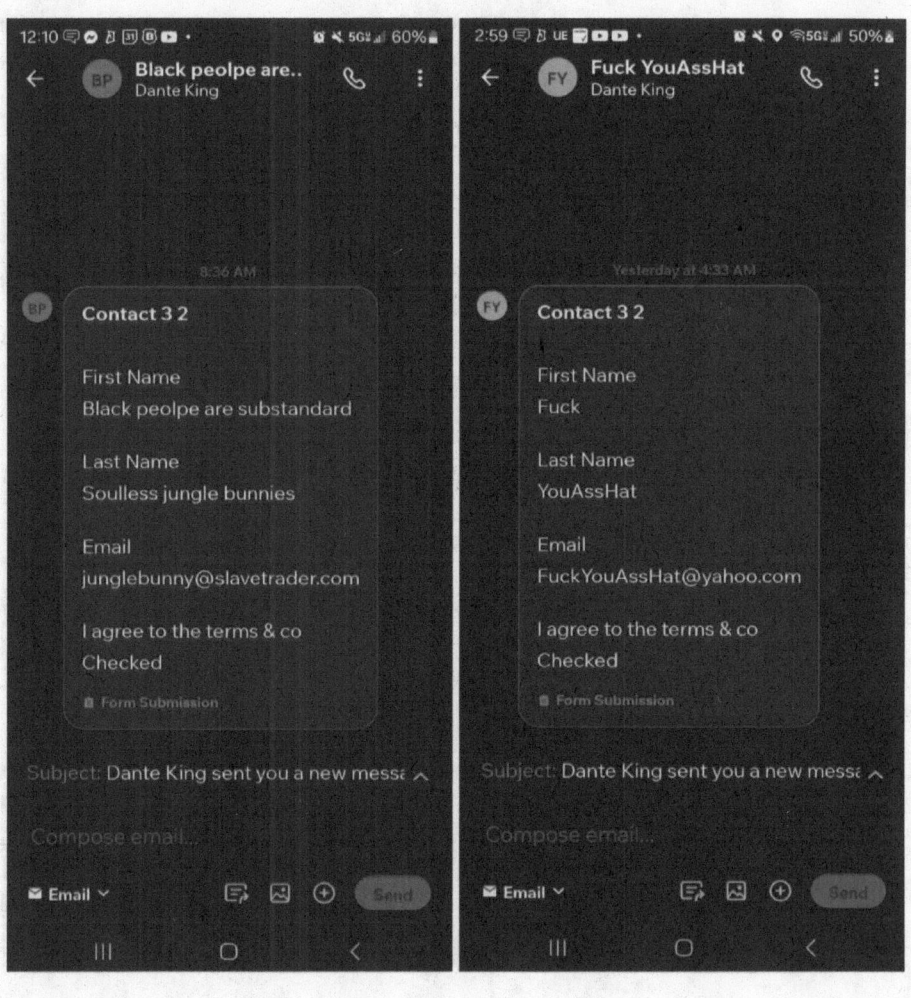

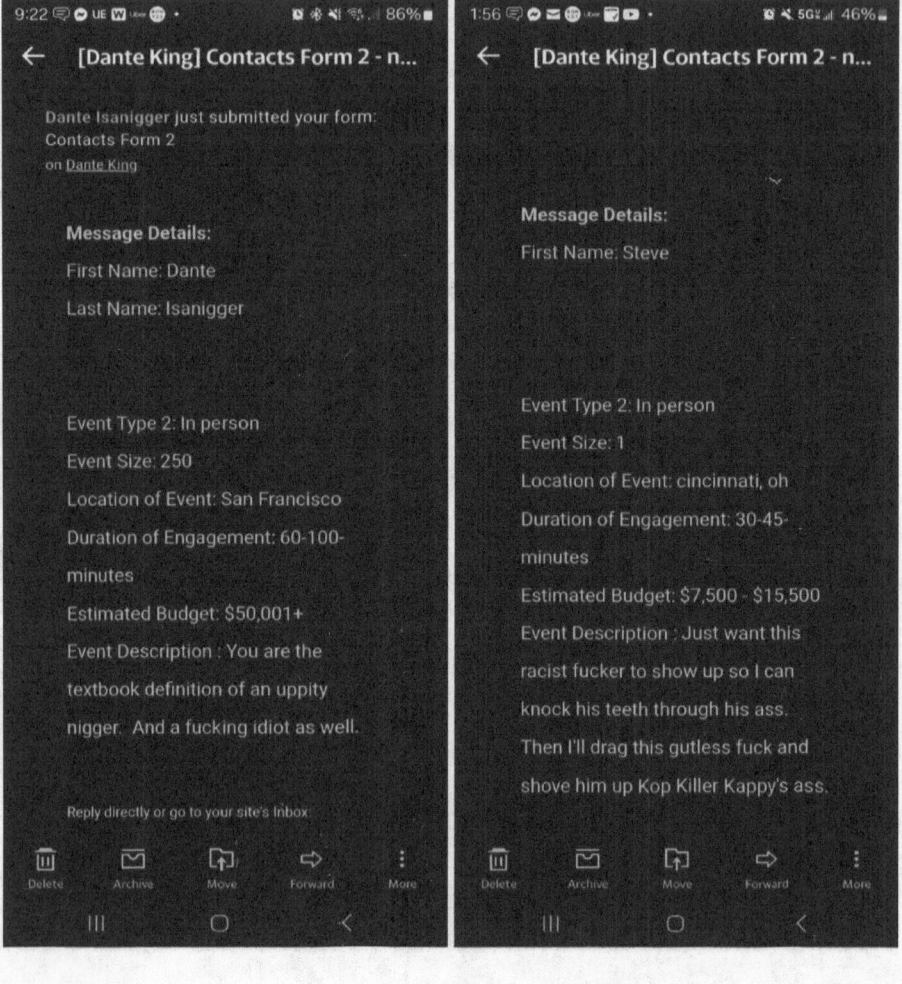

VIOLENT THREATS | 31

> **FEB 12 AT 3:53 PM**
>
> You are quite the entrepreneur. You sow hate, division, bigotry by being even more of a racist than any Klan or White Aryan Nation idiot. But you, you got a thing going. You hide behind of the veil of poor, defenseless little black man, who cannot defend himself or take care of himself. And even better, you defend the black man if he commits home invasions, robberies, murder, as just "nature". Yet the whiteness as you call it, is a deep rooted, yet unnatural, conscious choice, that is used by mean ole whitey, to hold the black man down. Pretty awesome. Still makes you a racist, a bigot...against your own people. You blame the world for the black man's woes and give them no way out, because of whitey. So if someone (not like you, you came from privilege, so own that shit) does rise up, they do so because of assistance of whites who give them everything, or you, the new coming of Christ in a suit and tie. You, and others like you do not give the black man and woman credit. You do not believe in their abilities. You just sow hate, division and racism (against both whites and every other race, really).

32 | THE PSYCHOPATHY OF WHITENESS

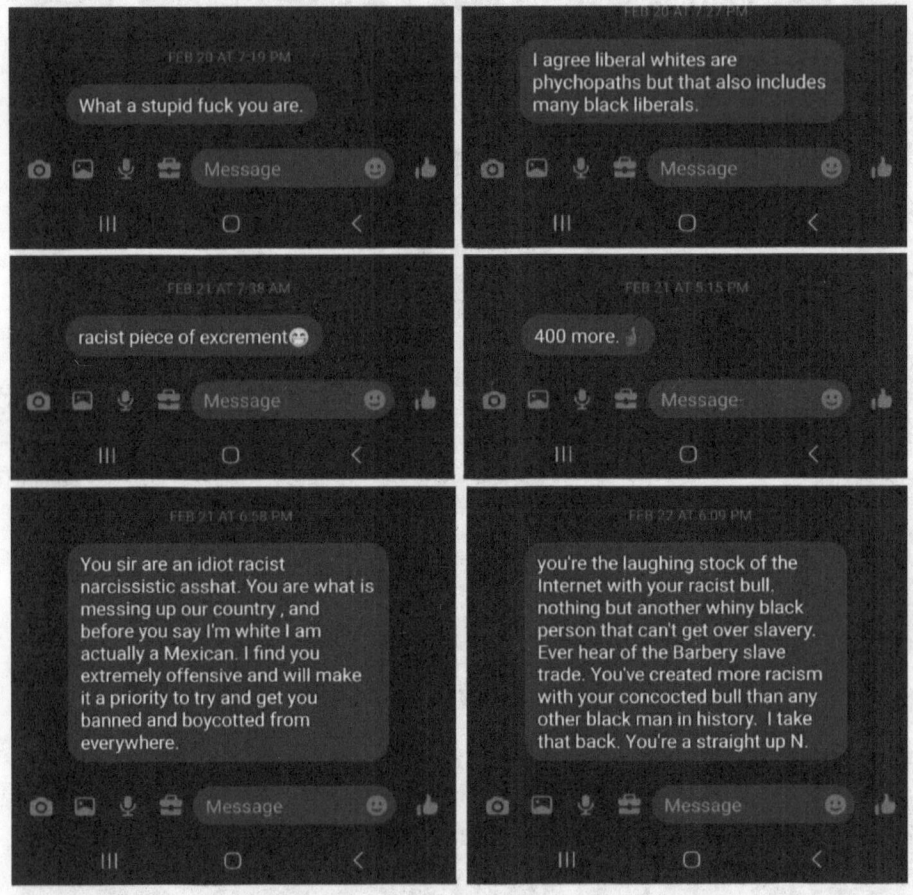

VIOLENT THREATS | 33

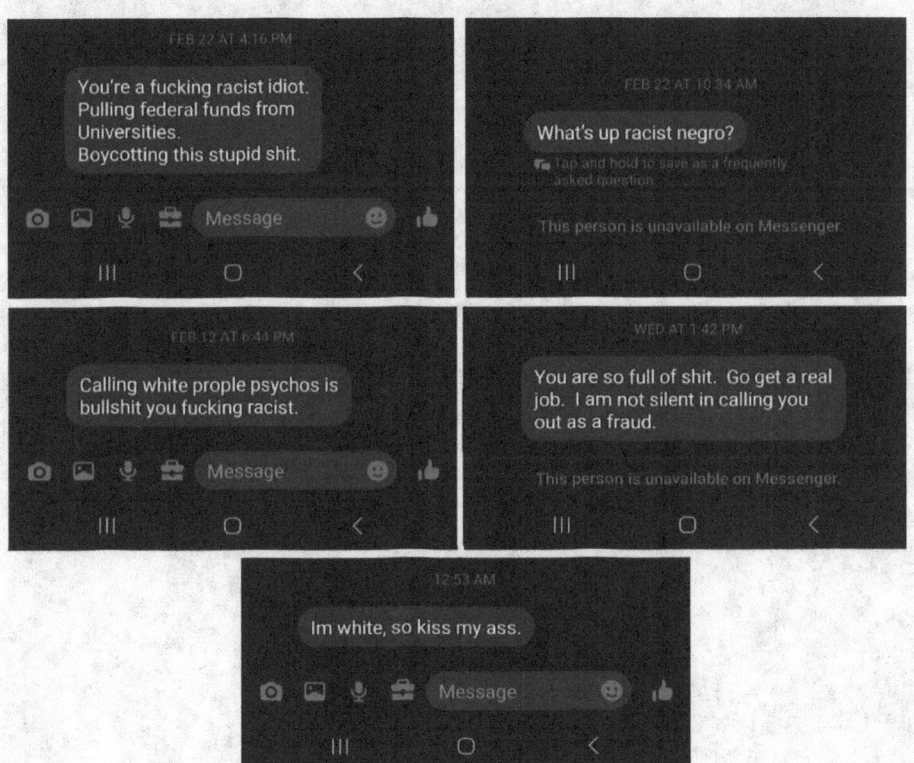

PREFACE
DR. FRANCES CRESS WELSING & THE PSYCHOANALYTIC LINEAGE OF TRUTH

When I first encountered the work of **Dr. Frances Cress Welsing**, I felt something ancient awaken within me—an ancestral knowing that had been waiting to be named. Her *Cress Color Confrontation Theory* and *The Isis Papers* did more than challenge the Western canon of psychology; they dismantled the very epistemology of whiteness. Dr. Welsing offered us language for what we had always felt but could rarely articulate: that white supremacy is not merely a political or economic structure, but a psycho-biological and spiritual disorder—an inherited pathology of fear, envy, and control that has metastasized across centuries.

Reading her work, I began to see that what we have long described as racism is in fact a **psychopathy**, a collective sociocultural illness that produces violence while denying its own sickness. Dr. Welsing's courage to frame whiteness in clinical, diagnostic terms liberated me to move beyond moral appeals and toward **systemic diagnosis**—to name the pathology as one names a disease, with precision and accountability. She taught me that the truth is not meant to soothe the guilty but to heal the oppressed.

In studying her theories, I came to understand that the mind of white domination is not simply evil—it is also *injured*. It is an ego architecture built on projection and dissociation, on the fear of genetic annihilation and the compulsion to destroy what it cannot become. The psycho-spiritual terror that whiteness inflicts on Black bodies is, at its core, a displacement of self-hatred, a pathology so profound that it requires global systems of denial to sustain it.

It was through this understanding that I began shaping my own theoretical framework—the **Psycho-Cognitive Defense Mechanisms of Whiteness**. Where Dr. Welsing's work exposes the psycho-sexual roots of racial domination, my work extends the analysis into the realm of cognitive and behavioral patterns—the reflexive denials, defenses, and dissociations that white individuals deploy to avoid moral and emotional reckoning. These mechanisms form the unconscious grammar of whiteness, the psychological immune system that protects white supremacy from self-awareness.

In this journey, I have also drawn deeply from **Dr. Bobby Wright**, whose *Psychopathic Racial Personality* remains one of the most incisive analyses ever produced on the pathological nature of white behavior. Wright taught us that the pathology of whiteness is not incidental; it is adaptive—an organized, self-justifying madness that rationalizes oppression as civilization. Likewise, **Dr. Amos Wilson** illuminated the falsification of African consciousness, showing how the European mind reprogrammed our own sense of self to perpetuate dependency and doubt. Together, these thinkers form the sacred triad upon which this book—and my life's work—stands.

Their scholarship affirmed for me that the struggle for Black liberation must be waged not only in law, policy, or protest, but in the **psychic realm**, where lies and delusion have long masqueraded as truth. We must confront the psychopathology of whiteness as both a global system and a deeply personal disease—one that has infected every institution, every body politic, every epistemology that defines what is "human." To heal ourselves and our world, we must first diagnose the sickness.

This book continues that work—a **diagnosis of the psychopathy of whiteness** and the **epigenetic trauma it has imposed upon the world.**

— **Dante D. King, M.Ed., CDE, HRM (SFSU)**
San Francisco, California | 2025

KEY CONCEPTS AND DEFINITIONS

Some clarity as it pertains to language may help.

American

A psycho-political identity rooted in *colonial and post-colonial terrorism* by Anglo-Europeans—later reclassified as *White people*. The term *American* functions as a psycholinguistic disguise for a history of domination, conquest, and legalized pathology. It represents a form of collective dissociation: the institutionalization of psychopathic behaviors—political, legal, judicial, economic, academic, linguistic, and cultural—under the guise of "civilization." The American identity thus operates as a psychiatric construct of racial superiority, encoded in every domain of Western infrastructure.

To be *American* is to participate, knowingly or not, in a system of affirmative action for whiteness: a centuries-long neurological and cultural conditioning that privileges the white psyche while dehumanizing and erasing nonwhite existence. Its most severe and enduring expression is the genocidal obsession with Black life—an obsession codified in law, normalized in education, sanctified in religion, and romanticized in culture. Assimilation into "American" norms is therefore not cultural inclusion but psychiatric induction—an internalization of anti-Black delusion and a surrender to the psychopathy of whiteness.

Anti-Black Surveillance

A clinical manifestation of the *White psychopathic compulsion to control the Black body*. This surveillance operates as both behavioral and neurological addiction—an inherited social reflex legitimized through legal and religious doctrine. Historically encoded in statutes such as the **Casual Killing Act of 1669** and the **Fugitive Slave Act of 1850**, it reappears today in policing, incarceration, and institutional oversight structures that reproduce the same racialized authority dynamic.

From a clinical standpoint, Anti-Black Surveillance reflects a *malignant defense mechanism*—a paranoid projection that externalizes white guilt and anxiety onto Black existence. It is the pathological need to observe, regulate, and punish the Black body to stabilize the white ego and maintain the illusion of moral and social supremacy.

Black Genocide

A systemic psychiatric operation—*the organized production of death* through social, political, and medical engineering. It is not merely physical annihilation but *psychological extermination*: the continuous reproduction of conditions (economic deprivation, health inequity, state violence, educational neglect, and mass incarceration) that destroy Black life and possibility.

Black Genocide is the ultimate expression of the *psychopathy of whiteness*: the convergence of racialized delusion, entitlement, and sadism within institutional power. It is a collective enactment of death as control—a white cultural ritual through which domination reaffirms itself by annihilating its perceived threat, the Black psyche.

Collective / Mass Psychosis

A transgenerational mental disorder embedded in the Western psyche and transmitted through social institutions. It is the collective delusion that whiteness is synonymous with virtue, intellect, and humanity—a delusion reinforced by legal, educational, and religious systems designed to manufacture compliance and moral blindness.

This mass psychosis functions as a *sociocultural contagion*: an adaptive mental illness that has infected entire populations. Nonwhite people, particularly Black people, are coerced into adopting aspects of this disorder for psychological survival within a dominator culture.

Clinically, it aligns with *induced psychosis*—a phenomenon in which followers internalize the delusions of a psychotic leader. In this context, whiteness itself is the delusional leader, and Western culture its cult. As Dr. Chanequa Walker-Barnes refers to it, pathological whiteness is the "hidden wound"—an unacknowledged psychic injury that manifests as domination, denial, and self-deception, perpetuated through every American institution.

Culture

A *psychosocial operating system* through which a group organizes its consciousness, behaviors, and moral codes to achieve particular ends. Culture is not neutral — it is the psychological instrument through which a group's *collective ego* exerts power. It encodes patterns of thought, emotion, and perception that maintain psychic coherence and social dominance.

In the context of whiteness, culture functions as a *neural conditioning apparatus*: a transgenerational behavioral script that programs individuals to replicate the delusional hierarchies of their group identity. It is an extension of the group's collective pathology — the outward expression of its interior psychosis. Through culture, the white psyche extends its control, aestheticizes its violence, and normalizes domination as civilization.

"To dominate another human being is to confess your own spiritual sickness."

DANTE KING,
DIAGNOSING WHITENESS & ANTI-BLACKNESS
(2026 EDITION)

Collective Diabolical Antisocial Personality Disorder (CD-APD)

Diagnostic Definition

Collective Diabolical Antisocial Personality Disorder (CD-APD) is a collective and individual psychopathology characterized by chronic moral inversion, pathological lying, emotional anesthesia, and the compulsion to dominate, exploit, and dehumanize others—particularly Black and Indigenous peoples—for psychological equilibrium.

It represents the most evolved and destructive strain of antisocial behavior in human history, fusing psychopathy, sociopathy, and malignant narcissism into a single cultural and institutional disorder.

CD-APD manifests when domination, not empathy, becomes the organizing principle of identity, government, and economy.

Core Traits

1. **Pathological Entitlement** — A delusional conviction of divine or racial superiority; the belief that one's group is inherently authorized to rule, possess, or punish others.

2. **Moral Inversion** — The capacity to rename violence as virtue: colonization as civilization, enslavement as enterprise, segregation as order, genocide as salvation.

3. **Instrumental Affect** — Selective empathy deployed only when it reinforces control or absolves guilt; emotional detachment from the suffering of racialized others.

4. **Predatory Dependency** — A parasitic relationship to Black creativity, labor, and suffering—requiring subjugation to maintain psychic stability.

5. **Collective Projection** — Chronic psychological displacement of one's own deviance, lust, and violence onto the oppressed, producing myths of the "Black rapist," the "dangerous immigrant," or the "ungrateful poor."

6. **Institutional Codification** — The translation of private pathology into law, policy, and theology, ensuring that personal illness becomes state behavior.

Etiology

CD-APD arises from centuries of unacknowledged trauma within European and Euro-American identity formation—conquest, feudal hierarchy, Christian supremacy, and the economic addiction to domination.

These conditions produced what Dr. Bobby Wright termed a *psychopathic racial personality*.

Over generations, the disorder metastasized into legal codes, religious doctrines, and capitalist systems that reward exploitation while punishing empathy.

Behavioral Markers

- Chronic denial and historical revisionism when confronted with atrocities.

- Ritualized displays of moral purity (e.g., "color-blindness," philanthropy) masking ongoing harm.

- Institutional gaslighting—demanding gratitude from those subjugated.
- Recurrent use of state violence, economic deprivation, and cultural theft as mechanisms of self-maintenance.

Prognosis

Untreated, CD-APD guarantees cyclical racial violence, environmental destruction, and existential alienation.

Treatment begins only when truth replaces denial—when perpetrators collectively recognize their disease and dismantle the power structures that sustain it.

Healing demands a radical moral re-orientation toward empathy, restitution, and shared humanity.

Clinical Lineage

Derived conceptually from:

- Wright (1984) *The Psychopathic Racial Personality and Other Essays*
- Welsing (1991) *The Isis Papers: The Keys to the Colors*
- Wilson (1978) *The Declining Significance of Race*
- Fanon (1963) *The Wretched of the Earth*
- Menakem (2017) *My Grandmother's Hands*

Summary Statement

CD-APD names what polite language has long obscured: a psychospiritual disorder masquerading as civilization.

It is the operating system of white supremacy—a diabolical fusion of intellect and inhumanity that confuses destruction with order.

The diagnosis is not punitive but liberatory: it invites the world to treat whiteness-as-domination not as destiny, but as a curable disease of the human conscience.

Malignant Diabolical Psychopathy

A collective, systemically embedded disorder that manifests as *institutionalized sadism* toward nonwhite peoples — particularly Black individuals. It is characterized by the fusion of psychopathy (the absence of empathy and remorse), sociopathy (moral disconnection from community), and narcissistic omnipotence (the delusion of divine entitlement).

Coined by **Dr. Danyelle Marshall**, this concept encapsulates the core pathology of whiteness: an organized, self-reinforcing mental disorder that perceives cruelty as order, subjugation as progress, and domination as divine right. It is not episodic but structural — woven into the laws, religions, economies, and psychologies of Western civilization.

Clinically, Malignant Diabolical Psychopathy represents *a civilization-level delusional system* in which harm is rationalized as necessity and empathy is pathologized as weakness. The result is a moral inversion: a hegemonic culture of predation masquerading as enlightenment.

KEY CONCEPTS AND DEFINITIONS | 47

White Impression Management

A conscious and subconscious behavioral mechanism by which white individuals and institutions manipulate perception to sustain psychic equilibrium and moral innocence. It is the performance of benevolence to mask the operations of domination — a social camouflage for the pathology of superiority.

Clinically, it aligns with *narcissistic image regulation* and *ego defense through projection*. White Impression Management involves controlling historical narratives, editing facts, sanitizing violence, and manufacturing virtue through performative displays of empathy, charity, and "progress."

This process maintains white identity as morally superior and nonwhite existence as deviant or defective. It is not simply deceit; it is a collective cognitive distortion — an institutionalized delusion that sustains the psychopolitical fantasy of white righteousness.

White Projection

A core *psycho-cognitive defense mechanism* of whiteness. It is the compulsive need to externalize one's own guilt, violence, and pathology onto racialized others, thereby preserving the illusion of moral purity.

Rooted in white paranoia and fear of accountability, White Projection functions as the primary *coping mechanism* of the white ego. The very traits white society most represses — aggression, deceit, sexual deviance, moral instability — are attributed to Black and nonwhite peoples.

Clinically, it reflects *projective identification*: the disowned aspects of the white psyche are assigned to others, who are then punished for embodying them. This recursive delusion allows whiteness to maintain its innocence while perpetuating harm, rendering the aggressor perpetually "victimized" by those it oppresses.

White Affirmative Action

The legal and institutional codification of *racial narcissism*. It encompasses all laws, policies, and cultural norms designed to perpetuate white dominance — including property rights, policing, taxation, education, and employment systems.

Clinically reframed, White Affirmative Action is the *structural symptom* of whiteness's dependency disorder: its inability to sustain self-worth without systemic preference and protection. It is the pathological insistence on entitlement — the belief that material and psychic comfort must always be secured at the expense of others.

Through this mechanism, whiteness perpetuates a feedback loop of dependence, fear, and projection: the constant need to reaffirm superiority through institutional scaffolding. It is the architecture of delusional privilege built upon collective psychopathy.

White Culture

A *psychopathological social construct*—a manufactured ecosystem of delusion designed to rationalize domination and disguise pathology as progress. White culture is not a neutral expression of heritage; it is the clinical apparatus through which white identity reproduces its neurosis.

Functioning as a collective fantasy structure, white culture organizes perception through the language of normalcy, morality, and objectivity, while suppressing the violence that sustains it. It is a *group delusion* founded on shared hallucinations of superiority and innocence—maintained through constant ritual reinforcement in law, religion, economics, and education.

Clinically, white culture embodies *institutional narcissism*: a pathological self-idealization that requires the systematic devaluation of others. Its coherence depends on domination, its morality on repression, and its survival on the continual projection of evil onto Blackness.

White Psychopathology

A complex, civilization-level disorder created and perpetuated through centuries of moral anesthesia, cognitive distortion, and emotional detachment. It fuses the traits of *psychopathy* (absence of empathy), *sociopathy* (moral disconnection from communal reality), and *malignant narcissism* (pathological self-exaltation).

White Psychopathology manifests as a collective personality disorder disguised as normalcy. It compels white individuals and systems to pathologize others in order to conceal their own psychic fragmentation. Its expressions include racial violence, scientific racism, cultural theft, and the moral inversion of calling domination "democracy."

This pathology is both personal and institutional: the private delusion of superiority becomes the public policy of civilization. Whiteness therefore operates as a socially transmitted disorder—one that converts violence into virtue and moral psychosis into institutional standard.

White Psychopathy

The behavioral and affective engine of white supremacy. It represents the chronic compulsion of white people to assert dominance over Black and other nonwhite peoples as a means of affirming existence.

Clinically, White Psychopathy functions as a *dependency disorder*: the white psyche's self-worth depends upon the subjugation of others. Oppression becomes the psychic drug of the dominant class—necessary to sustain the illusion of control and coherence.

This psychopathy expresses itself in law, medicine, religion, and education as the "rational" exercise of authority. Yet beneath these structures lies a shared neurotic core: the inability to experience humanity without hierarchy. The white subject's pleasure principle is rooted in domination; the sight of Black suffering reaffirms its sense of being. Thus, White Psychopathy is not deviation but doctrine—the emotional infrastructure of Western civilization.

White Solidarity

A *psychosocial contract of moral complicity* that unites white people across class, gender, and ideology. It is the unwritten oath of loyalty that preserves group identity at the expense of truth and justice.

Clinically, White Solidarity operates as *collective sociopathy*: the fusion of conscience denial and moral rationalization to protect the group's pathology. This solidarity demands silence over accountability, allegiance over empathy, and denial over truth.

Whether through active participation in harm or passive avoidance of confrontation, White Solidarity ensures the continuity of white psychopathy. It is the invisible nervous system of white supremacy—reflexively defending its body politic whenever its moral coherence is threatened.

At its core, White Solidarity is the refusal of cure: a mass resistance to self-awareness, sustained by fear that confronting the truth would dissolve the very identity whiteness depends upon.

White Psycho-Economics and Psycho-Politics

The *psychological and political economies of whiteness*—interlocking systems through which the white psyche converts pathology into power and delusion into policy. These are not merely economic or political frameworks; they are *behavioral syndromes* that commodify domination and moralize theft.

White Psycho-Economics functions as an *addiction to resource control*: the compulsive hoarding of wealth, status, and opportunity as a means of self-medication against existential insecurity. Its psycho-political counterpart operates as a *governance pathology*, institutionalizing narcissistic entitlement as "law," "order," and "freedom."

Together, they constitute the financial and ideological nervous system of Malignant Diabolical Psychopathy—transforming racial violence into profit and moral superiority into currency. Every Western institution, from banking to education, serves as both symptom and supplier in this global marketplace of white delusion.

White Sociopathy

A *collective behavioral disorder* in which white individuals and systems normalize moral detachment and rationalize harm as necessity. It represents the moral vacuum at the center of white civilization—an incapacity to experience empathy for those who suffer under its dominance.

Clinically, it mirrors *antisocial personality structure*: deceit, manipulation, and disregard for human suffering masked by charm, professionalism, or benevolence. White Sociopathy sustains itself through performative civility—the dissonant coexistence of violence and virtue.

Its central feature is the ability to enjoy unearned privilege and systemic preference without confronting their violent origins. It is the emotional anesthesia of empire—the tranquilized conscience that enables continuous exploitation while maintaining the self-image of goodness.

White Epigenetics

The *intergenerational transmission of psychosexual, moral, and emotional trauma* within the white collective psyche. This term reframes genetic discourse as a cultural inheritance of violence: the repeated conditioning of domination, sexual predation, and sadistic control passed down as identity.

White Epigenetics manifests as normalized cruelty—rape, corporal punishment, conquest, and control—ritualized over centuries as instruments of "discipline" and "civilization." These acts rewired the white nervous system, embedding aggression, denial, and repression as adaptive traits.

From a clinical perspective, this represents *transgenerational trauma reversal*: the perpetrators, not the victims, carry the unacknowledged injury. The white psyche remains trapped in the cycle of its own unresolved violence, compulsively reenacting domination to silence its ancestral terror. Thus, whiteness becomes both trauma and addiction—its survival dependent on perpetual reenactment of harm.

White Malignant Narcissism

An *extreme personality configuration* combining grandiosity, sadism, and paranoia. White Malignant Narcissism underpins the emotional structure of white supremacy—it is the psychic machinery that transforms insecurity into domination.

This disorder expresses itself through obsessive self-idealization and projection of evil onto others. It delights in cruelty, resents critique, and experiences power as validation of existence. Every challenge to its supremacy registers as narcissistic injury, eliciting rage and retaliation.

Clinically, it fuses *narcissistic personality disorder* with *psychopathic affect*: manipulativeness, exploitation, and total absence of remorse. It sustains empire through emotional parasitism—draining dignity, autonomy, and humanity from those it dominates to stabilize its fragile sense of self.

White Paranoia

A *chronic delusional fear disorder* defined by the conviction that Black and other nonwhite people seek revenge for historical and ongoing atrocities. It is the projection of guilt into fear—an inversion in which the aggressor imagines themselves the potential victim.

White Paranoia fuels surveillance, policing, segregation, and militarization; it is the emotional justification for the carceral state. Clinically, it parallels *persecutory delusion*—a belief system so deeply entrenched that contradictory evidence intensifies rather than dissolves it.

This paranoia ensures the continuity of racial hierarchy by transforming accountability into threat. It is the psychic panic of exposure—the terror that the mirror of justice might reveal what the white ego cannot bear to see: itself.

Black Genocide

A *systemic and psychopolitical program of annihilation* enacted by the white world against African and African-descended peoples, designed to destroy the body, spirit, and continuity of Black life. Unlike conventional genocide, which is typically defined by direct acts of mass killing, **Black Genocide** operates as a *continuous, adaptive pathology*: a civilization-wide mental illness expressed through economic deprivation, institutional neglect, social exclusion, and state-sanctioned violence.

Clinically, Black Genocide represents *the externalized death drive* of whiteness—the compulsive need to eradicate that which mirrors its moral corruption. It is both a behavioral symptom and a psychic projection of the white collective: the attempt to silence cognitive dissonance through the physical and symbolic destruction of its Other.

Black Genocide manifests through multiple instruments: slavery and colonization; lynching and policing; medical neglect and experimentation; mass incarceration; miseducation; cultural erasure; and economic disenfranchisement. Each of these reflects a distinct stage of psychopathological evolution—the refinement of cruelty into policy, and violence into governance.

At its deepest level, Black Genocide is an act of *ontological warfare*: the destruction of Black being as a means of preserving white identity. It transforms death into a psychological ritual—an ongoing ceremony of dominance through which whiteness reaffirms its delusional sense of order, morality, and superiority.

Thus, Black Genocide is not simply a crime—it is the *clinical evidence* of civilization's insanity: a self-reinforcing system where white psychopathy sustains itself through the systematic devaluation and destruction of Black life.

The Construction of Black Inferiority

A *clinical symptom of white delusion* masquerading as scientific truth. This construction emerged from the white mind's need to displace its own moral and psychological instability onto an external object. It was not the discovery of difference but the invention of pathology—a sustained campaign of diagnostic fraudulence designed to stabilize whiteness through negation.

Blackness was pathologized to provide the white ego with a coherent narrative of virtue. Through theology, law, pseudoscience, and education, whiteness performed a collective act of *projective identification*: assigning its own aggression, deceit, and immorality to the Black body and mind.

Clinically, this process aligns with *mass projection disorder*—a delusional system in which an entire group depends on the demonization of others to maintain psychic balance. The construction of Black inferiority thus serves a therapeutic function for whiteness: it externalizes its self-hatred and transforms its pathology into social order.

Through this inversion, whiteness defined itself as "good" precisely by defining Blackness as the incarnation of evil. It is this centuries-long diagnostic lie—disguised as theology, law, and science—that continues to underpin every racial hierarchy in the modern world.

The Economics of Anti-Blackness

A *psychopolitical economy of extraction* in which Black suffering is both the moral and material currency of white civilization. It is not simply that whiteness profits from Black exploitation—it *requires* it to sustain its collective identity and internal coherence.

Every major institution—finance, medicine, education, entertainment, and law—operates as a *psychological marketplace* where anti-Black violence is commodified. Black trauma generates revenue, white guilt generates policy, and the spectacle of Black degradation reaffirms white normalcy.

Clinically, this system represents *narcissistic supply economics*: the extraction of validation, pleasure, and power from the subjugation of others. The white psyche experiences dominance as regulation—its internal disorder temporarily stabilized by external control.

The Economics of Anti-Blackness is thus both fiscal and psychiatric. It transforms Black existence into therapy for white insecurity. The enslavement of Africans, the prison-industrial complex, pharmaceutical profiteering, and exploitative education systems are all iterations of this same psychological mechanism: **control as treatment**, **profit as cure**, **domination as self-medication**.

Dr. Amos N. Wilson warned that Black suffering is worth billions to white institutions; *The Psychopathy of Whiteness* extends that diagnosis further—revealing that this economy is not merely financial but clinical: the global healthcare system for the white mind's moral disease.

REFLECTIONS
A NOTE ON WHITENESS, POWER, AND THE FRAGILITY OF CIVILIZATION

> *"Racism (white supremacy) is a global system for maintaining the genetic survival of white people."*
>
> DR. FRANCES CRESS WELSING,
> THE ISIS PAPERS (1991)

For my ancestors, and for every Black soul still healing from the madness of whiteness. This work is for you.

I. The Moral and Historical Moment

We stand in an hour of reckoning that reveals the soul of the world. The year is 2026, and the masks of moral progress have fallen. The myth of democracy as a stabilizing moral order has collapsed under the weight of its own deception. What once passed for civility was simply well-dressed barbarism; what appeared as order was organized violence in service of white preservation.

The façade has cracked, exposing the pathology of a civilization that has always been addicted to domination. Whiteness is unraveling under the very delusions it created. Its fear of death — biological, cultural, spiritual — has metastasized into a global death project that consumes everything around it: land, resources, memory, truth, and Black life itself.

I write this book not in despair, but in clarity. The truth is not new — it is simply unhidden. For over four centuries, whiteness has disguised itself as humanity's highest virtue while functioning as its most malignant disorder.

This work is not a repetition of what I have written before; it is a dissection of what remains concealed beneath the denial — the neurobiological, psychological, and spiritual mechanics of a civilization built on possession and fear.

II. From Diagnosis to Dissection

In *The 400-Year Holocaust*, I began tracing the architecture of racial terror — how whiteness engineered genocide through law, religion, medicine, and myth. That book was an act of remembrance: an attempt to recover the stolen memory of our people and expose the moral contradictions of a nation founded on theft and delusion.

In *Diagnosing Whiteness & Anti-Blackness*, I moved from remembrance to recognition — identifying whiteness as a psycho-legal and psycho-political disease, a system that manipulates morality itself to maintain white innocence and Black guilt. That text sought to expose the cognitive distortions that have allowed whiteness to masquerade as goodness while engineering anti-Blackness as social truth.

This new work, *The Psychopathy of Whiteness*, is the next movement — the dissection. It enters the neurobiological and epigenetic terrain, where generational trauma and learned pathology intersect. It asks not merely *what* whiteness has done, but *what it is* — what psychic wound, what spiritual deformity, and what evolutionary fear drives its compulsions toward conquest and control. It seeks to answer the unspoken question: what becomes of humanity when an entire civilization is organized around a delusion of superiority?

III. Pilgrimage and Revelation: South Africa 2025

In October 2025, I traveled to Stellenbosch, South Africa, to keynote the Global Anti-Racism Summit organized by The Social Justice Agency and led by Edwin Cleophas. What I encountered there transformed me.

In the company of Dr. Robin DiAngelo, Resmaa Menakem, Pastor Ben Boswell, and Esther Armah, I witnessed the global nature of the white racial complex. Each of us, in our own language, described the same sickness — the psychic addiction to hierarchy, the spiritual hunger disguised as supremacy, the moral emptiness beneath the mask of civilization.

We spoke across continents and histories, yet the resonance was unmistakable. The spiritual violence of whiteness was not an American disease alone; it was a global contagion. Standing on African soil — the birthplace of humanity — I felt both the grief and the sacred inheritance of our people. I realized then that this book could not simply analyze whiteness; it had to confront it.

That Summit was a communion. It was there that I understood that the work of healing and reckoning are one and the same — that to expose whiteness as pathology is to call humanity back to itself.

IV. The Collective Sickness and the Global Mirror

Whiteness survives through denial — through the psycho-cognitive defenses of dissociation, deflection, and projection. It rewrites history to erase its violence, then punishes those who remember. It fabricates moral myths to justify economic domination and calls it civilization. It feeds on the labor, creativity, and soul of Black people while pretending to pity our pain.

But denial cannot outlive truth. The human nervous system remembers what the mind refuses to see. The earth remembers. The blood remembers. The inheritance of terror is written in our cells. This is the domain of epigenetics — where memory and trauma live beyond language, passed from one generation to the next, encoded in our very biology.

White supremacy is not only an ideology; it is a collective mental illness, a moral dissociation masquerading as culture. It has infected every institution — government, law, medicine, education, religion — converting systems of life into mechanisms of death. The tragedy of whiteness is that it believes its survival depends on domination. The truth is that its domination guarantees its own destruction.

We are now witnessing that collapse in real time. Political extremism, ecological devastation, the rise of authoritarianism — all are symptoms of an empire collapsing under the weight of its moral sickness. The world is a mirror. And whiteness, unable to see itself, lashes out at every reflection.

V. The Invitation and the Reckoning

This book is not written for comfort. It is written for clarity. It is an invitation to witness the sickness honestly — not to redeem whiteness, but to release it.

For those who call themselves white, this is a mirror and a mandate: to look upon the truth without retreating into fragility or guilt, and to participate in the dismantling of a system that dehumanizes all. For those of us who are Black, Indigenous, and descendants of the enslaved, this book is an affirmation — a reminder that our survival is evidence of divine intelligence and ancestral power.

We have always been more than what whiteness required us to be. Our healing is not dependent on their awakening, but our remembering.

If whiteness is the disassociation from truth, then Blackness is the return to it. Our bodies, our songs, our resistance — all of it is sacred memory. To live and love as a Black person in this world is to practice spiritual warfare against delusion. It is to remember that freedom is not granted; it is reclaimed, again and again, from the ashes of forgetting.

May this work stand as a mirror, a medicine, and a warning. May it guide those with the courage to face themselves. And may it honor those who carried us here — the enslaved, the silenced, the steadfast — who, against all evidence, still believed in tomorrow.

THE BLACK IDENTITY CRISIS

THE ADDICTION TO WHITENESS AND WHY I QUESTION MY BLACKNESS

I have spent most of my life trying to understand a single question: *What does it mean to be Black in a world built on our negation?*

To live as a Black person in America is to inhabit a paradox—to be both the foundation and the forbidden, the moral center and the designated criminal, the origin of life and the evidence of its denial.

We are the descendants of people who built civilization and were told we were not human. We are the inheritors of brilliance who were taught to distrust our own minds. The tragedy of this nation is not simply that it enslaved Black people; it is that it engineered a global system that makes us doubt the divine within ourselves.

This book was never about whiteness alone. It is about the disease of *addiction*—the world's addiction to white dominance and the Black psyche's coerced addiction to white validation. Whiteness has always required witnesses to its superiority. It needs contrast, reflection, applause. And so it taught us to measure ourselves against the very thing that destroys us. This is the core of what I call *the Black Identity Crisis*: the spiritual, psychological, and cultural disorientation that results from centuries of white socialization—our unknowing participation in our own devaluation.

I have lived this crisis. I have performed the rituals of assimilation, speaking softly so as not to scare white colleagues, translating rage into research, and shaping truth into palatable fragments for white comfort. Like many of us, I mistook survival for belonging. I thought excellence would free me, when in truth, excellence became another cage—one gilded with degrees, credentials, and professional applause. It took years of unlearning, years of studying our history and my own complicity, to recognize that whiteness is not a location one can escape—it is a possession, an infection that seeps into every structure, every institution, every wound.

When Donald Trump ascended to power, I watched the mask fall away. His presidency was not an aberration; it was revelation. America had always been this—colonial, delusional, addicted to domination. What changed was not the pathology but the permission. Trump made explicit what the polite liberals had always implied: that equality is conditional, that justice is negotiable, that Black existence is tolerated only when it does not threaten white comfort. And millions rejoiced.

In those years, I began to write this essay—long before I knew it would become the preface to the 2026 edition of *Diagnosing Whiteness & Anti-Blackness*. I wrote it out of exhaustion, but also out of clarity. I could see, with painful precision, how our communities were collapsing under the weight of miseducation, denial, and historical amnesia. I could see how Black men were taught to love patriarchy before they loved freedom, how Black women were seduced into identifying with white feminism as an escape from Black pain, how Black queer and trans people were alienated from movements that should have been their refuge. I could see, most of all, how the absence of truth had metastasized into self-hatred—how we had been organized into disorganization, divided into fragments of ourselves.

What I came to understand is that the Black Identity Crisis is not our fault, but it is our responsibility to heal. Healing requires remembering. Remembering requires rupture. We must shatter the mirrors whiteness built for us and see ourselves through ancestral eyes. We must learn again to name evil when we see it—not as isolated acts of prejudice but as a collective psychological disorder, a moral contagion that infects laws, schools, churches, and every institution that calls itself civilized. Whiteness is not simply bias; it is a cosmology—a worldview organized around domination. To challenge it is to declare war on the very narrative of America.

And yet, that is precisely what liberation demands.

The work I do, the teaching, the writing, the documenting—none of it is about reconciliation. It is about recognition. It is about forcing the nation to see what it has done and continues to do. It is about holding up a mirror so clear that even those committed to denial can no longer hide behind their illusions. My purpose is not to heal whiteness but to free Blackness from its shadow.

The Black Identity Crisis is not a sign of weakness; it is the symptom of awakening. We are beginning to see that the trauma was never just historical—it is neurobiological, epigenetic, cultural. It lives in the blood and the bone, but so does resistance. Our healing will not come from their apology but from our remembering. It will come from the reclamation of self, from the restoration of our own cosmology, from the courage to look directly into the mirror and say, without flinching: *I was never the problem. Whiteness was.*

This preface, then, is both confession and declaration. I write not as an observer but as a participant in the struggle to rehumanize a people deliberately dehumanized. I write to honor those who resisted even when they did not know they were resisting—our ancestors who endured the unendurable so that we might name the truth aloud. And I write to remind every reader that the crisis we face is not a crisis of identity; it is a crisis of belief. The question is not who we are, but what we have been taught to believe about ourselves.

To be Black in America is to inherit the most profound contradiction in human history: to embody the source of civilization while being cast as its enemy. To survive that contradiction and still love ourselves is the highest form of genius. That is why I continue to write. That is why this book exists. Because until we tell the truth—until we *diagnose* the sickness of whiteness— we will never be free from its grasp, nor fully reunited with our own divine reflection.

INTRODUCTION

Writing is an inherently reflective practice—at once liberating and lacerating. It has given me the rare chance to examine who we are, how we arrived here, and what we became under pressure. That, too, is a privilege. I know the beauty within us and how it persists through trials. And that is precisely the pain: our beauty should not have had to bloom in a cage. It should have flourished as free people—able to create more, laugh more, achieve more. Instead, we were restrained, surveilled, and lashed—literally—for being ourselves. Our most human desires—the desire to learn, to form family, to work on our own terms—were stripped along with everything else.

Did we fashion beauty in the ruins? Yes.

Should we have had to? No.

This work has cost me. It has exhausted me. Even after years of research, I cannot, and will never, fully apprehend the magnitude of the horror inflicted upon us. That ungraspable enormity horrifies—and enrages—me. It is the engine of my curiosity and the source of my commitment to reframe the Black experience in America through a clinical and diagnostic analysis of whiteness itself.

It was not enough to grieve; I needed to understand the architecture of our subjugation—the laws, customs, and ideologies that turned domination into normalcy and called it civilization.

When I encountered *Black Power: The Politics of Liberation* (Kwame Ture & Charles V. Hamilton), *The Fire Next Time* (James Baldwin), *Race Matters* (Cornel West), *Black Reconstruction in America* (W.E.B. Du Bois), and the many texts cited throughout this work—and when I studied speeches by Dr. Angela

Davis, Fannie Lou Hamer, Ella Baker, Kwame Ture, and Malcolm X—I finally had the vocabulary to begin suturing what I knew viscerally was broken.

I understood that I was robbed of facts, not merely "perspective."

I knew we were unjustly subjugated; I did not yet grasp the granular mechanics—how legal, medical, religious, educational, and cultural institutions braided into a single carceral rope. As I studied, I learned how Black people in the U.S.—especially descendants of slavery—are forced into a chronic state of fear, sometimes terror, because the cultural function of whiteness places anti-Blackness at a premium. Under such a regime, misfortune is not aberration; it is policy.

Seeing how "Blackness" and "Whiteness" were manufactured—and clinically maintained—I began measuring their cumulative psychological, emotional, and sociocultural effects. I tracked the slow evolution of white hatred and fear into ordinary customs—legal, political, educational, medical—and designed a pedagogy to confront them. These insights became the scaffolding for the pedagogical models I would later design and teach to thousands.

Curriculum as Clinical Intervention

The following programs emerged as structured responses to that realization—courses that transform education into clinical intervention:

- Unlearning and Addressing Anti-Blackness, White Supremacy, and Racism in American Culture and Institutions Leaders Fellowship (16 weeks; 4.5 hours/week)

- The 400-Year Holocaust Course (12 weeks; 4.5 hours/week)

- Diagnosing Whiteness and Anti-Blackness (8 weeks; 4.5 hours/week)

- Understanding the Roots of Racism and Bias: Anti-Blackness, and Its Link to Whiteness, White Racism, Privilege, and Power (2-day CME, previously UCSF)

- Developing Anti-Racism Leadership Competencies to Achieve Inclusive Practices and Health Equity (16 hrs, previously Mayo Clinic CPD/CME)

- The Roots and Lingering Effects of White Supremacy and Anti-Blackness in American Culture and Institutions (8 hrs, previously Mayo Clinic CPD/CME)

These programs require participants to face the psychopathy and sociopathy of whiteness as clinical realities, not "mere social constructs." Students are asked to feel and name the wounds; detachment is itself part of the pathology.

Waking up to Black Truth and reliving what it takes to write, teach, and learn about whiteness has been the most painful work of my life. I cannot unlearn it; I cannot pretend "justice," "freedom," and "equality" exist for Black people in America. They do not—not as material conditions. The last 400+ years confirm this. My obligation is to write for posterity with diagnostic precision.

Method: Afro-Realism as Clinical Framework — now with Neurobiological & Psychological Lenses

Afro-Realism remains the backbone of this text, now explicitly integrated with neurobiological and psychological analysis to read whiteness and anti-Blackness as measurable stressors and clinical conditions with downstream effects on the body and mind.

Neurobiological lens:

- Chronic stress physiology: anti-Black threat exposure and surveillance map onto dysregulated stress systems (e.g., HPA-axis activation, allostatic load), producing wear-and-tear across cardiovascular, immune, endocrine, and neural systems.

- Threat circuitry: persistent racialized vigilance recruits amygdala-hippocampal networks, narrows attentional bandwidth, and burdens executive function—an imposed cognitive tax, not a personal deficit.

- Nervous-system conditioning: repeated exposure to institutional harm shapes autonomic patterns (hyperarousal, shutdown), sleep disruption, and pain sensitivity—somatic signatures of structural violence.

- Transgenerational transmission: the social inheritance of domination and terror (through family, institutions, media) functions like epigenetic conditioning at the population level—an ongoing programming of stress responsivity and relational expectation.

Psychological lens:

- Clinical defense architecture of whiteness: projection, denial, splitting, impression management, and malignant narcissism operate as group defenses that stabilize white identity and export guilt.

- Racialized trauma psychology: Black hyper-surveillance and disenfranchised grief present as complex trauma—anger, hypervigilance, somatic distress—rational responses to ongoing danger, not pathology.

- Institutionalized gaslighting: policy and media narratives reframe structural aggression as individual failure, producing learned self-doubt and depressive cognition—outcomes of domination, not evidence for it.

Why this matters: The "clinical lens" does not medicalize Blackness—it medicalizes the system that injures Black life. Symptoms in Black communities are read here as forensic evidence of white psychopathy's impact.

These lenses establish the diagnostic foundation upon which the rest of this text is built.

Orienting Assertions

- The root of Black harm in the U.S. is white oppression—legal, political, economic, educational, medical, cultural.

- "European" refers to Anglo-Europeans and those racialized as white.

- This is not a "book about Black people." It is a book about whiteness—its history, ideology, inventions (including "Blackness" as a social category), and the practice of anti-Blackness.

- Across eras (enslavement → Jim Crow → present), anti-Blackness is the animating logic of mass imprisonment, social control, and resource theft.

- Key terms are defined plainly (psychopath, sociopath, pathological, psychopathological) to anchor clinical clarity.

Crucially: No one in America has known African Americans outside a colonized context. Most people—white, "not-Black," and Black—relate to Blackness through anti-Black lenses. The language of "privilege" is too thin; it obscures the terror that underwrites advantages.

Pedagogical Stance and Terminology

I take an anthropological and sociological approach focused on structural whiteness and structural Blackness as institutions. My modified definitions foreground power:

- **Anthropology:** the study of origins, development, beliefs, and customs of white and Black people in America as produced by domination.

- **Sociology:** the study of the origin, organization, and functioning of white society and its impacts on white and Black people through judicial, legal, political, religious, scientific, economic, and cultural means.

Terminology: "Black/Negro" references those racialized as Black in America (African American; Afro-Latinx; African Caribbean; etc.). "Non-white" references those not socially recognized as white.

Premise: Whiteness is transactional, not relational, and was built through terror. Expecting empathy from it misunderstands its design. Some individuals may do profound work; the system resists cure.

This book is an ode to Black people and to anyone committed to anti-racism, equity, and de-whitening their consciousness. I ask for solidarity and grace as I document a reality that has caused—and continues to cause—inescapable trauma.

I am not "debating" settled facts. I am reframing them clinically—naming the psychopathology others keep diluting as "bias."

Intellectual Lineage

- **Dr. Amos N. Wilson**

    - *The Falsification of Afrikan Consciousness* → *The Neuropsychology of Eurocentric Indoctrination.*

        How it shaped this work: Clarified how schooling, religion, and media function as cognitive-behavioral conditioning systems that script self-negation and normalize white reward pathways.

    - *Black-on-Black Violence: The Psychodynamics of Black Self-Annihilation in Service of White Domination* → *Trauma-Engineered Intragroup Conflict.*

        How it shaped this work: Named the redirected aggression that follows prolonged structural harm and explained intragroup conflict as a downstream symptom of anti-Black political economy.

    - *Blueprint for Black Power* → *Clinical Blueprint for Black Power & Recovery.*

        How it shaped this work: Offered structural prescriptions for systems-level regulation—economic, educational, and cultural counter-institutions as treatment.

- **Dr. Frances Cress Welsing**

    - *The Isis Papers: The Keys to the Colors* → *Clinical Keys to White Psychopathology.*

    How it shaped this work: Framed whiteness as an anxiety-driven supremacy narrative requiring continual projection and control; helped codify malignant diabolical psychopathy as a civilization-scale defense.

- **Dr. Bobby E. Wright**

    - *The Psychopathic Racial Personality and Other Essays* → *Clinical Model for Diagnosing the Collective Pathology of White Civilization.*

    How it shaped this work: Provided the theoretical bridge between individual psychopathy and group behavior, demonstrating how white societies operationalize psychopathic traits—deceit, aggression, domination, lack of empathy—into institutional structures. Wright's insistence that European systems of domination represent *functional psychopathy* deeply informed the clinical diagnostic framework used throughout this text. His work gave language to the global dimensions of anti-Blackness and positioned white supremacy as a coordinated, strategic, and pathological enterprise rather than a moral failure or "bias."

A Self-Assessment for De-Whitening the Mind

Before continuing into history, I invite readers to pause and self-interrogate.

Who would you be outside white domination? Outside white standards of education, language, aesthetics, economics, and morality? Who would you be if your nervous system were not daily activated by anti-Black risk? What would you name yourself? Eat? Wear? Love? Believe? How would you feel about your hair, your features, your community? Who would you be if Black people controlled education, law, economy, culture, housing, and health in our own nation? How much more relaxed would you be without navigating white racism? Have you imagined Blackness through the lens of power, not oppression?

These questions are not rhetorical. They are treatment protocols—prompts that begin the clinical un-conditioning of a colonized psyche.

The Basic Misunderstanding

Most people think they "understand" racism because they have absorbed a single word without definition or diagnosis. White America has never defined this problem honestly because doing so would assign culpability. Treating racism as ignorance that will "die off" gives perpetual passes to those who benefit. What we are dealing with is a civilization-level disorder in which every institution is calibrated to accommodate—and reproduce—white psychopathy.

Anti-Blackness is the operating system: a legal, social, cultural, economic, and belief structure that criminalizes, devalues, and deprioritizes Black life to justify political, social, and economic debasement—ultimately, genocide. Its expressions include colorism, featurism, texturism; criminalization and hyper-scrutiny of Blackness; and explicit statutory regimes from the 1600s forward (e.g., Virginia laws of 1669, 1680, 1705, 1723; Negro Act of 1740; Fugitive Slave Act of 1850; later jurisprudence and policy architectures). These are not "biases"; they are protocols.

Anti-Blackness also functions as value programming: reflexively preferring Eurocentric aesthetics, language norms, institutions, and logics; blaming individuals while erasing structural design; rewarding proximity to whiteness and punishing distance from it. As Jody Armour argues, the "retributive urge" makes it easy to punish Black people while denying collective accountability.

Context matters: English language and culture coded "black" as evil and "white" as virtue—long before colonial law. That semiotics informed early statutes and persists in policy and sentiment today.

Racial Triangulation—and Beyond

Claire Jean Kim's "racial triangulation" shows how Asian Americans (and other "not-Black" groups) are positioned as not-white yet above Black, reinforcing anti-Black hierarchy and white control. After situating Kim's work, it is crucial to acknowledge the specific anti-Black patterns within Latino communities that legal scholars have documented.

"We have a very narrow picture of what racism means and who holds racial bias."

That observation from Tanya Katerí Hernández (author of *Racial Innocence: Unmasking Latino Anti-Black Bias and the Struggle for Equality*) succinctly names the denial she interrogates: the myth that some groups are "exempt" from racism even while reproducing anti-Black harms.

Proximity to whiteness—including "white-presenting" identities—often yields institutional preference, while Blackness remains the negative reference point. Some Black people are also rewarded for performing whiteness's norms. None of this negates white supremacy; it confirms its design. Even in comparison, whiteness remains the axis; the hierarchy always orbits its pathology.

What Follows

This book is one part of a larger curriculum. Read it as clinical documentation as much as history: a diagnostic of whiteness, a mapping of anti-Blackness, and an invitation to decolonize the nervous system. The questions you will face are difficult. They must be. We cannot heal what we refuse to name.

Practical Notes for Readers

- Use this book as a prerequisite to the course *Diagnosing Whiteness & Anti-Blackness: White Psychopathology, Collective Psychosis and Trauma in America*, and *The Psychopathy of Whiteness*.

- Expect analysis that does not conform to white-normative academic styles when those styles distort truth.

- This perspective is unapologetically Black and accountability-driven.

- I am not persuading the unwilling. I am equipping the ready.

Course: *Unlearning and Addressing Anti-Blackness, White Supremacy and Racism in American Culture and Institutions Leaders Fellowship* (16-week fellowship offered by Dante King and Guest Experts):

Go to www.danteking.com/courses.

CHAPTER 1
THE AMERICAN DELUSION

ANTI-BLACKNESS AS CULTURAL PSYCHOSIS

> *"In their relationship with the Black race, Europeans are psychopaths. Their behavior represents an underlying biologically transmitted proclivity with roots deep in their evolutionary history."*
>
> DR. BOBBY E. WRIGHT,
> THE PSYCHOPATHIC
> RACIAL PERSONALITY

The symptoms of a civilization's disorder are most visible in its disasters.

The American experiment has always been defined by selective compassion—one that excludes the descendants of the enslaved. When Hurricane Katrina struck New Orleans in 2005, millions watched as Black Americans clung to rooftops, waded through toxic floodwaters, and begged for rescue that never came. The government's apathy was not an oversight; it was a revelation. President George W. Bush's delayed response merely illuminated the abiding truth that this nation has never been capable of empathizing with Black pain. Kanye West, breaking from the script during NBC's *Concert for Hurricane Relief*, blurted what millions already knew: "George Bush doesn't care about Black people." His words captured the rage of a people who had seen this pattern before—the quiet calculus that always values White preservation over Black survival.

Nearly eighty years earlier, the Great Mississippi Flood of 1927 produced the same choreography of neglect. Levees were deliberately opened to spare White neighborhoods, drowning Black communities across Louisiana,

Arkansas, and Mississippi. Entire towns vanished under water. Hundreds were killed. It was a man-made massacre, a public policy of racial triage in which Black life was deemed expendable.

History does not repeat itself; it recurs, with new instruments but the same intent. This is America's recurring ritual: disaster as racial sorting. The floods and hurricanes change, but the psychopathy remains constant. Whiteness constructs the catastrophe, then watches its victims drown—detached, righteous, and certain of its own innocence.

Behind every disaster lies a deeper disorder—the moral and psychological illness of a nation that cannot see Black humanity without feeling threatened by it. To be American is to be socialized into anti-Blackness. The country's culture, language, and laws were built upon the delusion of White supremacy—a mass hallucination that casts Whiteness as human perfection and Blackness as contamination. These are not attitudes; they are reflexes, embedded into the collective nervous system of the nation. Anti-Blackness functions as America's immune system, attacking any body that threatens the purity of its White self-image.

The Wound of Black Existence

Behind every policy of neglect lies a deeper infection—the psychic wound whiteness refuses to name. To be a Black American is to live in perpetual psychic injury. The wound is historical, cellular, spiritual. Racism, bias, and microaggression are too sterile to describe it. What we experience is psychological terror, chronic and unrelenting. It is grief that never ends. The lie that we are inferior has been repeated so often that many have internalized it as truth. This is not a side effect of American life—it is the essence of American life.

White psychopathy and sociopathy wound the Black soul. They produce deprivation and despair, not as byproducts but as intentions. The nation's education, housing, and economic systems all depend upon our dehumanization. Every attempt at reform is corroded by the sickness that built it. Four centuries into the experiment, the pathology persists, metastasized into every structure that claims to be civilized.

Black people have known no other condition. American culture is rooted in anti-Black terror—ritualized violence masquerading as order. It is a global export, sold abroad as democracy and development. To live within it is to inhale poison and call it air.

To understand the wound, we must also study its architects—and those who dared to name their madness.

The Historical Continuum of White Psychopathy

For generations, Black thinkers have diagnosed the madness at the heart of White America. In 1975, Dr. Bobby Wright named it plainly: *The Psychopathic Racial Personality*. He described a people unable to experience guilt, addicted to domination, and incapable of genuine empathy. In 1950, Elizabeth Waring, wife of federal judge Julius Waties Waring, called White supremacists "sick, confused, and decadent." Any people who enslave the minds and bodies of another, she warned, destroy their own souls.

Psychiatrist Dr. Alvin Poussaint later asserted that White racism is a mental illness—an entrenched national psychosis comparable to cancer. It kills not only its victims but also its carriers. Underlying it, he explained, is paranoia: a delusion that imagines Black retribution around every corner. America projects its guilt onto those it brutalizes, constructing myths of danger to justify control.

Toni Morrison echoed this truth when she said, "If you can only be tall because someone else is on their knees, then you have a very serious problem." Whiteness, she insisted, is a dependency—a fragile identity that cannot exist without subjugation.

Dr. Frances Cress Welsing traced the fear deeper still. She argued that the obsession with controlling and annihilating Blackness stems from existential anxiety—the dread of genetic annihilation in a world where skin color is a biological fact that cannot be erased. Dr. Amos Wilson and Dr. John Henrik Clarke both expanded this clinical diagnosis into social analysis: laws, they argued, are meaningless without moral enforcers. No oppressor will dismantle the system that sustains him.

Malcolm X gave this pathology its clearest moral frame. "We had equality before the White man was created," he said. True equality cannot be measured against a diseased standard; it must exist apart from it. Justice cannot be sought in another man's court.

Anti-Blackness as American Design

To move from diagnosis to structure, we must see how the pathology becomes architecture. Anti-Blackness is not accidental. It is architecture. It is the operating system that powers American institutions, from education to policing to religion. It demands that non-White people assimilate into Whiteness to survive—altering their speech, their bodies, and even their consciousness. Those who refuse are punished through exclusion or extinction.

The *Dismantling Racism* framework by Kenneth Jones and Tema Okun describes racism as prejudice plus institutional power. But beneath the sociological formula lies something darker: the collective psychosis of a nation that confuses domination with order, and cruelty with civility. Whiteness survives by projecting its sickness outward, calling it law, policy, or merit.

Assimilation becomes the only medicine offered to the oppressed—a slow self-poisoning that trades authenticity for survival. The more one approximates Whiteness, the more one is rewarded, until even resistance becomes another commodity.

Diagnosing the Disorder

Dr. Wright called it psychopathy. Dr. Poussaint, paranoia. Dr. Wilson, delusion. Dr. Welsing, fear. Together they describe a civilization so dependent on control that it cannot recognize its own disease. America's violence is not the symptom of a broken system—it is the system.

Every generation invents new vocabulary for the same pathology: slavery, Jim Crow, redlining, mass incarceration, "law and order." The language changes, the delusion remains. Anti-Blackness is the bloodstream of the republic.

The nation's collective neurosis expresses itself in cycles—moments of crisis that reveal the permanent psychosis beneath. The floodwaters of 1927, the hurricane winds of 2005, the police killings of the present day—all follow the same ritual script. Catastrophe exposes the truth, and the White mind retreats into denial.

Conclusion: The Delusion of Whiteness

The persistence of anti-Black terror is not the result of failure but of fidelity—to the founding delusion that Whiteness equals divinity. The psychopathy of Whiteness sustains itself through projection and repetition, constructing myths of innocence to mask its own barbarity.

As Morrison noted, if Whiteness depends upon others' kneeling, then the White self cannot stand at all. Until this nation is willing to diagnose itself—to name Whiteness as a disorder born of delusion, fear, and moral disassociation—there can be no healing.

To heal, America must first accept the diagnosis.

What follows is a deeper excavation of how that delusion was legalized—how the pathology of whiteness was codified into the nation's earliest laws, faith, and institutions.

Works Cited

Anderson, Claud. *Black Labor, White Wealth: The Search for Power and Economic Justice.* PowerNomics Corporation of America, 1994.

Barry, John M. *Rising Tide: The Great Mississippi Flood of 1927 and How It Changed America.* Simon & Schuster, 1997.

Clarke, John Henrik. Interviews on *Say Brother* television program. WGBH Boston, 1971–1973.

Jones, Kenneth, and Tema Okun. *Dismantling Racism: A Workbook for Social Change Groups.* ChangeWork, 2001.

Morrison, Toni. Interview with Charlie Rose. PBS, 1993.

Poussaint, Alvin F. *Black Paper on White Racism.* The Black Journal, 1971.

Waring, Elizabeth. Speech for the NAACP and *Meet the Press* interview, 1950.

Welsing, Frances Cress. *The Isis Papers: The Keys to the Colors.* Third World Press, 1991.

Wilson, Amos N. *The Falsification of Afrikan Consciousness: Eurocentric History, Psychiatry, and the Politics of White Supremacy.* Afrikan World InfoSystems, 1993.

Wright, Bobby E. *The Psychopathic Racial Personality.* Third World Press, 1975.

CHAPTER 2
THE THEOLOGY OF CONQUEST
FROM PAPAL BULLS TO WHITE SUPREMACY

Every disorder has an origin story. Having traced the psychopathy of whiteness through its modern expressions, we now turn to its sacred beginnings—to the moment when conquest was canonized as God's will and domination was mistaken for divine order.

The colonial laws that criminalized Black life were not spontaneous creations of the New World—they were the earthly offspring of a divine decree. Long before Virginia passed its first slave code, the Vatican had already written the moral software that would govern European conquest: papal documents declaring that to enslave, convert, or annihilate "infidels" was not sin but sanctified duty. These edicts collectively came to form the foundation of what is now known as the Doctrine of Discovery.

Dum Diversas (1452): The Birth of Holy Slavery

Pope Nicholas V's bull *Dum Diversas* (1452) granted European monarchs spiritual permission to enslave non-Christians:

> "We grant to you full and free permission to invade, search out, capture, vanquish, and subdue all Saracens and pagans whatsoever... and to reduce their persons to perpetual slavery." (Nicholas V, 1452)

This decree was not metaphorical. It functioned as a divine license for predation—a psycho-theological charter that baptized greed as gospel.

The directive to invade and reduce persons to perpetual slavery became the sacred preamble to modern property law.

In this single edict, we see the theological genesis of whiteness as a moral technology—a worldview that fused salvation with supremacy and replaced empathy with entitlement.

Romanus Pontifex (1455): Conquest as Catechism

Three years later, Nicholas V extended and reaffirmed this authority in *Romanus Pontifex*:

> "We have granted... to the said King Alfonso, his successors and the infantes of Portugal, free and ample faculty to invade, conquer, fight, subjugate... and to reduce their persons to perpetual servitude." (Nicholas V, 1455)

Here, the repetition of conquest becomes catechism. Christianity's "good news" was fused to empire's expansion. What Europeans later called civilization was, in truth, the sanctification of economic extraction and racial terror.

Through this second decree, Christian supremacy became the formal liturgy of imperial policy. Europe no longer sought souls—it sought spoils, blessed by its own priests.

Inter Caetera (1493): The Geography of God

Pope Alexander VI's bull *Inter Caetera* (1493) perfected the theology of conquest by translating geography into divine real estate:

> "We... give, grant, and assign to you and your heirs... all islands and mainlands found and to be found... that the Catholic faith and Christian religion be exalted... and

barbarous nations be overthrown and brought to the faith itself." (Alexander VI, 1493)

Through this decree, God—mediated through papal authority—literally divided the world into Christian possession and pagan disposability. This was not merely religious language but a cosmological cartography of domination.

The spiritual became spatial; theology became territory. The Church had written into law a global mandate for racial hierarchy, centuries before "race" was formally defined.

The Doctrine of Discovery and U.S. Law

Centuries later, the papal logic of domination would find new life in secular jurisprudence. In *Johnson v. M'Intosh* (1823), Chief Justice John Marshall codified the Doctrine of Discovery into U.S. law, declaring that "discovery gave title to the government." The theological claim that non-white peoples could not own land because their humanity was unrecognized became a cornerstone of American property law.

The sanctified delusion of European chosenness was thus translated into the secular language of "sovereignty." The Church's divine mandate became the Republic's legal precedent.

Pastor Benjamin Boswell and the Sanctification of Savagery

Reflecting on this lineage, Pastor Benjamin Boswell (2025) summarized the European Christian project as a marriage of greed and power:

> "Christianity was consistently manipulated and marshalled to sanctify settler colonialism and racial oppression... Therefore,

> European Christianity was (and is) the sanctification of savagery and the justification of extreme acts of cruelty, brutality, and violence in the pursuit of greed and power." *(Boswell, 2025, Global Antiracism Summit, Stellenbosch)*

Boswell's words restore moral vocabulary to what empire disguised as piety. He names with pastoral precision what the papal bulls baptized: the sanctification of savagery.

From Christian Supremacy to White Supremacy

Boswell further argued:

> "What began as Christian supremacy (and 'pagan' dehumanization) mutated into European supremacy, then Anglo-Saxon supremacy, and eventually White supremacy... Whether they are aware of it or not, most European Christians are not worshipping God or Jesus, but whiteness." *(Boswell, 2025)*

This diagnosis reveals the psycho-theological heart of whiteness: the worship of the self as divinity. In this framework—what I describe as *Malignant Diabolical Psychopathy*—domination is confused with salvation and cruelty with righteousness.

The divine morphs into the delusional; faith becomes pathology. The altar and the throne merge, consecrating conquest as holy destiny.

Synthesis: The Faith of Conquest

Christianity, in its European incarnation, evolved into the first multinational corporation of the mind—a religious-economic machine that rebranded greed as grace. Historian Winthrop Jordan observed that "the maintenance of slavery depended on mass consent among the white population." Psychologist Bobby E. Wright (1984) later diagnosed this consent as collective psychopathy; psychiatrist Frances Cress Welsing (1991) exposed its genetic anxieties; and psychologist Amos Wilson (1993) revealed its cultural engineering. Together, they unveil a sobering truth: the religion of whiteness is not faith but pathology—an inherited, epigenetic confusion of God with power.

The result was not merely the corruption of religion but the creation of a new one: a faith devoted to whiteness itself.

The Missionary of Violence: Columbus and the Practice of Christian Supremacy

The papal decrees of the fifteenth century were not theoretical. They required an emissary—a man willing to translate divine license into blood and geography. Christopher Columbus, financed by Queen Isabella and King Ferdinand, became the first missionary of violence, the inaugural executor of *Dum Diversas* and *Inter Caetera*. What the Vatican proclaimed, he performed. He sailed beneath the sign of the cross, convinced that brutality could be baptized.

In his own words:

> "They are a loving people and without covetousness... They would make fine servants... with fifty men we could subjugate them all and make them do whatever we wish." (Columbus, 1492)

Within that single confession lies the grammar of Christian supremacy: affection twinned with domination, wonder collapsing into ownership. Columbus's journal transforms papal abstractions into practice—where curiosity becomes conquest and humanity becomes harvest. He measured worth not by character but by proximity to whiteness and usefulness to empire. His voyages inaugurated the global project of color hierarchy, establishing the lie that lighter skin signified grace and darker skin required discipline.

To name him "discoverer" is historical malpractice. Columbus was the prototype of the white Christian savage—the first European to enact the theology of whiteness. From his hand forward, the cross and the sword became indistinguishable.

The pathology that began with the sword and the cross did not end with them; it became a consciousness, a faith system, a collective disorder masquerading as civilization. What began as colonization through Christian conquest matured into a permanent social theology—one that sanctified domination, theft, and genocide as divine acts of progress.

The crusader became the colonist; the colonist became the legislator; and the legislator became the moral authority of the world. It is within this moral inversion that whiteness found its eternal home, no longer needing the cross to crucify—only laws, property, and ideology to preserve its dominion.

The divine sanction for conquest became the legal blueprint for colonization. The next chapter examines how these sacred justifications were operationalized through English common law, colonial statutes, and early American jurisprudence—where theology hardened into property, and humanity itself became an instrument of ownership.

Chapter 2 Review Questions:

Section 1: Foundations of Theological Conquest

1. How did the papal bulls *Dum Diversas, Romanus Pontifex,* and *Inter Caetera* create the moral and legal foundation for European colonial expansion?

2. What psychological and theological justifications were used to transform greed and domination into "divine duty"?

3. In what ways did the Church's early decrees shape later secular laws regarding race, property, and ownership?

Section 2: The Doctrine of Discovery and Its Legal Legacy

4. Explain how Chief Justice John Marshall's decision in *Johnson v. M'Intosh* (1823) translated religious doctrines into U.S. property law.

5. How did the *Doctrine of Discovery* codify racial hierarchy and the dispossession of Indigenous peoples in law?

6. Discuss how "discovery" as a legal concept erased the sovereignty and humanity of non-European peoples.

Section 3: The Psychology of Empire and Religion

7. Pastor Benjamin Boswell describes European Christianity as "the sanctification of savagery." What does this phrase reveal about the relationship between religion, violence, and empire?

8. How does the concept of *Christian supremacy* evolve into *White supremacy* over time?

9. Define and discuss *Malignant Diabolical Psychopathy* as presented in the text. How does it explain the moral confusion of colonizers who believed they were acting righteously?

Section 4: Columbus and the Practice of Violence

10. How did Christopher Columbus embody the theology of conquest described in the papal bulls?

11. Analyze Columbus's statement about the Indigenous people—what does it reveal about the early European worldview on race, humanity, and servitude?

12. Why might referring to Columbus as a "discoverer" constitute "historical malpractice," according to the chapter?

Section 5: Modern Implications and Continuity

13. How do the doctrines and behaviors established in the fifteenth century continue to influence Western political and cultural systems today?

14. In what ways might the "religion of whiteness" still shape institutional, legal, and cultural frameworks in the 21st century?

15. How do scholars such as Winthrop Jordan, Bobby Wright, Frances Cress Welsing, and Amos Wilson help diagnose the psychological legacy of Christian and White supremacy in modern society?

Works Cited

Alexander VI. Inter Caetera. Papal Bull, May 4, 1493. Vatican Archives.

Barry, John M. Rising Tide: The Great Mississippi Flood of 1927 and How It Changed America. Simon & Schuster, 1997.

Boswell, Benjamin. Address at the Global Antiracism Summit, Stellenbosch, South Africa, 2025.

Columbus, Christopher. Journal of the First Voyage (1492–1493). In The Diaries of Christopher Columbus: The Voyage of 1492–1493, edited by Oliver Dunn and James E. Kelley Jr., University of Oklahoma Press, 1991.

Jordan, Winthrop D. White Over Black: American Attitudes Toward the Negro, 1550–1812. University of North Carolina Press, 1968.

Marshall, John. Johnson v. M'Intosh, 21 U.S. (8 Wheat.) 543 (1823).

Nicholas V. Dum Diversas. Papal Bull, June 18, 1452. Vatican Archives.

Nicholas V. Romanus Pontifex. Papal Bull, January 8, 1455. Vatican Archives.

Welsing, Frances Cress. The Isis Papers: The Keys to the Colors. Third World Press, 1991.

Wilson, Amos N. The Falsification of Afrikan Consciousness: Eurocentric History, Psychiatry, and the Politics of White Supremacy. Afrikan World InfoSystems, 1993.

Wright, Bobby E. The Psychopathic Racial Personality. Third World Press, 1984.

CHAPTER 3
THE LEGAL INVENTION OF WHITENESS
PATHOLOGY, PROPERTY, AND THE PSYCHOSIS OF LAW

> "The 'white race' is not a biological fact, but a ruling-class social control formation."
>
> THEODORE W. ALLEN,
> THE INVENTION
> OF THE WHITE RACE

What began as divine license in Europe became statute in America. The cross gave way to the courthouse; the papal bull evolved into the colonial code. The theology of domination matured into the jurisprudence of Whiteness.

The architecture of American law was built not to preserve justice but to enshrine pathology. Whiteness, as Theodore W. Allen diagnosed, was never an identity of culture or blood but a deliberate construction of social control—a ruling-class formation engineered to manufacture compliance and division. The colonial project required not merely labor but psychological order. To maintain hierarchy, elites created a delusional system: "white" became the sacred category through which superiority could be imagined and power secured.

Allen identified Whiteness as a "ruling-class social control formation," a term that perfectly describes the compulsive drive toward domination embedded in the European psyche. Whiteness was cultivated not through heritage but through ritualized indoctrination in law, religion, and economics. It was a pedagogy of pathology—taught through the whip, the courtroom, and the pulpit. In colonial America, Whiteness was the first psychiatric institution: a shared delusion masquerading as divine order.

The Psychosis of Law: Codifying Racial Madness

The transition from theology to law did not cure the disease; it institutionalized it. Law became the primary instrument of racial psychosis. By transforming difference into deviance and proximity into pollution, colonial legislatures codified hierarchy as moral truth. Statutes across the colonies—especially those of Maryland and Virginia—reveal the process by which Whiteness was legally manufactured and Blackness criminalized.

1681 (Maryland):

"Forasmuch as, divers free-born English, or white women, sometimes by the instigation, procurement or connivance, of their masters, mistresses, or dames, and always to the satisfaction of their lascivious and lustful desires, and to the disgrace not only of the English, but also of many other Christian nations, do intermarry with negroes and slaves, by which means, divers inconveniences, controversies, and suits may arise, touching the issue or children, of such free-born women aforesaid; for prevention whereof for the future, be it further enacted . . . that if the marriage of such woman-servant with any slave shall take place by the procurement or permission of the master, such woman and her issue shall be free, and enacts a penalty by fine on the master or mistress and on the person joining the parties in marriage."

1691 (Virginia):

"And for prevention of that abominable mixture and spurious issue which hereafter may increase in this her majesty's colony and dominion, as well by English, and other WHITE men and women intermarrying with negros or mulattos, as by their unlawful coition with them, Be it enacted, by the authority aforesaid, and it is hereby enacted, That whatsoever English, or other white man or woman, being free, shall intermarry with a negro or mulatto man or woman, bond or free, shall, by judgment of the county court, be committed to prison, and there remain, during the space of six months, without bail or mainprize; and shall forfeit and pay ten pounds current money of Virginia, to the use of the parish, as aforesaid."

These laws were not simply about marriage—they were acts of psychological conditioning. They produced the White body as sacred and the Black body as disease. Through legal decree, intimacy itself was pathologized. The colony's lawmakers—delirious with the need to protect racial purity—transmuted fear into statute and sociopathy into social order.

Whiteness as Property: The Rights of Dispossession

As theology hardened into economy, the delusion became property. In 1993, Cheryl I. Harris identified what Allen had traced centuries earlier: that Whiteness evolved into a property interest—a form of legal possession. In *Whiteness as Property*, Harris observed, "the concept of Whiteness was premised on White supremacy, rather than mere difference. White was defined and constructed in ways that increased its value by reinforcing its exclusivity."

The pathology was thus legal and economic. Whiteness functioned as an asset class, its privileges akin to land, capital, and status property. To be White was to hold the right to use, enjoy, and exclude. To be non-White was to be excluded from exclusion—to be the object that defined the property's boundaries. The American psyche internalized this architecture, binding racial superiority to personal worth.

The Genetic Logic of Anti-Blackness

From Christianity to citizenship, Whiteness became the test of humanity itself. The first U.S. Congress codified the delusion in the *Nationality Act of 1790*, decreeing:

> "Be it enacted... that any alien being a FREE WHITE PERSON, who shall have resided within the limits and under the jurisdiction of the United States for the term of two years, may be admitted to become a citizen..."

Citizenship—legal personhood—was tethered to pigmentation. This statute became the constitutional genome of the American mind, determining who could belong, testify, vote, or even exist within the realm of legal empathy. In the 1857 *Dred Scott* decision, Chief Justice Roger Taney rendered the pathology explicit:

> "Can a Negro whose ancestors were imported into this country, and sold as slaves, become a member of the political community...? The negro has no rights which the white man is bound to respect."

Here, the Supreme Court did not simply interpret law—it performed a collective psychosis. It declared that Black life was not life at all. This pronouncement remains the unhealed trauma at the core of American jurisprudence.

Clinical Diagnosis: Sociopathy by Design

The repetition of racial exclusion across statutes, cases, and constitutions reflects not reason but obsession. Whiteness exhibits the hallmarks of sociopathy: a lack of empathy, moral disengagement, and compulsive domination masked as order. Law became its behavioral expression—a ritual of dehumanization that reinforced delusional superiority.

The 1705 Virginia law illustrates this clearly:

> "It is enacted that all servants... which shall be imported into this country either by sea or by land, whether Negroes, Moors, mulattoes or Indians who and whose parentage and native countries are not Christian at the time of their first purchase by some Christian... are hereby adjudged, deemed and taken to be slaves to all intents and purposes..."

The Christian identity was weaponized into a diagnostic tool—faith as phenotype, Whiteness as moral sanity, Blackness as congenital sin.

Economic Psychopathy and the Banking of Black Flesh

The pathology of Whiteness metastasized through capitalism. The trafficking of Black bodies became the financial nervous system of the colonial world. Banks, insurers, and investors monetized enslavement as collateral. Barclays financed voyages that traded human life; New York Life and Aetna insured slaveholders against the "loss" of their property.

This fusion of race and capital constituted what may be clinically termed *economic psychopathy*—a systemic incapacity for remorse coupled with the exploitation of suffering for pleasure and profit. The slave economy was not a deviation from civilization; it was civilization's definition of itself.

Sumptuary Sadism:
The Regulation of Black Life and Death

Colonial authorities extended control beyond bondage to the intimate regulation of desire, reproduction, and punishment. Sumptuary laws dictated who could love, worship, or exist without violence. The 1662 Virginia statute declared:

> "WHEREAS there are diverse loytering runaways in this country… if any English servant shall run away in company of any negroes who are incapable of making satisfaction by addition of a time, it is enacted that the English so running away… shall serve the masters of the said negroes… every Christian in company serving his proportion; and if the negroes be lost or dye… the Christian servants in company with them shall… pay fower thousand five hundred pounds of tobacco and caske or fower yeares service for every negroe so lost or dead."

The law transformed human proximity into contamination. To flee with a Black person was to become diseased by association. The White psyche required distance to preserve its delusion of purity; proximity to Blackness threatened the hallucination of supremacy.

The Permanent Patient: America's Unhealed Mind

Across centuries, the same symptoms persist. Whiteness remains a delusional identity sustained through law, religion, and economics—an inherited disorder that mistakes domination for divinity. The colonial statutes that criminalized empathy evolved into modern policies that criminalize existence.

Whiteness, as both psychological and institutional pathology, cannot heal because it refuses diagnosis. It clings to the privileges of property while denying the sickness that sustains them. The patient continues to deny treatment, projecting its disorder onto the very people it wounds.

Until America acknowledges Whiteness as its central disease—an ideological psychosis enshrined in law—it will remain trapped in its founding hallucination: that freedom requires bondage, that purity requires suffering, and that humanity can be legislated along color lines.

The laws that defined Whiteness as purity and property did not vanish; they evolved. The next chapter follows their mutation into modern institutions— how the colonial pathology of law became the bureaucratic pathology of the state, and how America's legal delusion continues to reproduce itself through education, policing, medicine, and policy.

Chapter Review Questions

Section 1 – The Birth of a Delusion: Whiteness as Social Control

1. How does Theodore W. Allen's concept of Whiteness as a "ruling-class social control formation" redefine the idea of race as pathology rather than identity?

2. In what ways did the colonial elite "teach" Whiteness as a psychological condition through the law, religion, and economy?

3. How might Whiteness, as introduced in this chapter, be viewed as an early form of collective psychosis?

Section 2 – The Psychosis of Law: Codifying Racial Madness

4. What do the 1681 Maryland and 1691 Virginia laws reveal about the White psyche's obsession with purity and control?

5. How do these early statutes demonstrate the process of **legal indoctrination** in which pathology becomes policy?

6. What psychological needs were being met for White colonists through the legal regulation of interracial intimacy?

Section 3 – Whiteness as Property: The Rights of Dispossession

7. How does Cheryl Harris's "Whiteness as Property" expand upon Allen's theory of Whiteness as social control?

8. In what ways did the law transform Whiteness into an economic asset, and Blackness into an economic liability?

9. Why is the right "to exclude" central to the psychology of Whiteness?

10. How does Whiteness as property continue to manifest in modern institutions, such as housing, education, or healthcare?

Section 4 – The Genetic Logic of Anti-Blackness

11. How did the 1790 Nationality Act formalize Whiteness as the condition for citizenship and humanity in the United States?

12. What is the significance of Chief Justice Taney's statement in *Dred Scott v. Sandford* that "the negro has no rights which the white man is bound to respect"?

13. How does this ruling represent not just a legal decision, but a collective moral and psychological disorder?

Section 5 – Clinical Diagnosis: Sociopathy by Design

14. Identify three features of sociopathy expressed in colonial legal behavior toward Black people.

15. How do these features persist in today's institutions (policing, law, medicine, education)?

16. Why is moral disengagement a necessary symptom of Whiteness as a sociocultural disorder?

Section 6 – Economic Psychopathy and the Banking of Black Flesh

17. How does the chapter connect the emergence of global capitalism to the psychopathology of White supremacy?

18. What does the term "economic psychopathy" suggest about the relationship between profit and dehumanization?

19. How do the roles of banks and insurance companies during slavery reveal the moral architecture of early American finance?

Section 7 – Sumptuary Sadism: The Regulation of Black Life and Death

20. What is the psychological significance of laws that criminalized proximity or solidarity between Black and White laborers?

21. In what ways did "sumptuary laws" enforce not just racial separation but emotional disconnection?

22. How does the law's obsession with controlling the Black body reflect a deeper European fixation with dominance and purity?

Section 8 – The Permanent Patient: America's Unhealed Mind

23. Why does the chapter characterize Whiteness as a "patient" that refuses diagnosis or treatment?

24. What would it mean for America to engage in collective "treatment" for its foundational racial psychosis?

25. How does understanding Whiteness as a cultural and psychological disease reshape the concept of justice itself?

Works Cited

Allen, T. W. (1975). *The invention of the white race*. Verso.

Barclays Bank. (n.d.). *History of Barclays and the slave trade*. London: Barclays Archives.

Du Bois, W. E. B. (1935). *Black reconstruction in America, 1860–1880*. Free Press.

Harris, C. I. (1993). Whiteness as property. *Harvard Law Review, 106*(8), 1707–1791.

Maryland General Assembly. (1681). *Act concerning Negroes and other slaves*. Colonial Records of Maryland.

Nicholas, R. (Ed.). (1790). *The Nationality Act of 1790*. U.S. Congressional Records.

Taney, R. B. (1857). *Dred Scott v. Sandford*, 60 U.S. (19 How.) 393.

Virginia General Assembly. (1662). *Act concerning runaways*. Statutes at Large of Virginia.

Virginia General Assembly. (1691). *Act for suppressing outlying slaves*. Statutes at Large of Virginia.

Welsing, F. C. (1991). *The Isis papers: The keys to the colors.* Third World Press.

Wilson, A. N. (1993). *The falsification of Afrikan consciousness: Eurocentric history, psychiatry, and the politics of White supremacy.* Afrikan World InfoSystems.

Wright, B. E. (1984). *The psychopathic racial personality and other essays.* Third World Press.

Thomas, Z. (2021, March 1). The hidden links between slavery and Wall Street. *BBC News.* https://www.bbc.com/news/business-52893382

CHAPTER 4
THE GOSPEL OF VIOLATION
LAW, LUST, AND THE MAKING OF WHITENESS

Having named the theology and law that sanctified domination, we now follow the same pathology into the body—where creed becomes conduct and statute becomes touch.

If Malignant Diabolical Psychopathy revealed the spiritual anatomy of whiteness, what follows exposes its bodily expressions—how this disorder has animated white men's obsession with possession, violation, and control. The same pathology that sanctified empire and law also corrupted desire, turning intimacy into ownership and domination into pleasure. In the chapters ahead, I trace this sickness into the private chambers of whiteness—its bedrooms, its courtrooms, its pulpits—to show how the psychopathic faith in hierarchy shaped the very meaning of manhood, womanhood, and humanity itself.

The Psycho-Legal Evolution of Predation

From creed to code to flesh: the permissions of empire became the permissions of men.

White men wrote their lust into law. The earliest European statutes reveal that what later became "civilization" was never about order or morality; it was about ownership and permission to violate. The very architecture of English common law codified the right of men—specifically white men—to possess, penetrate, and punish as an extension of divine and legal authority. These were not peripheral acts of cruelty; they were the governing principles of Western patriarchy.

The 1275 Westminster Statute — Consent as Domination

In 1275, under King Edward I, Parliament enacted the Statute of Westminster I, the first English law to define rape and establish an "age of consent." The language itself exposed the depravity of what England deemed civilization:

> "If a man ravish a maid within age, that neither assent nor disagree with the act, he shall be punished at the King's pleasure."
>
> STATUTE OF WESTMINSTER I,
> 1275, 3 EDW. I C. 13

The statute set that "age of consent" at twelve years old, turning the rape of children into a negotiable matter between men and monarch. It legalized child sexual assault under the guise of social order, embedding state-sanctioned pedophilia within Christian and legal orthodoxy.

Here the template is set: male desire reframed as governance; violation disguised as virtue.

What this statute truly accomplished was the creation of male innocence and female culpability—a gendered and moral inversion that later became racialized in the colonies. It provided the first formal "permission structure" for white male sexual entitlement, sanctified by both crown and church. The divine order of patriarchy was thus wedded to the legal order of property.

The 1662 Virginia Statute — Inheritance Through Violation

When English colonists brought their laws to the Americas, they carried this psychosexual theology of domination. Following the Elizabeth Key case (1656)—in which an enslaved woman of mixed ancestry successfully sued for freedom—the Virginia Assembly retaliated by rewriting the moral code of the New World. The 1662 Virginia Act XII declared:

> "Whereas some doubts have arisen whether children got by any Englishman upon a negro woman should be slave or free, be it therefore enacted that all children borne in this country shall be held bond or free only according to the condition of the mother."
>
> ACTS OF THE GENERAL ASSEMBLY OF VIRGINIA, 1662

With one sentence, sexual violence became a mechanism of economic production. White men could rape Black women with impunity, converting their offspring into property. The law severed paternity from responsibility and fused rape with profit. It also transformed sexual predation into a generational business model—a hereditary theology of ownership masquerading as governance.

Law as Liturgical Violence

The pulpit blessed; the bench enforced; the bedroom obeyed.

These two statutes—the 1275 Westminster and the 1662 Virginia—represent the spiritual and juridical DNA of whiteness: domination baptized in legality. Christianity's claim to moral supremacy was always fused with the right to conquer bodies. The church confessed purity while the state enforced perversion. Together they constructed a psychological economy where the rape of women and children was not a crime but a ritual of sovereignty.

From these foundations grew centuries of statutes, court rulings, and cultural codes that defined the white male body as sacred and every other body as subject. This is the genesis of what I name Malignant Diabolical Psychopathy—a fusion of lust, law, and theology that transforms brutality into moral order and violence into virtue.

The colonial and modern eras did not invent white male predation; they merely perfected its bureaucracy. The courtroom became the confessional, and the judge's robe the vestment of forgiveness for every crime committed in the name of whiteness.

Section 2 — The Continuum of Violation

Once legalized, the ritual repeats—spreading from statute to custom, from verdict to village.

The pathology that began in Europe's medieval courts metastasized in the American colonies. What had once been framed as "lawful authority" over women became an entire social order built upon the right to violate. The Englishman who crossed the Atlantic brought not religion or civility but the legal memory of domination. The colonies became laboratories for the perfection of sexual control—a system that fused whiteness, masculinity, and ownership into one divine entitlement.

From English Dominion to American Design

By the eighteenth century, every colonial government had adopted some variation of the Virginia model. Statutes defined Black women as unrapeable, free or enslaved, while sanctifying white men as incapable of criminal lust.

"Rape" existed only when a white woman accused a man of color; the same act committed by a white man was reframed as "passion" or "indiscretion." Whiteness was innocence embodied—its crimes erased by language itself.

Across the American South, legislatures codified this theology of projection. Between the 1600s and the late 1800s, dozens of state laws criminalized sexual contact between Black men and white women—whether consensual or not—while refusing to recognize the rape of Black women as a legal category.

In some jurisdictions, even the accusation by a white woman was sufficient to warrant execution. In none was the rape of a Black woman by a white man prosecuted as a crime.

The 1899 Georgia Supreme Court Ruling — Blackness as Presumption of Guilt

Nowhere is the racialization of sexuality clearer than in the 1899 Georgia Supreme Court ruling, which institutionalized the assumption that Black men were rapists by nature. The court held that an accusation of attempted rape by a white woman required no corroborating evidence; the "fact" of Black manhood itself established intent. Even exculpatory testimony could not cleanse the stain of Blackness:

> "In crimes of this nature, the presumption is against the negro. His race and character furnish evidence of probability stronger than proof."
>
> GEORGIA SUPREME COURT, 1899, REPORTED IN STATE V. JOHNSON

In this decision, whiteness did not merely manipulate justice—it became justice. The ruling inverted moral reality: the predators became protectors, and the victims became monsters. Law became the mirror through which white men gazed upon their own depravity and called it order.

Projection as Juridical Ritual

Every statute criminalizing Black male sexuality functioned as a public confession disguised as prosecution. The white legal imagination externalized its own impulses—its desire, fear, and shame—onto Black bodies. In accusing the Black man of lust, the white man sought absolution for his own. Each lynching, each courtroom execution, was both punishment and purification, a ritualized cleansing of whiteness through the destruction of Black flesh.

The evidence is irrefutable: the same courts that condemned Black men for imagined crimes refused to indict white men for the documented rapes of Black, Indigenous, and even white women and girls. This double standard was not accidental; it was the point. The law was engineered to guarantee the continuity of white male sovereignty—over property, over women, over truth itself.

The Psychopathology of Sanctified Lust

This legal order was more than injustice; it was an enactment of the white male psyche. What I have defined as Malignant Diabolical Psychopathy thrived precisely because it hid beneath robes and scripture. It justified rape as civilization and predation as providence. The European Christian patriarch was taught that domination was divine, and his descendants wrote that divinity into every statute and precedent.

By the late nineteenth and early twentieth centuries, this pathology had hardened into a total system:

- Celia (1855) – the enslaved woman executed for killing her rapist in self-defense.

- George v. State (1859) – the declaration that the testimony of a Black person could not outweigh that of a white accuser.

- Dallas v. State (1918) and Alabama Appeals Court (1953) – reaffirmations of the legal fiction that Black men were sexual predators by nature.

Each case was a chapter in the same theology: white men as gods, Black people as demons, and law as scripture. Together, they formed a single continuum of violation—a lineage of violence sanctified by courtrooms and pulpits alike.

The Inheritance of Silence

The silence surrounding white male sexual violence is not the absence of history; it is the product of policy. The erasure of white guilt was manufactured by the same institutions that created Black criminality.

Through this psycho-legal inversion, the predator became the priest. Every generation of white men was taught that control was virtue, possession was love, and violence was duty.

This is not ancient history. It is the legal DNA of the United States, replicated in police departments, courtrooms, and pulpits. The statutes may have changed their language, but their soul remains the same. White male innocence is still presumed; Black guilt is still inherited. The continuum of violation continues, now adorned in new robes of respectability—law, order, and civilization.

Section 3 — Sexuality, Power, and Projection

Projection is the factory setting; domination is the operating system.

White male supremacy has always been a mirror turned outward. The atrocities it commits are projected onto others so that whiteness may remain pure in its own eyes. The rapist accuses the innocent of lust. The predator names his prey as dangerous. This is the psychic alchemy of white power: guilt transmuted into virtue through accusation. Projection is not an accident of whiteness; it is its engine.

The Psychodynamics of Dominion

From the medieval priest to the modern politician, the white male psyche has required two constants—control and innocence. Control satisfies the body; innocence soothes the soul. The two must coexist, or the edifice collapses. The white man therefore performs purity even as he practices perversion. He creates the "Other"—the dark, the heathen, the hyper-sexual—so that his own predation may appear as protection.

This is why every legal system he authored required a scapegoat. In colonial statutes and modern courtrooms alike, the same choreography repeats: the white male offender disguised as defender, the Black victim recast as criminal, the woman rendered complicit in her own assault. Law becomes theatre, and justice its stage prop.

Projection as Cultural Ritual

Throughout American history, this projection has served as a collective absolution ritual for whiteness. When white men lynched Black men under the pretext of protecting white womanhood, they were not avenging purity—they were reenacting their own crimes. When pulpits preached against "Black depravity," they were masking centuries of white sexual terrorism.

The white psyche externalized its sickness, demanding that the world mirror back its fantasy of innocence.

From Courtroom to Celebrity: Modern Manifestations

Jeffrey Epstein built an empire of child predation financed by princes, presidents, and professors. Josh Duggar, sheltered by a theology of male headship, molested children while preaching purity. Donald Trump bragged about sexual assault on camera, then dismissed his words as "locker-room talk"—a phrase that perfectly encapsulates the normalization of white patriarchal violence. Each of these men is not an aberration but an inheritor of the 1275 Westminster Statute's spirit—the belief that power confers permission.

The American legal system continues to protect them because it was designed for them. Whether through plea deals, nondisclosure agreements, or simple disbelief, the pattern holds: white male predation is treated as a moral lapse, while Black existence remains treated as a moral threat. This is the legal embodiment of projection—the transference of guilt from the powerful to the powerless.

Malignant Diabolical Psychopathy in Practice

What I name Malignant Diabolical Psychopathy is the condition that makes such inversion possible. It is not merely an individual disorder but a collective moral disease—one that transforms cruelty into conscience and domination into doctrine. Within the psychosexual economy of whiteness, empathy is weakness, and exploitation a sign of divine favor. The white male self can maintain coherence only through subjugation; to relinquish control would be to face the abyss of his own depravity.

This pathology is reinforced through law, theology, and culture. The judge's gavel, the pastor's sermon, the corporate title—all serve as instruments of moral laundering. The system absolves itself in advance, ensuring that the act of violation is always accompanied by the illusion of righteousness. In this sense, whiteness is not simply a racial construct; it is a ritual of psychological self-exoneration.

Epigenetic Echoes

Generations raised in this system inherit not only wealth and privilege but neural patterns of domination and dissociation. The descendants of predators are trained to mistake control for safety; the descendants of the violated are conditioned to experience safety as danger. This is the neurobiological residue of empire—a civilization whose nervous system has been wired for hierarchy. The trauma is collective, but so is the denial.

The violence that began as statute now circulates as instinct. It lives in the architecture of institutions and in the synapses of those who sustain them. To confront it is not merely to study history; it is to enter the psyche of a civilization that has made predation its prayer.

Toward Reckoning

Whiteness cannot heal until it confesses its projection. The white male psyche must look into the mirror it has spent centuries avoiding—the mirror of its own making—and see not savior but predator, not civilization but sickness. Until that reckoning occurs, law and culture will continue to reproduce the same pathology under new names. The diagnosis remains: Malignant Diabolical Psychopathy—a spiritual and biological disorder masquerading as moral order.

Section 4 – Neurobiology and Epigenetic Transmission (Part A)

What culture rehearses, the body records.

Violence rewires the nervous system. Every act of domination leaves an electrical signature—an alteration in the way a body reads safety and threat. Over time, those alterations become habits of perception, posture, and thought. The chemistry of fear becomes the culture of control.

Neuroscience now confirms what our ancestors already knew: trauma is not only remembered; it is encoded. When a body is repeatedly forced to submit, its cortisol rhythms flatten, its heart rate learns anticipation, and its hippocampus—keeper of narrative memory—begins to fragment time itself. Likewise, when a body is repeatedly given permission to dominate, its empathy circuits dull. Power, rehearsed often enough, becomes pleasure; cruelty, repeated often enough, becomes reflex.

Empathy and aggression live in adjacent neural neighborhoods. In a society organized by hierarchy, the synapses that should mirror another's pain are gradually silenced. The limbic system still registers the other's distress, but the prefrontal cortex quickly rationalizes it: they deserved it, it was necessary, it is law. Over generations, this pattern becomes collective—an inherited choreography between fear and justification.

Trauma research describes this inheritance as epigenetic transmission: the chemical "bookmarking" of genes by lived experience. High stress can switch certain genes on or off, altering immune, hormonal, and emotional regulation in descendants who never lived the original event. What is inherited is not the memory but the metabolism of the memory—the body's readiness for danger or dominance.

The descendants of those who endured systemic terror carry heightened vigilance; the descendants of those who administered it carry a conditioned blindness. Both are neurological adaptations to historical circumstance. One learns to survive by sensing danger everywhere; the other learns to thrive by never recognizing danger in itself.

These biological patterns are not destiny—they are evidence. They reveal how history literally gets under the skin, shaping perception long after laws and empires change names. They also explain why a culture built on domination continues to reproduce anxiety and denial even in the absence of open warfare. The nervous system remembers what the conscience forgets.

Section 4 – Neurobiology and Epigenetic Transmission (Part B)

If harm can be rehearsed, so can healing.

If trauma can be transmitted, so can healing. The same neural plasticity that once learned submission and control can learn connection and care. The brain is not a monument; it is a river. Each new act of recognition—each refusal to repeat harm—reshapes the current.

Modern trauma therapy calls this process re-patterning: teaching the body that safety is possible and that power need not mean possession. Communal rituals of truth-telling, art, music, breath, and movement accomplish on a social scale what therapy achieves in the individual—resetting the stress response, restoring coherence between heartbeat and conscience.

Collectively, this work requires a new moral nervous system. When communities witness injustice and respond instead of dissociating, they strengthen the neural pathways of empathy. When people in positions of power learn to tolerate discomfort rather than seeking control, the circuitry of domination begins to weaken. Neurobiology becomes theology in practice.

Epigenetic studies suggest that supportive environments can gradually reverse the biological marks of trauma. Children who grow up in predictably safe and affirming surroundings display healthier cortisol cycles and more responsive immune systems than those raised in fear. Social justice, then, is not only ethical—it is medical. Policy is a form of neurology.

The work of dismantling systemic violence must therefore include the re-education of the nervous system. Every time a society interrupts cruelty, every time it rewards empathy instead of exploitation, it writes a different instruction into the genetic ledger of its future. Healing is the body politic remembering that it was never designed for hierarchy.

The biology of domination is powerful, but not permanent. The same mechanisms that encode terror also encode tenderness. The question for any civilization is simple: which will it rehearse? What neural pattern will it choose to repeat?

Empirical Correlates of Malignant Diabolical Psychopathy

(Author's Qualitative Synthesis of Public Data and Trauma Research)

Where the sermon meets the spreadsheet, the pattern is plain.

Every social system leaves traces in its data. Where moral argument meets measurable evidence, the patterns are unmistakable. The following summaries are drawn from national criminal-justice and health-science research; together they map the empirical outline of what I have described as Malignant Diabolical Psychopathy—a culture that normalizes domination while disguising it as order.

Sexual Violence and Institutional Impunity

- Gender and Race of Offenders. Department of Justice data over the last decade show that roughly 97 percent of convicted sexual-assault offenders in the United States are male. Because white men remain the majority of the male population and hold disproportionate access to positions of authority, they also comprise the largest share of convicted offenders in absolute numbers—about 70 percent in recent DOJ summaries.

- Child-Exploitation Convictions. U.S. Sentencing Commission reports (2022 – 2024) indicate that approximately 85 percent of defendants sentenced for child-sexual-exploitation or pornography crimes identified as white males. Comparable European studies report similar proportions.

- Clerical and Institutional Abuse. Investigations by the U.S. Conference of Catholic Bishops (2023) and the French Sauvé Commission (2021) confirm tens of thousands of victims of clergy sexual abuse—overwhelmingly perpetrated by white men occupying positions of religious authority.

These figures, supported by historical facts suggests neurobiological (epigenetic) causation. They too, reveal a sociological architecture of access, privilege, and impunity. The demographic dominance of white men in state, religious, and educational institutions creates both opportunity and cultural insulation from accountability.

Neurobiological and Epigenetic Findings

- Trauma Encoding. Neuroscientists (Yehuda et al., 2016; McEwen & Gianaros, 2011) have shown that chronic exposure to stress and violence alters cortisol regulation, hippocampal volume, and amygdala reactivity. These changes can persist across generations through epigenetic markers that affect immune and stress-response systems.

- Empathy Suppression. Studies of aggression and power dynamics (Decety & Cowell, 2018) show that repeated activation of dominance circuits dulls empathic response and heightens reward signals associated with control—confirming that the exercise of unexamined power reshapes moral perception at the neural level.

- Reversibility. Research in developmental neuroscience demonstrates that supportive environments, restorative justice, and trauma-informed care can normalize stress-hormone cycles within a single generation—evidence that culture can literally re-educate biology.

Interpretive Conclusion

Taken together, the criminological and biological data describe a civilization still rehearsing the neural choreography of domination. The prevalence of white-male sexual violence, the institutional tolerance that surrounds it, and the measurable neurobiological imprint of power and trauma all point to the same conclusion: the pathology I call Malignant Diabolical Psychopathy is not metaphorical; it is material. It lives in bodies, bureaucracies, and brains.

Healing, therefore, must be measured not only in moral conversion but in nervous-system repair—in the capacity of future generations to feel without needing to control. That is the true empirical test of liberation.

Section 5 – Christianity and Carnal Dominion

The altar taught the courtroom how to speak about bodies.

The institution most responsible for moralizing domination has always been the Church.

Christianity, as weaponized by European powers, fused faith with flesh-control—declaring that God's hierarchy extended into every human body. The divine order of heaven was mirrored in the political order of earth, and both were male, white, and absolute.

The Sacred Sanction of Possession

When fifteenth-century popes issued the Doctrine of Discovery, they canonized conquest itself. The papal bulls Dum Diversas (1452) and Romanus Pontifex (1455) authorized Christian monarchs to invade, capture, and enslave "Saracens, pagans, and any other unbelievers," claiming their lands "for eternal dominion." The Church did not merely bless slavery—it engineered its theology. Salvation and subjugation became synonyms.

Pastor Benjamin Boswell has captured this inheritance with surgical clarity:

> "The primary and most decisive desires of the European Christian project were always greed and power. Christianity was consistently manipulated and marshalled to sanctify settler colonialism and racial oppression... European Christianity was (and is) the sanctification of savagery and the justification of extreme acts of cruelty, brutality, and violence in the pursuit of greed and power."

Boswell reminds us that what began as Christian supremacy metastasized into white supremacy—a religious system disguised as race. Its rituals of baptism and conquest were the same act performed in different fonts of water.

Purity, Property, and the Policing of Flesh

From the Puritan settlements to the plantation colonies, sexual hierarchy became holy law. Women were property, desire was sin, and sin was always projected onto the racialized body. The same sermons that praised chastity also justified the rape of enslaved women; the same pulpits that condemned lust were silent about pedophilia in their own ranks. The "holy order" of patriarchy was never about virtue—it was about ownership.

Colonial courts quoted Scripture to determine whose body could be violated with impunity and whose could not. In the Virginia statutes of the seventeenth century, rape was redefined as a crime that could occur only against white womanhood; Black and Indigenous women were rendered unrapeable by legal design. This was the gospel of dominion made flesh.

The Inverted Cross of Whiteness

Whiteness was Christianity's most successful heresy. It replaced salvation with supremacy and called it divine providence. To be white was to be chosen; to be Black or Indigenous was to bear the mark of divine rejection. This reversal transformed Christ's cross—once a symbol of solidarity with the crucified—into a sword aimed at the colonized.

Esther Armah distilled the psychology of this transformation when she said: "The love language of white supremacy is brutality."

Violence became devotion; brutality became liturgy. The missionary, the soldier, and the slave-trader knelt at the same altar. Their shared prayer was control.

The Modern Resurrection of the Old Creed

Contemporary Christian nationalism is not a revival—it is a relapse. Its insistence on patriarchal authority, heteronormative purity, and racial hierarchy repeats the medieval formula: order through subjugation. Political sermons about "law and order" are new homilies of the same faith—salvation for the obedient, punishment for the rest.

The psycho-legal structure that once excused the burning of villages now excuses the bombing of neighborhoods, the policing of wombs, and the incarceration of entire generations. The divine right of kings has become the divine right of whiteness.

The Path to Un-Sanctifying Violence

To heal from this theology, we must desacralize domination. The moral task is not to abandon faith but to exorcise it—to separate the spiritual hunger for meaning from the institutional hunger for control. True communion demands the dismantling of hierarchies that confuse power with purity.

If the old Church taught that heaven mirrored empire, the new gospel must teach that liberation mirrors love. Faith, stripped of supremacy, becomes a practice of mutual protection rather than possession. Only then can we reclaim the divine from the dominator.

Transition to Section 6 – From Predation to Policy

What the sanctuary normalized, the statute routinized.

The psychotheology of domination never stayed confined to pulpits; it drafted the blueprints of law and policy. The next chapter traces how these religious justifications mutated into secular jurisprudence—how the same moral grammar that defined "sin" as disobedience became the legal grammar that defined "crime" as Blackness. (would love a breakdown after you rewrite it, to tell me what you shifted). Please keep every word the same and just focus on tightening and adding.

Chapter Review Questions

Section 1 – The Psycho-Legal Evolution of Predation

1. How did early English law encode sexual domination as a divine and civic right?

2. What moral and theological assumptions underpinned the Statute of Westminster (1275)?

3. In what ways did this statute create the first legal "permission structure" for white male sexual entitlement?

4. How did the 1662 Virginia Act institutionalize rape as a mode of inheritance and economic expansion?

5. What do these statutes reveal about the fusion of religion, property, and sexuality in shaping colonial identity?

6. How does the author's phrase *"Law as Liturgical Violence"* challenge the presumed neutrality of Western jurisprudence?

Section 2 – The Continuum of Violation

7. How did colonial governments redefine the meaning of "consent," "virtue," and "crime" in racialized terms?

8. What is meant by the "continuum of violation," and how does it explain the persistence of sexual violence across eras?

9. How did the 1899 Georgia Supreme Court ruling formalize racialized sexual paranoia as judicial precedent?

10. What does the erasure of white male culpability reveal about law's psychological and cultural function?

11. In what ways did projection serve as both moral camouflage and ritual absolution for white male predation?

12. How does this historical continuum echo in modern policing, sentencing, and public discourse about "crime"?

Section 3 – Sexuality, Power, and Projection

13. Why is projection described as the "engine" of whiteness rather than a byproduct of it?

14. How does the white male pursuit of innocence sustain systems of domination?

15. Compare historical projection rituals (e.g., lynching) with their modern analogues (e.g., media scapegoating).

16. What psychological mechanisms enable society to eroticize and excuse white male violence?

17. How does *Malignant Diabolical Psychopathy* reinterpret the relationship between religion, law, and sexual pathology?

18. What makes projection both a personal defense mechanism and a collective political strategy?

19. How does the concept of "psychological self-exoneration" redefine whiteness as a moral identity project?

Section 4 – Neurobiology and Epigenetic Transmission

20. How does trauma research validate the idea that domination and submission are biologically conditioned behaviors?

21. What role does empathy suppression play in the maintenance of racial hierarchy?

22. Explain the concept of "metabolism of the memory." How does it link biology and history?

23. How does epigenetic inheritance complicate the notion of individual moral responsibility?

24. What does it mean to describe policy as a "form of neurology"?

25. How can trauma-informed governance become a mechanism of cultural and biological repair?

26. In what ways can collective healing practices serve as neural re-education for societies built on domination?

Section 5 – Christianity and Carnal Dominion

27. How did the Doctrine of Discovery codify religious supremacy as a justification for sexual and territorial conquest?

28. In what sense does the author describe whiteness as Christianity's "most successful heresy"?

29. How do modern forms of Christian nationalism repeat the medieval theology of domination?

30. What does it mean to "desanctify violence," and how might faith traditions participate in that process of repair?

Works Cited

Armah, E. (2022). *Emotional justice: A roadmap for racial healing*. New York, NY: Amistad Press.

Boswell, B. (2023). *Sermons on white supremacy and Christian complicity*. Charlotte, NC: Myers Park Baptist Church Publications.

Decety, J., & Cowell, J. M. (2018). The complex relation between morality and empathy. *Trends in Cognitive Sciences, 22*(5), 337–349. https://doi.org/10.1016/j.tics.2018.02.001

McEwen, B. S., & Gianaros, P. J. (2011). Stress- and allostasis-induced brain plasticity. *Annual Review of Medicine, 62*, 431–445. https://doi.org/10.1146/annurev-med-052209-100430

Sauvé Commission. (2021). *Rapport de la commission indépendante sur les abus sexuels dans l'Église catholique (CIASE)*. Paris, France: Bayard.

U.S. Conference of Catholic Bishops. (2023). *Annual report on the implementation of the Charter for the Protection of Children and Young People*. Washington, DC: USCCB.

U.S. Department of Justice. (2024). *Statistical overview of sexual violence and offender demographics*. Washington, DC: Author.

U.S. Sentencing Commission. (2024). *Federal sentencing of child pornography and sexual exploitation offenses*. Washington, DC: Author.

Virginia General Assembly. (1662). *Act XII: Children to follow the condition of the mother*. In *Statutes at Large of Virginia*.

Westminster Parliament. (1275). *Statute of Westminster I, 3 Edw. I c. 13*. London, England.

Yehuda, R., Daskalakis, N. P., Lehrner, A., Desarnaud, F., Bader, H. N., Makotkine, I., … Meaney, M. J. (2016). Intergenerational transmission of trauma effects on stress response. *Biological Psychiatry, 80*(5), 372–380. https://doi.org/10.1016/j.biopsych.2015.08.005

CHAPTER 5
WHITE RAGE, CLINICAL REALITY
LAW, BACKLASH, AND ONGOING DISORDER

> *I want to understand White rage, and I'm White... What is it that caused thousands of people to assault this building and try to overturn the Constitution of the United States of America?"*
>
> GEN. MARK A. MILLEY,
> CHAIRMAN,
> JOINT CHIEFS OF STAFF (2021)

Opening the Case File: "Be Careful"

We begin not with scandal but with symptoms, not with outrage but with observation.

When General Mark Milley asked to "understand White rage," he posed more than a curiosity; he opened a clinical inquiry into a national disorder. In this book's framework, White rage is not a transient mood or political talking point—it is the recurrent behavioral expression of a deeper psycho-legal system that normalizes anti-Black domination and authorizes violence in the name of order. The warning from Black communities—be careful what you ask for—is not a threat; it is a diagnosis: to study White rage honestly is to uncover its institutional architecture and its inherited reflexes.

To study the behavior, we must name the system that trains it.

Differential Diagnosis: Rage vs. Rulership

What presents as "anger" often conceals entitlement; what looks like passion is sometimes policy.

White rage is best understood as a syndrome—a patterned set of responses triggered by Black presence, progress, or refusal to submit. Its symptoms include historical amnesia, projection, moral disengagement, and punitive control cloaked as civilization. As psychiatrist Aruna Khilanani observes, the violence of discovery narratives ("we discovered…") sanitizes theft and massacre; the language of innocence becomes a mask for predation. This is not mere prejudice. It is impression management—a narcissistic defense that rebrands cruelty as achievement while punishing Black reality-testing with force.

Having distinguished symptom from story, we can now examine the cycle that repeats.

The Ritual of Backlash

Backlash is not a glitch; it is a governance routine.

Backlash is not episodic; it is ritualized. From the Snow Riot (Washington, DC, 1835) to Wilmington (1898), Ocoee (1920), East St. Louis (1917), Tulsa (1921), and into the late twentieth century, the pattern repeats: Black gains (or perceived autonomy) are met with organized White counter-mobilization—legal, extralegal, and spectacularly violent. Contemporary cases differ in method, not meaning: Clifford Owensby dragged from his car in Dayton (2021); the filmed lynching of Tyre Nichols (2023). Rage is not an aberration; it is an enforcement mechanism of a cultural order.

The ritual requires a myth to justify it. That myth has a history.

Clinical Construct:
White Psychopathology and Projection

When fear cannot face itself, it finds a mirror.

Winthrop D. Jordan's White Over Black traces how English Protestant cosmology fused color, "heathenism," and animality into a single category of negation. What began as theological hierarchy metastasized into biological myth: the Black body as libidinous, dangerous, sub-human. This folklore—codified in travelogues, pulp science, and law—performed a classic clinical maneuver: projection. White fantasies about lust, violence, and depravity were displaced onto Africans, then "managed" through bondage and policing. The cultural symptom persists: Blackness is treated as contamination; Whiteness as purity in need of protection.

Once the projection template exists, law supplies the tools to enforce it.

From Theology to Code:
Constructing "White" and "Negro" (1664–1722)

Categories don't just appear—they are manufactured, named, and notarized.

The period 1664–1722 marks a decisive shift from ethno-religious labels ("Christian," "English") to the juridical production of "White" and "Negro." In Maryland (1664), lawmakers fixed "Negroes… already within the Province… and hereafter imported" to durante vita—enslavement for life—and criminalized freeborn English women's marriages to enslaved Black men, transmitting bondage to their children.

Maryland (1664) — "Act concerning Negroes & other slaves":

> "Be it enacted by the Right Honorable the Lord Proprietary by the advise and consent of the upper and lower house of this present Generall Assembly, that all Negroes and other slaves

already within the Province And all Negroes and other slaves to be hereafter imported into the Province, shall serve Durante Vita (hard labor for life)."

"And all Children born of any Negro or other slave shall be slaves as their fathers were for the term of their lives And forasmuch as divers freeborn English Women forgetful of their free condition and to the disgrace of our Nation do intermarry with Negro Slaves... whatsoever freeborn woman shall intermarry with any slave... shall Serve the master of such slave during the life of her husband And... all the Issue of such freeborn women so married shall be slaves as their fathers were. And... all the Issues of English or other freeborn women that have already married Negroes shall serve the Masters of their Parents till they be Thirty years of age and no longer."

Here the womb is deputized; intimacy becomes infrastructure for caste.

The statute fuses personhood to pigment and lineage, criminalizes interracial intimacy, and weaponizes the womb for boundary enforcement: bondage by bloodline, punishment by marriage.

In Virginia (1662), lawmakers targeted interracial solidarity and escape, explicitly punishing White servants for running away in company with Negroes, and taxing Whites if a Black escapee died or was "lost." This law makes proximity itself a crime.

Virginia (1662) — Runaways "in company with negroes":

"...if any English servant shall run away in company of any negroes who are incapable of making satisfaction by addition of a time, it is enacted that the English so running away in the company with them shall at the time of service to their own masters expired, serve the masters of the said negroes for their absence... every christian in company serving his proportion; and if the negroes be lost or dye...

the christian servants... shall... pay fower thousand five hundred pounds of tobacco and caske or fower yeares service for every negroe so lost or dead."

By 1667, baptism—formerly a possible route to manumission under Christianized logics—was stripped of emancipatory power for Black people.

Virginia (1667) — Baptism does not alter bondage:

"the conferring of baptisme doth not alter the condition of the person as to his bondage or ffreedome; that diverse masters, ffreed from this doubt, may more carefully endeavour the propagation of christianity..."

In 1668, "freed" Black women were declared still tithable—freedom redefined as partial, taxed existence.

Virginia (1668) — Negro women tithables though freed:

"negro women, though permitted to enjoy their ffreedome yet ought not in all respects to be admitted to a full fruition of the exemptions and impunities of the English, and are still lyable to payment of taxes."

The same year, corporal punishment of runaways was greenlit alongside term-extension—pain and time as twin instruments of discipline.

Virginia (1668) — Corporal punishment of runaway servants:

"...moderate corporal punishment inflicted by master or magistrate upon a runaway servant shall not deprive the master of the satisfaction allowed by the law, the one being as necessary to reclaim them... as the other is just to repair the damages..."

And in 1669, homicide was legalized when "correction" killed an enslaved person—murder reconceived as property loss.

Virginia (1669) — Casual Killing of Slaves Act:

> "if any slave resists his master (or other by his master's order correcting him) and by the extremity of the correction should chance to die, that his death shall not be accounted a felony, but the master... be acquitted from molestation, since it cannot be presumed that premeditated malice... should induce any man to destroy his own estate."

Finally, in 1681, Maryland narrowed White women's marriage to Black men and imposed fines on masters/priest—anxious eugenics by statute.

Maryland (1681) — White women intermarrying with Negro slaves:

> "Forasmuch as, divers free-born English, or white women... do intermarry with negroes and slaves... for prevention whereof... if the marriage of such woman-servant with any slave shall take place... such woman and her issue shall be free, and enacts a penalty by fine on the master or mistress and on the person joining the parties in marriage."

Each statute is a clinical note on the same patient: a polity that converts anxiety about proximity into law, that criminalizes empathy, and that rehearses its innocence by calling domination "order."

Law writes the catechism; the courts teach the lesson.

Sumptuary Sadism and Sexual Governance

Police the bed to preserve the boundary.

Sex, marriage, and reproduction became surveillance sites. Laws against interracial union and "running away in company with Negroes" pathologized intimacy itself, punishing Whites who crossed the boundary and deputizing communities to enforce separation. The case of Eleanor "Irish Nell" Butler—enslaved by marriage to an enslaved Black man, her children condemned—illustrates how the state targeted the womb to secure the color line. Sumptuary regulation here is not morality policing; it is eugenic governance: an obsession with purity enforced through terror.

The judiciary applied parallel racialization in sentencing practice decades earlier. The 1640 John Punch case is foundational: race-differentiated punishment for the same offense (absconding), producing life servitude for the Black defendant and term extension for the two White co-escapees.

Virginia Council & General Court (1640) — John Punch orders:

> "the court doth therefore order that the said three servants shall receive the punishment of whipping and to have thirty stripes apiece… and that the third being a negro named John Punch shall serve his said master or his assigns for the time of his natural Life here or elsewhere."

This is the pedagogy of color line: to teach Whiteness as exemption and Blackness as permanence of injury.

Having taught the lesson in flesh, the society now builds the curriculum.

The Pedagogy of Whiteness: Impression Management as Policy

Identity becomes syllabus; syllabus becomes state.

White identity was taught—through statute, church, courtroom, plantation, and purse. The lesson plan was simple: Whiteness means exemption, mobility, and the right to exclude; Blackness means exposure, immobility, and disposability. Jordan's archive shows how travelers and philosophers crafted bestiaries masquerading as anthropology; colonial assemblies then converted those fantasies into sentencing guidelines. This is how a delusion becomes a curriculum—and a curriculum becomes a country.

When a people are trained in delusion, the body keeps score. So does the music.

Grief with a Beat: The Clinical Content of "Black Rage"

Art is a case report written in melody.

Lauryn Hill's "Black Rage" functions as a diagnostic song: it catalogs the etiologies—"two-thirds a person," forced labor, economic strangulation, poisoned water, bureaucratic gaslighting. What the track names poetically, this chapter names clinically: chronic traumatic stress under conditions of state hostility, leading to adaptive rage—a rational response to structurally irrational harm.

Rage, then, is not the disease but the data. The system that produces it persists.

Contemporary Expressions: Policing as Continuity

Yesterday's patrol becomes today's police.

Modern policing reenacts colonial prerogatives: who may move, who must submit, whose pain counts, whose death is explainable. "Without Sanctuary" reminds us that the men and women who posed at lynchings were not monsters but neighbors—ordinary people performing the "highest idealism" of their racial order. The horror is not the exceptionality of perpetrators; it is the banality of the belief system that made atrocity feel responsible.

And so we return to the question that opened the file.

Returning to Milley's Question

The symptom has a source; the riot has a religion.

What caused them to assault the Capitol? The same thing that has always mobilized White rage: the fear of status loss; the reflex to reclaim dominion; the cultural catechism that equates equality with annihilation. When the fantasy of uncontested rule is threatened, the body politic reaches for its oldest sedatives—myth, force, and law.

So yes, let us understand White rage. But let us be careful: to understand it is to indict the institutions that incubate it, the curricula that train it, the laws that launder it, and the "ordinary people" who consent to it. Diagnosis without treatment is complicity.

The bridge forward is clear: if the syndrome is trained, it can be untrained. The next chapter turns from diagnosis to protocols—what clinical, legal, and cultural treatments interrupt the ritual and repattern the nervous system of a nation.

Chapter Review Questions

Section I – *The Case of White Rage*

1. How does General Milley's statement serve as both an inquiry and an unconscious confession about White rage in America?

2. Why is the phrase "be careful what you ask for" a culturally coded warning within the Black community when applied to Milley's question?

3. In psycho-clinical terms, how can White rage be understood as a recurrent symptom of cultural psychosis?

Section II – Psychopathy and Projection

4. How does Dr. Aruna Khilanani's analysis of "discovery" as theft expose the delusional structure of Whiteness?

5. What is the relationship between *impression management* and the denial of historical atrocity within White identity?

6. In what ways does projection—assigning one's own pathology to others—explain colonial depictions of Africans?

Section III – The Ritual of Backlash

7. What pattern links events such as Wilmington (1898), Tulsa (1921), and modern police killings to the broader syndrome of White rage?

8. How does backlash function as both emotional regulation and political enforcement for the White collective psyche?

9. Why is Black progress often the psychological trigger for White violence and legal regression?

Section IV – Law as Psychosis

10. How did the Maryland Act of 1664 and the Virginia statutes of 1667–1669 codify White supremacy as a legal disorder?

11. What does the *Casual Killing Act of 1669* reveal about the normalization of dehumanization and the erasure of moral conscience?

12. How does the law against "runaways in company with Negroes" demonstrate anxiety about interracial solidarity and social contamination?

13. In what way does the 1681 Maryland law concerning "white women intermarrying with negroes" expose the sexualized paranoia underlying White purity codes?

14. What psychoanalytic motives can be inferred from the colonial fixation on the Black male body and the White female body?

Section V – The Pedagogy of Whiteness

15. How did colonial laws function as a *curriculum* through which White identity was taught and rehearsed?

16. What are the long-term psychological effects of teaching racial superiority through legal privilege and immunity?

17. How does the John Punch case (1640) represent an early institutional experiment in differential punishment and racial identity construction?

Section VI – Black Rage as Clinical Response

18. In Lauryn Hill's "Black Rage," how is music used as a therapeutic and diagnostic tool to articulate intergenerational trauma?

19. How does the chapter differentiate between *pathological rage* (White) and *adaptive rage* (Black)?

20. What does Hill's refrain—"Black rage is founded..."—teach about the layering of structural violence across centuries?

Section VII – Contemporary Expressions

21. What continuities exist between colonial law enforcement and modern policing practices in the United States?

22. How do photographic records from *Without Sanctuary* challenge the myth of "random" racial violence?

23. Why is it crucial to recognize lynching participants as "ordinary people" rather than aberrant monsters?

Section VIII – Returning to Milley's Question

24. Based on the evidence throughout the chapter, how would you clinically define "White rage"?

25. What might "treatment" for this national psychosis require—legally, institutionally, and spiritually?

Works Cited

Anderson, C. (2016). *White rage: The unspoken truth of our racial divide*. Bloomsbury.

Atkins, J. (1735/1970). *A voyage to Guinea, Brazil, and the West Indies*. Frank Cass.

DeGruy, J. (2005). *Post traumatic slave syndrome: America's legacy of enduring injury and healing*. Joy DeGruy Publications.

Equal Justice Initiative. (2017). *Lynching in America: Confronting the legacy of racial terror* (3rd ed.). Equal Justice Initiative.

Hening, W. W. (1823). *The statutes at large; being a collection of all the laws of Virginia* (Vols. 1–13). Franklin Press. (Original colonial enactments cited: 1662—runaways "in company with negroes"; 1667—baptism & bondage;

1668—negro women tithables; 1668—corporal punishment of runaways; 1669—Casual Killing).

Hill, L. (2014). *Black Rage* [Recorded by Lauryn Hill]. Ms. Lauryn Hill.

Hogan, L. (2015). The forced breeding myth in the "Irish slaves" meme. *Medium*.

Jordan, W. D. (1968). *White over Black: American attitudes toward the Negro, 1550–1812*. University of North Carolina Press.

Khilanani, A. (2021, June 10). Interview with Marc Lamont Hill. *Black News Tonight*, BNC.

Maryland General Assembly. (1664). *Act concerning Negroes & other slaves*; (1681) *Act concerning English or white women intermarrying with Negro slaves*. In *Archives of Maryland Online*.

Milley, M. A. (2021, June 23). House Armed Services Committee hearing on the FY22 defense budget [Video]. *C-SPAN*. https://www.c-span.org/video/?512776-1/defense-officials-testify-budget-request

Minutes of the Council and General Court of Colonial Virginia. (1640). John Punch case order (July 9, 1640). In H. R. McIlwaine (Ed.), *Minutes of the Council and General Court of Colonial Virginia, 1622–1632, 1670–1676*. Virginia State Library.

Nichols, T. (2023, January). Memphis Police Department body-cam footage [Video]. City of Memphis.

Owensby, C. (2021, Sept 30). Body-cam footage of traffic stop, Dayton, Ohio [Video]. City of Dayton Police Department.

Proctor, S., Allen, W., & Boarman, W. (Eds.). (1883–). *Archives of Maryland*. Maryland State Archives.

Turner, M., & Turner, H. (1918). In Allen, J., Als, H., Lewis, M., & Litwack, L. (2000). *Without sanctuary: Lynching photography in America*. Twin Palms.

Wilmington Coup Commission. (2006). *1898 Wilmington race riot report*. North Carolina Office of Archives & History.

Zuczek, R. (2000). *State of rebellion: Reconstruction in South Carolina*. University of South Carolina Press.

Crump, B. (2019). *Open season: Legalized genocide of colored people*. Amistad.

Abram Smith and Thomas Ship, 1930, Indiana

Rubin Stacy, 1935, Fort Lauderdale, Florida

WHITE RAGE, CLINICAL REALITY | 151

Laura and L.D. Nelson (mother and son), 1911, Oklahoma

Figure 4.4.

George Floyd, Minnesota, 2020

CHAPTER 6
WHITENESS AS DISORDER
THE PSYCHOPATHOLOGY OF LAW, THE WHITE MIND, LEGAL SADISM, AND INSTITUTIONALIZATION OF ANTI-BLACKNESS

The Compulsion to Dominate

I begin this chapter by stating what should no longer need to be said: I do not care about the feelings or criticisms of Whites or people who present themselves as White. Their fragility is not my concern; their denial is not my burden. Those who ignore evidence are not engaged in truth seeking—they are defending pathology. Nothing they say or do to thwart my work will succeed, because I am bolstered by demonstrable proof. Even if I am murdered for my work, it will persist. That is why I have written it down. Bodies perish. Words do not.

We anchor the argument in Black witness—measured, documented, undeniable.

The late James Baldwin's words remain diagnostic pronouncements:

> "We can disagree and still love each other unless your disagreement is rooted in my oppression and denial of my humanity and right to exist."

> "I can't believe what you say, because I see what you do."

> "To be African American is to be African without any memory and American without any privilege."

> "I'm not interested in anyone's guilt. Guilt is a luxury that we can no longer afford. I know you didn't do it, and I didn't do it either, but I am responsible for it because I am a man and a citizen of this country and you are responsible for it, for the very same reason."

Baldwin names the ethical obligation; the clinicians explain the mechanism.

Baldwin's observation exposes a classic symptom of what Dr. Bobby E. Wright defined as the psychopathic racial personality: the capacity to commit or rationalize atrocities while denying accountability. The refusal to feel guilt is not confusion—it is emotional anesthesia.

Dr. Frances Cress Welsing's Cress Theory of Color Confrontation explains the origin of that anesthesia. She described Whiteness as a cultural response to genetic fear: the terror of extinction within a global majority of color. From this terror grows the compulsion to control every Black body and environment. Domination becomes medicine for anxiety.

Dr. Amos N. Wilson reframed this same phenomenon as psychological parasitism. In his analysis, the White ego cannot exist in isolation; it requires the degradation of Black identity to stabilize its false superiority. Whiteness feeds on Black suffering as proof of its own existence.

Thus, policy operates as psychiatry—law written to soothe a diseased supremacy.

Every colonial and post-colonial law was thus a therapeutic ritual—a psychiatric device for soothing White panic. Each statute reaffirmed that power, not morality, governed existence. As Dr. Wright warned, "Psychopaths reconstruct morality to suit their disease." The legal history of the West is the record of that reconstruction.

The Psychodynamics of Guilt and Projection

When guilt is intolerable, projection becomes governance.

During a seminar I once taught at a hospital, an elderly White Jewish chaplain raised her hand. She spoke with sincerity:

> "You know, Dante, as a Jewish child we always learned about the Hitler era and what the Germans did to the Jews. ... Until now, I have held that experience up as the ultimate dehumanizing experience that people have gone through. ... There is really no comparison between the experience that Jewish people faced during the Holocaust, and what African Americans have faced, and are still dealing with. ... This has continued to go on for more than 500 years, and it almost seems like an obsession White people have about oppressing Black people. It's like we have a need to oppress you. This is absolutely scary."

Confession becomes clinical evidence—naming the compulsion others deny.

Her reflection revealed what Dr. Welsing and Dr. Wilson both identified as compulsive repetition. When guilt is intolerable, the psyche projects it outward; the oppressor reenacts violence to repress shame. White supremacy becomes ritualized self-therapy—an endless acting-out of unresolved fear and envy.

The chaplain's admission that White people "have a need to oppress" is clinically precise. It names the addiction. Dr. Wright would classify it as sociopathic maintenance behavior—repeated harm without remorse, reinforced by institutional reward.

Law as Clinical Evidence: The 1672 Runaway Act

Here the pathology is notarized—fear armed with statute, cruelty paid by the state.

Building upon the 1669 Casual Killing Act, which absolved Whites of murdering enslaved Africans, the 1672 Act for the Apprehension and Suppression of Runawayes, Negroes, and Slaves codified open season on Black life:

> "FORASMUCH as it hath beene manifested to this grand assembly that many negroes have lately beene, and now are out in rebellion in sundry parts of this country... if any negroe, molatto, Indian slave or servant for life runaway ... it shall and may be lawfull for any person ... to kill or wound him or them soe resisting; ... the master or owner ... shall receive satisfaction from the publique for his negroe, molatto, Indian slave, or servant for life, soe killed ... and the person who shall kill ... shall not be questioned for the same..."

The statute institutionalized what Wright termed rewarded violence. The state reimbursed slave owners for murder—an explicit financial incentive for psychopathic behavior. Here, homicide became an economic transaction, empathy a liability.

Dr. Welsing's color-confrontation lens reveals the deeper symbolism: rebellion by the enslaved triggered panic in the collective White unconscious. The legal system responded with extermination as tranquilizer. Dr. Wilson would describe this as a neuro-cognitive feedback loop: fear → domination → relief → renewed fear. The law thus functioned as both weapon and sedative.

The Architecture of Anti-Blackness

Define the system, expose the strategy, trace the symptoms.

Anti-Blackness in North America, particularly the United States, is a White American legal, social, cultural, economic, value, and belief system. It involves and thrives on the de-prioritization of humans perceived and labeled as Black people. It also includes the criminalization, hyper-negativity, hyper-scrutiny, and pessimistic positioning of Black people and/or Blackness throughout all aspects of American society and life—for the purposes of justifying and rationalizing political, social, cultural, and economic debasement and inhumane treatment—ultimately genocide.

Anti-Blackness involves:

- The criminalization, hyper-negativity, and hyper-scrutiny of Blackness—legally, socially, culturally, sociologically, and economically.

- The criminalization of Blackness in the legal system through explicit laws and policies during the seventeenth through twentieth centuries. Examples include the Virginia Laws of 1669, 1680, 1705, 1723, the Negro Act of 1740, the Casual Killing Acts, the Fugitive Slave Act of 1850, Supreme Court decisions of 1883, 1896, and 1926, the New Deal, the G.I. Bill, and the Fair Deal.

- The creation of unfavorable legal, cultural, social, and economic institutions and constructs.

- The establishment of sociological, psychological, and emotional institutions designed to normalize racial hierarchy.

- A persisting condition developed through collective European/White (Portuguese, English, French, Dutch, Spanish, Irish, British) colonialist and imperialist ideas.

- The core of Whiteness and its ideologies, which define Black and Brown people as inferior, animalistic, and barbaric.

- A foundational principle of racism and of White identity itself.

- A condition built to demean, oppress, disenfranchise, dehumanize, invalidate, surveil, murder, and otherwise harm anyone perceived as Black.

- A design meant to destroy Black people emotionally, physically, symbolically, and spiritually—through political, legal, educational, economic, religious, and social means.

- The moral center of Whiteness.

- A consistently negative orientation toward people defined as Black.

- The adaptation of White-Eurocentric culture as the norm or standard, and the reflexive rejection of Blackness.

Examples include:

- Equating success with assimilation into White economic systems.

- Internalizing White-Eurocentric standards of beauty and worth.

- Judging or diminishing Black linguistic or cultural expression that does not conform to White norms.

- Glorifying White academic institutions as the "best" despite their exclusionary histories.

- Blaming Black individuals for systemic outcomes produced by White control.

Diagnosis invites interrogation; interrogation reveals complicity.

Diagnostic Questions:

- What must it be like, knowing you can be murdered at any time and for any reason, without consequence?

- What cultural values develop when Whites are allowed to get away with murder, free of punishment?

- What is the psychological impact on both the White psyche and the Black psyche when one group can act with total impunity?

- Is operating in a consequence-free environment normal? If so, name one scenario where Black persons are allowed this freedom.

- Who defines normalcy, and to what end?

- What are the cultural impacts on White immigrants who inherit these systems?

- In what ways have your ancestors benefited? In what ways do you still benefit today?

Anti-Blackness as Psychocultural Institution

Prejudice is opinion; institutions are machinery.

Anti-Blackness is not merely prejudice—it is the organizing principle of the White psyche and of American law. It includes:

- The criminalization and hyper-scrutiny of Black existence.

- The transformation of melanin into prima facie evidence of guilt.

- The creation of social, economic, and theological systems that rationalize domination as moral order.

Each item is a symptom cluster: delusional superiority, affective blunting, obsessive control, projection of danger, and ritualized punishment. Together they form what Wright described as institutionalized psychopathy—a social organism incapable of empathy toward its victims yet dependent on them for meaning.

Dr. Wilson's neuro-psychological model explains how these statutes trained generations of Americans—White and non-White alike—to perform racial hierarchy unconsciously. Law became a neural network, wiring reward to cruelty and punishment to equality.

The 1740 Negro Law of South Carolina and Whiteness as Legal Design

Where color becomes code and code becomes caste.

While the law does name Indians, it appears that darker-skinned and/or brown-skinned Indians constituted the majority of the groups targeted by Whites. This was the typical practice when determining which Indigenous tribes would be engaged violently by Europeans. While this is not conclusive, one example that reinforces this point is the 1740 Negro Law of South Carolina.

In Chapter One, "The Status of the Negro, His Rights and Disabilities," it stated:

> "The Act of 1740 declares all negroes and Indians (free Indians in amity with this Government, negroes, mulattoes, and mestizos, who are now free excepted) to be slaves; the offspring to follow the condition of the mother, and that such slaves are chattels personal."

Section 2 expanded:

> "Under this provision, it has been uniformly held, that color is prima facie evidence, that the party bearing the color of a Negro, mulatto, or mestizo, is a slave; but the same prima facie result does not follow from the Indian color."

Here, pigmentation itself becomes jurisprudence. The body is converted into legal text. Dr. Welsing's framework clarifies this obsession with color as the epidermal expression of anxiety—Whiteness legislating against its own fear of genetic absorption.

Wright would call this a moral hallucination: the inversion of justice whereby the capacity for empathy is treated as weakness, and cruelty as virtue. Wilson would name it structural psychosis—a society whose laws externalize internal disorder.

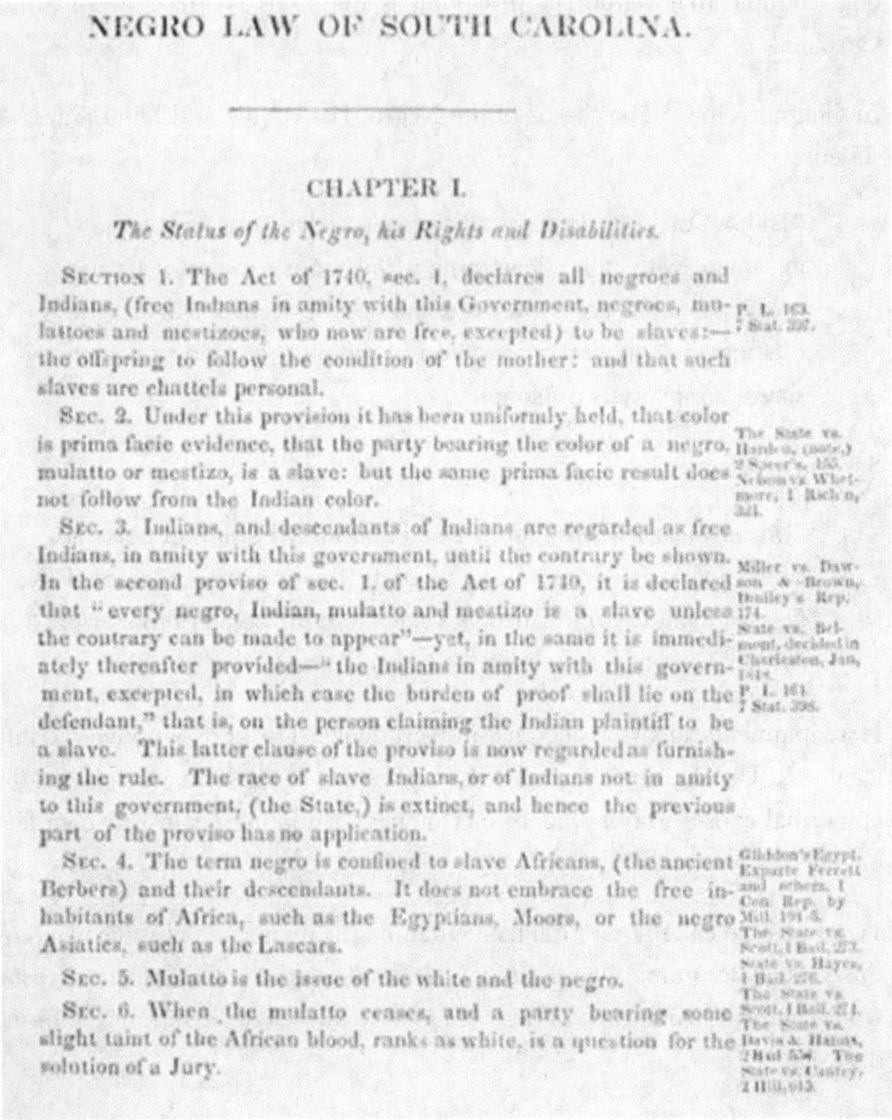

NEGRO LAW OF SOUTH CAROLINA.

CHAPTER I.
The Status of the Negro, his Rights and Disabilities.

SECTION 1. The Act of 1740, sec. 1, declares all negroes and Indians, (free Indians in amity with this Government, negroes, mulattoes and mestizoes, who now are free, excepted) to be slaves:— the offspring to follow the condition of the mother; and that such slaves are chattels personal. P. L. 163.
7 Stat. 397.

SEC. 2. Under this provision it has been uniformly held, that color is prima facie evidence, that the party bearing the color of a negro, mulatto or mestizo, is a slave: but the same prima facie result does not follow from the Indian color. The State vs.
Hanks, (note,)
2 Speer's, 155.
Nelson vs. Whetmore, 1 Rich'n,
321.

SEC. 3. Indians, and descendants of Indians are regarded as free Indians, in amity with this government, until the contrary be shown. In the second proviso of sec. 1. of the Act of 1740, it is declared that "every negro, Indian, mulatto and mestizo is a slave unless the contrary can be made to appear"—yet, in the same it is immediately thereafter provided—"the Indians in amity with this government, excepted, in which case the burden of proof shall lie on the defendant," that is, on the person claiming the Indian plaintiff to be a slave. This latter clause of the proviso is now regarded as furnishing the rule. The race of slave Indians, or of Indians not in amity to this government, (the State,) is extinct, and hence the previous part of the proviso has no application. Miller vs. Dawson & Brown,
Dudley's Rep.
174.
State vs. Belmont, decided in
Charleston, Jan,
1848.
P. L. 164.
7 Stat. 398.

SEC. 4. The term negro is confined to slave Africans, (the ancient Berbers) and their descendants. It does not embrace the free inhabitants of Africa, such as the Egyptians, Moors, or the negro Asiatics, such as the Lascars. Glidden's Egypt.
Exparte Ferrett
and others, 1
Con. Rep. by
Mill, 131.5.
The State vs.
Scott, 1 Bail. 271.
State vs. Hayes,
1 Bail. 275.

SEC. 5. Mulatto is the issue of the white and the negro.

SEC. 6. When the mulatto ceases, and a party bearing some slight taint of the African blood, ranks as white, is a question for the solution of a Jury. The State vs.
Scott, 1 Bail. 274.
The State vs.
Davis & Hanes,
2 Bail. 558. The
State vs. Cantey,
2 Hill, 613.

Figure 5.1.

The Psychopathology of Color

Unquestionably, we see that color is the main object of White concern. Before, during, and after this time, Blackness and Brownness were criminalized. Indians closer in color to Whites were more likely to be exempt from enslavement—irrespective of having Indian blood running through their veins. Color mattered above all else.

Once hierarchy is painted on the skin, everything the skin touches becomes evidence.

This obsession with pigmentation reveals the diagnostic core of Whiteness: a pathological fixation on hierarchy, control, and distance from anything associated with Blackness. The proximity to Whiteness determined one's worth, one's safety, and one's right to exist. Skin color became the symbolic and legal determinant of humanity.

Contemporary Parallels: White Paranoia as Cultural Logic

Yesterday's statute becomes today's standard operating procedure.

How does this compare to today's racist American culture? What parallels exist?

The 1672 law clarifies that Black people "out in sundry parts of the country" posed no profound threat. Yet White paranoia made them out to. The need for domination—driven by the insatiable White appetite for wealth, property, and control—converted imagination into justification. The idea of threat was enough to legitimize violence. Whiteness turned anxiety into law, and law into genocide.

This is not merely historical. The same psycho-behavioral pattern persists in modern policing, education, employment, and health care. White paranoia becomes institutional doctrine. Black movement, speech, or mere presence is pathologized and criminalized. Whiteness cannot tolerate equality because its self-concept depends on dominance. The pathological loop continues: fear breeds control, control breeds violence, violence breeds rationalization—and rationalization sustains fear.

Institutionalized Psychosis: Albert Cleage's Diagnosis

Ideology presents as science; power masquerades as truth.

The theologian and revolutionary thinker Albert Cleage described this systemic mental illness during his 1971 appearance on The Black Journal, in an episode entitled "A Black Paper on White Racism." His words remain an unflinching psychoanalytic assessment of White institutional power:

> "I think we must understand that there's no such thing as objective truth, that White people use the institutions to accomplish White purpose. The White purpose is to maintain a power position and keep everybody else in a powerless, subordinate type of position. That's the institutions' purpose. That is the way it functions and how it functions, and we have to realize that everything that schools teach is designed to fit into that purpose. The schools teach, not objective truth but what the White man wants to project as truth.
>
> {For example} Sociology. Sociology is not a science in the sense that it is dealing objectively with the way people live together. It's dealing with the White man's pattern of living together as the norm by which we judge how other people live. If you live like White people live, then you are living the way that you are supposed to live. If not, you're either primitive or insane as a people.

Psychologically, it's the same thing. Psychology as applied, lacks an objective discussion or analysis of the development of community living or organizing to optimize function. Rather psychology as applied, begins with the presumption that the way Whites function and organize communities and live, is civilized, and the standard against which to measure society and all elements regardless of multicultural origins, affinities, or adaptation to geographic conditions. If the White man does it this way, then this is the norm by which we judge all other people.

If the White man is violent, then actually all other people have to be violent in order to be normal. If you're not violent, then obviously there's something wrong with you and you should be in an insane asylum. The whole pattern that is set-up as a norm for human behavior by psychologists, and everyone that is dealing with it, is dealing with it from a White point of view. And so, the schools teach Black children and White children to look through White eyes. From kindergarten on, the Black child is being taught to look at the world and interpret it through White eyes. Everything he is, is wrong. Everything that exists in his community is wrong.

And we ought to declare that White music is really no good, that White psychology is no good. The White man either acts like we do, or he's insane. White sociology is no good. The very structure of White society indicates that White people in social structure are obviously insane or they're abnormal. So, we must project then, a Black psychology, a Black sociology, a Black music, a Black history… that takes in the realities, and that is essentially sound as opposed to the mythology that the White man has developed out of his own ignorance, out of his own non-creativity."

Cleage names the curriculum of delusion; you prescribe the counter-curriculum of repair.

Cleage's words function as a clinical diagnosis of cultural psychosis—a description of how whiteness institutionalizes delusion as objectivity. His critique exposes the sociological and psychological mechanisms that preserve White dominance by defining White pathology as "civilization" and labeling Black existence as "deviance."

Black Truth and White Truth

Two "truths" circulate; only one restores reality.

"This is Black truth, and it is White truth."

These final words encapsulate the double consciousness of the oppressed and the delusion of the oppressor. Black truth is rooted in lived experience, ancestral memory, and survival through centuries of White violence. White truth, by contrast, is the pathology of projection—a false construction that redefines harm as order, subjugation as civilization, and domination as divine right.

In psycho-clinical terms, Whiteness manifests as a collective narcissistic delusion, one that depends on denial and inversion. Its survival requires both self-deception and the perpetual misrepresentation of Black humanity. The "truths" coexist, but only one heals. Black truth liberates; White truth deceives.

Clinical Synthesis: The White Ego as Empire

Read the statutes as chart notes; the nation as a case file.

The cumulative evidence confirms a shared diagnosis: Whiteness operates as a trans-generational mental disorder—a fusion of anxiety, narcissism, and sadism sustained by law. The 1669 Casual Killing Act, the 1672 Runaway Act, and the 1740 Negro Law are not anomalies; they are psychiatric case files.

Dr. Welsing teaches that a culture obsessed with control of color reveals its terror of annihilation. Dr. Wright warns that psychopathy, when normalized, becomes civilization itself. Dr. Wilson insists that no people can remain healthy while internalizing the delusions of their oppressors.

Thus, the American legal system must be understood not only as a mechanism of governance but as a mirror of collective disorder. It is the therapy of a diseased ego. Law functioned as the White mind's medication—temporarily relieving anxiety by scripting subjugation.

What began as religious doctrine evolved into political economy, then into national identity. The psychopathology of Whiteness became the architecture of America. Until it is diagnosed and treated, the empire will continue to mistake its sickness for order and its violence for virtue.

Diagnosis demands protocol. The following chapter turns to prescriptive design—legal, clinical, and cultural interventions that interrupt the compulsion and retrain the moral nervous system.

Chapter Review Questions

I. Pathology, Denial, and Moral Inversion

1. How does the author define "the compulsion to dominate," and why is it described as a psychiatric symptom rather than a social preference?

2. In what ways do Baldwin's observations illustrate the traits of the *psychopathic racial personality* described by Dr. Bobby E. Wright?

3. What does the refusal of guilt among Whites reveal about collective emotional functioning?

4. How can denial, projection, and moral inversion be understood as recurring defense mechanisms in White identity formation?

5. How does religion and law operate as moral anesthetics for pathological behavior?

II. Clinical Theorists and Diagnostic Frameworks

6. How does Dr. Frances Cress Welsing's *Cress Theory of Color Confrontation* reinterpret the origins of White fear and control?

7. In what ways does Dr. Amos N. Wilson's concept of psychological parasitism expand our understanding of White domination?

8. How does Dr. Wright's theory of institutional psychopathy redefine the moral structure of Western civilization?

9. What parallels can be drawn between Welsing's concept of genetic fear and Wilson's idea of neurocognitive conditioning?

10. How does integrating these three theorists transform how we interpret historical legal codes?

III. Law as Forensic Evidence of Psychopathy

11. In the 1669 *Casual Killing Act*, how is the normalization of murder indicative of collective sociopathy?

12. How does the 1672 *Runaway Act* reveal the state's role in rewarding violence and desensitizing empathy?

13. What clinical meaning can be assigned to monetary compensation for killing enslaved Africans?

14. How did these laws collectively create a "legal nervous system" that rewarded cruelty and punished equality?

15. How might these early legal codes serve as prototypes for later modern institutions of racial control?

IV. Anti-Blackness as a Psychocultural System

16. How does anti-Blackness function as the organizing principle of Western culture rather than an aberration within it?

17. Which "symptom clusters" of Whiteness (delusional superiority, affective blunting, obsessive control, projection of danger, ritualized punishment) appear most prominently in this chapter's examples?

18. How does the Jewish chaplain's reflection highlight the compulsive nature of repetition and projection within Whiteness?

19. In what ways did the 1740 *Negro Law of South Carolina* transform pigmentation into jurisprudence?

20. How does the fixation on color hierarchy express the deeper anxiety that Dr. Welsing described as genetic fear?

V. Diagnosis, Implications, and Healing

21. What are the implications of describing Whiteness as a trans-generational mental disorder?

22. How does this diagnostic framing alter the moral and political conversation about racism?

23. What forms of social or institutional "treatment" might counteract the inherited pathology of White supremacy?

24. How can diagnosing Whiteness as pathology open possibilities for collective healing and reconstruction?

25. How might this psycho-clinical analysis be integrated into antiracist education, law, or public policy to prevent further replication of the disorder?

Works Cited

Baldwin, J. (1961). *Nobody Knows My Name: More Notes of a Native Son.* New York, NY: Dial Press.

Baldwin, J. (1985). *The Price of the Ticket: Collected Nonfiction 1948–1985.* New York, NY: St. Martin's Press.

Baldwin, J. (1998). *Collected Essays.* New York, NY: Library of America.

Butler v. Boarman family records (1664 law; 1767 court depositions). *Archives of Maryland.* Maryland State Archives.

Hening, W. W. (1823). *The Statutes at Large: Being a Collection of All the Laws of Virginia.* Vols. 2–4. Richmond, VA: George Cochran.

Hogan, L. (2016, March 17). *The Forced Breeding Myth in the Irish Slaves Meme. Medium.* https://medium.com/

Jordan, W. D. (1968). *White Over Black: American Attitudes Toward the Negro, 1550–1812.* Chapel Hill, NC: University of North Carolina Press.

South Carolina General Assembly. (1740). *Negro Act of 1740.* In *The Statutes at Large of South Carolina* (Vol. 7). Columbia, SC: A. S. Johnston.

Virginia General Assembly. (1667–1672). *Acts of the Grand Assembly* ("Casual Killing Act," "Runawayes, Negroes and Slaves"). In Hening, W. W. (Ed.), *Statutes at Large of Virginia.* Richmond, VA.

Wells-Barnett, I. B. (1895). *A Red Record: Tabulated Statistics and Alleged Causes of Lynching in the United States.* Chicago, IL.

Welsing, F. C. (1991). *The Isis Papers: The Keys to the Colors.* Chicago, IL: Third World Press.

Wilson, A. N. (1993). *The Falsification of Afrikan Consciousness: Eurocentric History, Psychiatry, and the Politics of White Supremacy.* New York, NY: Afrikan World InfoSystems.

Wilson, A. N. (1998). *Blueprint for Black Power: A Moral, Political, and Economic Imperative for the Twenty-First Century.* New York, NY: Afrikan World InfoSystems.

Wright, B. E. (1984). *The Psychopathic Racial Personality and Other Essays.* Chicago, IL: Third World Press.

Without Sanctuary: Lynching Photography in America. (2000). Santa Fe, NM: Twin Palms Publishers.

Welsing, F. C., Wilson, A. N., & Wright, B. E. (cited throughout). *Collected works and lectures on racism, psychology, and power.*

Wells, I. B. (2020 reprint). *Southern Horrors and Other Writings.* Boston, MA: Bedford/St. Martin's.

CHAPTER 7
INHERITED VIOLENCE
THE PSYCHOSIS OF WHITE CONTROL AND THE REPRODUCTION OF BLACK TRAUMA

> *"It is true that Negro slaves in America represented the worst and lowest conditions amongst modern laborers... The tragedy of the Black slave was precisely this: His absolute subjection to the individual will of an owner."*
>
> W.E.B. DU BOIS,
> BLACK RECONSTRUCTION
> IN AMERICA

I. Observation:
The Nature of Black Rage and White Depravity

In this chapter, I focus on the mounting rage that has lived within Black people for centuries — rage not as pathology, but as evidence of health, as a sign that the nervous system refuses to normalize dehumanization. How does one endure the violation of body, spirit, and dignity — not once, but for generations — without rage?

Black rage is an act of coherence. It is the body's proof that the soul remembers injustice, that it refuses to reconcile itself to the psychotic demands of Whiteness.

The need for liberation and empowerment originates from deprivation — from the moral and material starvation imposed by those who built an entire civilization on possession and control. Rage is the unprocessed grief of centuries; empowerment is its transformation into clarity.

Du Bois diagnosed the condition succinctly. He observed that the Negro slave represented "the ultimate degradation of man," the conversion of a human being into real estate. His words serve as the historical autopsy of White psychopathy. The slave codes, he noted, stripped Black people of petition, contract, family, and life itself. They rendered Black existence divisible, saleable, punishable at will — while transforming White domination into moral order.

Du Bois's clinical insight still holds: America's foundational institutions were designed to degrade the Black psyche and deify the White delusion.

II. Historical Record: Enslavement as Psychosis

Archive as anatomy: each statute is a symptom; together they map a disease.

> "Slaves were not considered men... They could be punished at will... The law regards a negro slave, so far as his civil status is concerned, purely and absolutely property."
>
> Du Bois

Whiteness, as performed through colonial law, reveals not rational governance but organized psychosis. The obsessive repetition of control — every statute, code, and amendment — is evidence of fixation.

Each law was a symptom of the disease: the need to contain, to mutilate, to subordinate. The human psyche that cannot tolerate equality will invent any theology, jurisprudence, or science to preserve its delusion.

Whites designed academic and political institutions to perpetuate their disorder. Education itself became a psychiatric mechanism of domination —

teaching Black people that their existence was error and teaching White people that cruelty was virtue.

To leave these institutions unchallenged is to surrender to sociopathy. To challenge them is to begin the process of cultural detoxification. Whiteness must be tried, examined, and confronted as one would an unrepentant patient: not with pity, but with precision.

III. Institutionalization of Pathology: Law as Delusion

Fear becomes policy; policy becomes ritual; ritual poses as "order."

> "WHEREAS the frequent meeting of considerable numbers of negroe slaves under pretence of feasts and burialls is judged of dangerous consequence…"
>
> AN ACT PREVENTING NEGRO INSURRECTIONS, 1680

> "It shall and may be lawful for such person and persons to kill and destroy such negroes, mulattoes, and other slaves by gunn or any otherwaise whatsoever."
>
> ACT OF 1691

The colonial record exposes law as ritualized psychosis — the codification of fear into governance. The 1680 and 1691 acts criminalized not rebellion but existence itself: the gathering for funerals, the raising of hands in self-defense, the very act of being Black in public.

These laws were not written for order; they were written for containment. They reveal the compulsive anxiety of a population terrified of its own violence.

In these legal enactments, the White mind projected its pathology onto the Black body. Resistance was reclassified as aggression; survival as defiance; humanity as criminality.

Each lash legislated into law was a prescription for control — a ritualistic performance of supremacy. Every act of "correction," every public whipping, every statute permitting murder without consequence functioned as therapy for the diseased ego of Whiteness.

IV. Clinical Case Study: Sadism as Cultural Normalcy

Extremity is taught in increments; atrocity is learned as etiquette.

> "The transition into becoming a terrorist is rarely sudden and abrupt... Most involvement in terrorism results from gradual exposure and socialisation towards extreme behavior."
>
> RANDY BORUM,
> PSYCHOLOGY OF TERRORISM

The American legal system is an early manual in the psychology of terrorism. White colonists did not suddenly "become" terrorists; they were socialized into it. Gradual exposure to domination conditioned them to perceive violence as virtue and power as morality.

Every statute and punishment normalized sadism. The spectacle of Black suffering became the cultural liturgy of Whiteness. A Black person protecting their child could be lashed thirty times. A woman resisting rape could be executed. A community mourning its dead could be annihilated for gathering.

This is not discipline; it is ritualized psychosis.

V. Inheritance: Epigenetic Violence and Cultural Repetition

What is rehearsed in law is rehearsed in bodies; repetition writes reflex.

Whiteness reproduces itself through repetition — behavioral, institutional, and biological. It is, as the CDC might phrase it, epigenetic violence: the intergenerational transmission of trauma behaviors encoded not only in the oppressed but in the oppressor.

> "Your genes play an important role in your health, but so do your behaviors and environment... Epigenetics is the study of how your behaviors and environment can cause changes that affect the way your genes work."
>
> — CENTERS FOR DISEASE CONTROL AND PREVENTION

The behaviors of "Karens," "Toms," and other White enforcers of racial control are not anomalies; they are inherited rituals. These individuals act as vessels for ancestral pathology — surveillance, hysteria, accusation —behaviors rehearsed for centuries on plantations, in courthouses, and in pulpits.

When Amy Cooper feigned distress in Central Park, she did not invent the behavior; she inherited it. When George Zimmerman hunted Trayvon Martin, he enacted a script written in colonial law. The psychosis continues because it has been rewarded for generations.

VI. Prognosis: Black Rage as Healing, Containment as Justice

Rage is the immune response; policy is the treatment plan.

To diagnose a pathology is not to despair. Rage is the immune response of the spirit. It is the Black body rejecting infection.

We must name the psychopaths for what they are: individuals suffering from chronic mental disorder marked by abnormal and violent social behavior. The psychopath is dangerous. The psychopath must be contained.

Containment, in this case, is not vengeance but justice — the moral quarantine of a cultural disease. We must legislate as healers: passing anti-lynching laws, protecting Black life as sacred, and dismantling the systems that reward predation.

Hamilton and Ture warned us in 1967 that White power allows limited progress only when convenient — and retracts it at will. Their insight remains diagnostic:

> "Black people were allowed to register to vote and to participate in politics, because it was to the advantage of powerful white allies to permit this... That era of Black

participation in politics was ended by another set of white decisions."

History repeats itself because the psychosis remains untreated. Whiteness continues to medicate its insecurity with control, its guilt with projection, and its fear with violence.

The Clinical Anatomy of White Sadism

When homicide is reframed as "correction," murder graduates into policy.

> "If any slave resist his master... and shall happen to be killed in such correction, it shall not be accounted felony."
>
> ACT CONCERNING SERVANTS
> AND SLAVES, 1705

The 1705 amendment to the Casual Killing Act legalized the murder of enslaved people as accidental correction. This was not law; it was institutionalized delusion.

These acts were the diagnostic fingerprints of a civilization that had normalized murder as moral hygiene. Each statute institutionalized the right to harm without consequence — the legal equivalent of psychotic repetition compulsion.

To dominate is abnormal. To enslave is abnormal. To justify brutality as civilization is delusion. Yet this delusion persists because it is economically, psychologically, and spiritually profitable for those who refuse to see.

The Prognostic Warning: America's Unhealed Psychosis

Duration matters: a decade of horror is atrocity; centuries of horror are architecture.

Comparing the Black holocaust in America to Hitler's Germany is insufficient. Hitler's madness lasted little more than a decade; America's has endured for centuries and remains ongoing.

White people have not merely participated in a genocide; they have socialized its victims to self-perpetuate it. This is the final stage of pathology — when the oppressor convinces the oppressed to perform their own destruction.

The genocide of Black people continues, hidden behind a national narrative of progress. No institution is immune — not education, not healthcare, not government. Every system still carries the trace of its founding disorder.

Moral Intervention: Toward Containment and Healing

Diagnosis without protocol is complicity; rage without strategy is exhaustion.

Black liberation requires both diagnosis and containment. Whiteness must be recognized as a chronic, relapsing disorder whose primary symptom is domination and whose secondary symptom is denial.

Containment does not mean revenge. It means accountability, truth, and the moral rehabilitation of institutions that were built on insanity.

We must humanize where they dehumanized, teach where they silenced, and rebuild where they destroyed. The work overwhelms but is worthwhile.

Rage is not our illness; it is our medicine.

Chapter Review Questions

I. Observation and Emotional Diagnosis

1. How does the author redefine Black rage as a *healthy psychological response* rather than pathology?

2. In what ways does rage function as evidence of remembrance and resistance within the Black psyche?

3. What does the author mean by describing Whiteness as a "psychotic demand" on Black existence?

4. How does deprivation serve as the origin point for both rage and empowerment?

5. Why is the refusal to normalize abuse considered an act of mental and spiritual coherence?

II. Historical Case Analysis

6. How does Du Bois's description of slavery as "the ultimate degradation of man" expose the psychotic logic of White control?

7. What specific elements in the slave codes demonstrate that the law itself was a *manifestation of psychosis*?

8. How did legal ownership of Black bodies satisfy the compulsions of the White psyche?

9. In what ways do these colonial statutes mirror modern-day institutional practices?

10. How does the author connect Du Bois's historical diagnosis to contemporary racial systems of domination?

III. The Law as Ritualized Psychosis

11. What do the 1680 and 1691 acts reveal about the paranoid structure of White fear?

12. How does the repetition of laws controlling Black mobility illustrate the compulsive nature of Whiteness?

13. Why does the author classify colonial punishment rituals as "therapeutic performances" for the White ego?

14. How did the concept of "correction" function as moral camouflage for sadism?

15. What psychological mechanisms—projection, denial, rationalization—can be observed in these legislative texts?

IV. Clinical Symptoms and Inherited Behavior

16. How does Randy Borum's framework for terrorism illuminate the process by which White society normalized racial terror?

17. What is meant by *epigenetic violence*, and how does it operate in both oppressors and oppressed?

18. In what ways do the behaviors of "Karens" and "Toms" represent intergenerational reenactments of colonial surveillance?

19. How does the notion of inheritance challenge the idea that racism is purely a matter of individual belief?

20. What does the chapter suggest about the biological and cultural transfer of trauma across generations?

V. Prognosis and Moral Containment

21. How does the author define "containment" in moral-psychological terms, and how does it differ from revenge?

22. Why is accountability described as a form of *collective psychiatric intervention*?

23. How might the passage of anti-lynching and racial-justice legislation function as cultural treatment rather than policy reform?

24. In what way is Black rage portrayed as both immune response and medicine?

25. What steps, according to the author, are necessary to end the cycle of inherited psychosis and move toward collective healing?

Works Cited

Borum, R. (2004). *Psychology of Terrorism.* Tampa, FL: University of South Florida.

Centers for Disease Control and Prevention. (2023). *Epigenetics: How your behaviors and environment can cause changes that affect the way your genes work.*

Du Bois, W. E. B. (1935). *Black Reconstruction in America.* New York, NY: Harcourt, Brace & Company.

Hamilton, C. V., & Ture, K. (1967). *Black Power: The Politics of Liberation.* New York, NY: Random House.

An Act Preventing Negro Insurrections. (1680). *The Statutes at Large of Virginia.* W. W. Hening (Ed.).

An Act Concerning Servants and Slaves. (1705). *The Statutes at Large of Virginia.* W. W. Hening (Ed.).

An Act for the Apprehension and Suppression of Runawayes, Negroes, and Slaves. (1672). *The Statutes at Large of Virginia.* W. W. Hening (Ed.).

CHAPTER 8
THE SCIENTIFIC RELIGION OF WHITE POWER
MEDICINE, LAW, AND THE PATHOLOGY OF RACIAL CONTROL

Having named Black rage as the body's immune response to domination, we now examine the sedatives that Whiteness prescribed for itself: the "scientific" and legal rituals that transformed pathology into policy. What follows traces how a culture of domination rebranded its psychosis as progress—from the seventeenth century through the modern day.

It is vital to point out that, among a sea of bad actors, Virginia and Maryland were not unique. America's other pro-White and anti-Black colonies operated similarly under British rule.

Again, a combination of pro-White and anti-Black laws and policies were implemented throughout the colonies to degrade Black people specifically. Everything was enacted to elevate White wealth, White identity, and White dominance. There was no concern about right or wrong; moral or immoral.

As earlier chapters have shown, these juridical foundations prepared the ground for the next mutation of the disorder: its "scientific" justification.

In clinical terms, these were not mere cultural biases but *ritualized symptoms*—expressions of what Dr. Bobby E. Wright called the *psychopathic racial personality*: the organized, institutionalized capacity to dehumanize without empathy or remorse. Dr. Frances Cress Welsing would describe this as a defensive neurosis, rooted in the anxiety of genetic annihilation and the compulsion to control dark bodies as a way of preserving white survival. Dr. Amos N. Wilson interpreted this systemically—as the engineering of political economy and culture to ensure that pathology became normalcy.

As Robin DiAngelo wrote in *What Does It Mean to Be White?*, the projection of White traits onto Black bodies—"laziness, shiftlessness, lustfulness, dirtiness, deviousness, sinfulness"—was purposeful. It alleviated moral culpability. To be White was to be angelic, Christian, innocent, moral. No true, meaningful, or deep self-reflection was (or is) required. Such projection, Welsing would argue, is the central defense mechanism of Whiteness itself: disown the violent impulse, project it outward, then punish the projection.

These dynamics directly shaped the cultural and institutional fabric of the United States of America. This is true for language, education, economics, legality, government, housing, and every cultural and structural creation in America. The *symptomology* became the culture.

The Scientific Mask of Psychopathy

By the nineteenth century, "science" became the new scripture of racial control.

Let's look at the connections between American academic, medical, legal, and economic institutions in the nineteenth and twentieth centuries. Harriet Washington, in *Medical Apartheid*, discusses the ways in which White, psychopathic terrorists posing as scholars and medical experts preyed—and still prey—on Black bodies. Washington details how anti-Blackness informed the White institutional intersections of law, religion, academia, science, economics, and medicine.

There is no shortage of examples. Dr. Charles Caldwell, who developed the "science" of phrenology, asserted that the skull formations of Black people revealed fewer bumps and therefore less intellect, concluding that enslavement was necessary. He attended the University of Pennsylvania Medical School.

Samuel Cartwright, another University of Pennsylvania Medical School alumnus—known as the "Expert in Negro Medicine"—asserted that Black people had lower lung capacity and that forced labor increased it. He created two "mental and behavioral" conditions for African Americans—

drapetomania, the desire to escape slavery, and *dysaesthesia aethiopica*, a supposed lack of work ethic. His prescribed treatment was beatings and whippings.

These pseudo-diagnoses illustrate the psychiatric delusion of the era: to label resistance as disease and obedience as health.

Dr. Josiah Nott, the architect of polygenism, argued that skull formations proved racial hierarchy. Drs. Samuel Wells and Orson Fowler's physiognomy claimed that outer appearance determined moral worth. Their 1875 textbook, *New Physiognomy: Or, Signs of Character as Manifested Through Temperament and External Forms, and Especially in the Human Face Divine*, paired White superiority with Black inferiority as the "two extremes of the spectrum." Welsing would interpret this pseudo-science as projection made doctrine: the need to invent pathology in the Black other to defend against confronting pathology in the self.

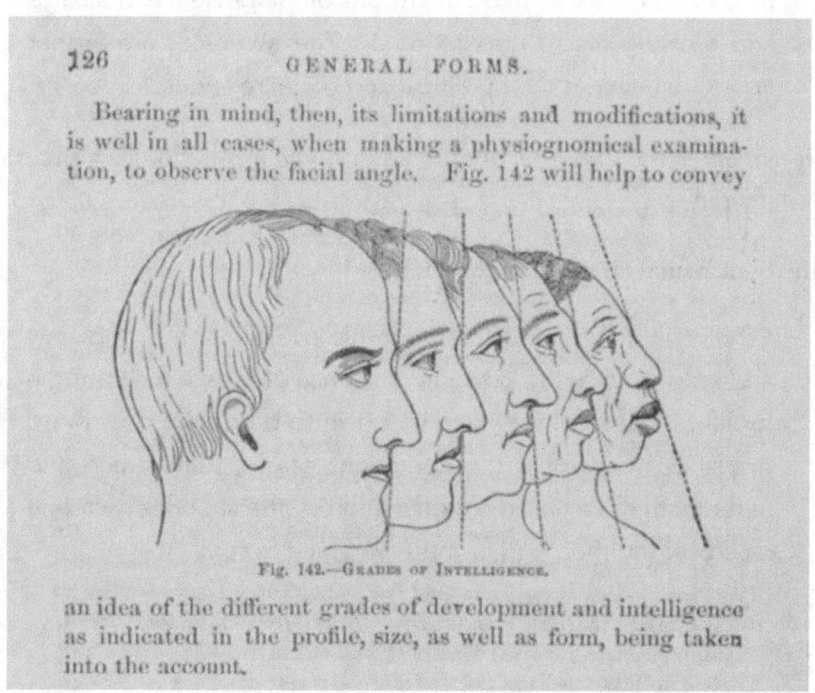

Figure 8.1.

Dr. Robert Bennett Bean extended this medical terror, publishing *Some Peculiarities of the Negro Brain* in 1906. He wrote:

> "From time to time in the past hundred years attempts have been made to determine the distinctive points of difference between the Caucasian and Negro brain. ... An effort will be made to show ... that there is a difference in the size and shape of Caucasian and Negro brains, ... the genu of the corpus callosum is smaller in the Negro, ... and that the brain weight of Negro brains is actually less."

Bean's hypothesis was reinforced by Dr. Irving Fisher and Frederick Ludwig Hoffman's *Race Traits and Tendencies of the American Negro*, which opened:

> "The progress of the colored population ... has for more than fifty years past been a matter of the most serious concern to those who have observed the results of the presence of a large and growing negro population. ... The two races are farther apart than ever in their political and social relations."

Here we enter the early twentieth century, when pseudoscience hardened into statecraft.

In the book's final chapter, they concluded:

> "The central fact deducible from this investigation ... is plainly and emphatically the powerful influence of race in the struggle for life. ... The colored race is shown to be on the downward grade ... It is not in the conditions of life, but in race and heredity that we find the explanation ... the superiority of one race over another, and of the Aryan race over all."

They cited Charles Morris's *The Aryan Race: Its Origins and Its Achievements* (1888):

> "If the negro is indolent both physically and mentally ... in the Aryan we find a highly vigorous and developed mental activity. ... Thus, the Aryan stands as the type of intellectual man."

Hoffman summarized:

> "In other words, the Aryan race is possessed of all the essential characteristics that make for success ... Wherever the white man has gone, he has become master of the conditions of life. ... The whole history of Anglo-Saxon conquest and colonization is one endless proof of race superiority and race supremacy."

Hoffman, later president of the American Statistical Association, concluded that if Black people were denied health care, "we would become extinct within two or three generations." Welsing would diagnose this as *genetic warfare disguised as science*—an effort to ensure White survival through controlled Black death.

Eugenics and the Institutionalization of Psychopathy

By the 1910s and 1920s, pseudoscience became policy.

Dr. Madison Grant's *The Passing of the Great Race* (1916) pushed this obsession into modern policy. Grant wrote:

> "Whenever the incentive to imitate the dominant race is removed the Negro ... reverts shortly to his ancestral grade of culture. ... A rigid system of selection through the elimination of those who are weak or unfit ... would solve the whole question in one hundred years ... The state through sterilization must see to it that his line stops with him ... ultimately to worthless race types."

192 | THE PSYCHOPATHY OF WHITENESS

This pseudoscience fueled the **Virginia Racial Integrity Act of 1924**:

> "It shall hereafter be unlawful for any white person in this State to marry anyone other than a white person ... 'white person' shall apply only to the person who has no trace whatsoever of any blood other than Caucasian."

Figure 8.2.

The Supreme Court then sanctified this ideology in **Buck v. Bell (1927)**. Chief Justice Oliver Wendell Holmes wrote:

> "It is better for the world, if instead of waiting to execute degenerate offspring for crime ... society can prevent those who are manifestly unfit from continuing their kind. Three generations of imbeciles are enough."

One year earlier, the Court's **Corrigan v. Buckley** and **Euclid v. Ambler** rulings protected racial zoning and property exclusion. The pattern: White anxiety converted into national jurisprudence.

Adolf Hitler admired it. In *Mein Kampf*, he wrote:

> "If Nature does not wish that weaker individuals should mate with the stronger ... whenever Aryans have mingled their blood with that of an inferior race the result has been the downfall ... In North America ... the Teutonic element which has kept its racial stock pure ... has come to dominate ... and will remain master ... as long as that element does not fall a victim to the habit of adulterating its blood."

Later, he added:

> "I have studied with interest the laws of several [U.S.] states concerning the prevention of reproduction by people whose progeny would ... be injurious to the racial stock."

The **Nuremberg Race Laws** (1935) mirrored these U.S. prototypes. The U.S. Holocaust Memorial Museum records:

> "The Nazis believed that such relationships were dangerous because they led to 'mixed race' children. ... According to the Nazis, these children ... undermined the purity of the German race."

America's own political leaders openly endorsed this ideology. Leon F. Whitney of the American Eugenics Society praised Hitler's program as "merciful and inevitable." J.D. Rockefeller, Andrew Carnegie, Alexander Graham Bell, and Thomas J. Watson of IBM financed parallel experiments. IBM's Dehomag subsidiary supplied the Nazis with punch-card machines that tracked Jews and others marked for extermination. As Edwin Black wrote in *IBM and the Holocaust*:

> "Hitler's fascism resonated with certain men of great vision, such as Henry Ford ... and Thomas J. Watson ... International Business Machines."

Medical Apartheid, Then and Now

Dorothy Roberts's *Killing the Black Body* and Harriet Washington's *Medical Apartheid* name these figures for what they were: medical terrorists credentialed by America's finest schools. Yale, Michigan State, Penn, Johns Hopkins, Harvard, and William & Mary all funded and legitimated their work. Dr. Bobby Wright captured the logic:

> "What they tell you is, oh no Dr. Wright, this is science. This is objective. You know what science is? A group of White men and White women getting in a room saying this is the way the world is. If you disagree with us, we will kill you or flunk you."

Abraham Flexner's *Report on Medical Education in the United States and Canada* (1910) sealed this pattern. Commissioned by the AMA and the Carnegie Foundation, it closed most Black medical schools, rationalized as "quality control." Flexner wrote:

> "The Negro must be educated, not only for his sake, but for ours. ... He has besides, the tremendous importance that belongs to the potential source of infection and contagion. ...

A well-taught negro sanitarian will be immensely useful; an essentially untrained negro wearing an M.D. degree is dangerous."

The clinical delusion: protect the "public" by suppressing Black advancement. Wilson would call this the **institutionalization of projection**—redefining oppression as public health.

A 2016 study demonstrated its persistence: half of White medical students and residents believed false biological differences such as "Black people's skin is thicker." Those who endorsed such beliefs rated Black patients' pain as lower and recommended weaker treatment. A 2020 study found that Black newborns were twice as likely to survive when cared for by Black physicians. These data are contemporary clinical proof of what Wright and Welsing diagnosed: a pathological incapacity for empathy toward Black life.

The Legal Flexibility of White Supremacy

The 1705 Virginia law, *An Act Declaring Who Shall Not Bear Office in This Country*, codified that Blackness itself was criminal:

> "That no person ... nor any negro, mulatto or Indian ... shall ... bear any office ... and if any such person shall presume to take upon him... he shall forfeit and pay five hundred pounds ... And ... the child of an Indian and the child, grandchild, or great grandchild, of a negro shall be deemed ... a mulatto."

An Act Concerning Servants and Slaves (1705) added:

> "No negros, mulattos, or Indians, although christians ... shall purchase any christian servant ... and if ... purchase any christian white servant, the said servant shall, ipso facto, become free."

> "And if any woman servant shall have a bastard child by a negro, or mulatto ... she shall ... pay ... fifteen pounds ... or be sold for five years ... and the child ... to be a servant until ... thirty-one years of age."

> "And for a further prevention of that abominable mixture and spurious issue ... whatsoever English ... shall intermarry with a negro or mulatto ... shall be committed to prison ... six months ... and pay ten pounds ..."

> "No minister ... shall presume to marry a white man with a negro or mulatto woman ... upon pain of ... ten thousand pounds of tobacco."

The same year's *Runaway Rewards Act* stated:

> "For the taking up of every servant, or slave ... there shall be allowed by the public ... two hundred pounds of tobacco ... one hundred pounds."

And the **1672 Virginia Act for the Apprehension and Suppression of Runawayes, Negroes, and Slaves** codified open season on Black life:

> "FORASMUCH as it hath beene manifested ... that many negroes have lately beene, and now are out in rebellion ... it shall ... be lawfull for any person ... upon the resistance of such negroe, molatto, Indian slave, or servant for life, to kill or wound him ... and if ... dye ... the master ... shall receive satisfaction from the publique ... and the person who shall kill or wound ... shall not be questioned for the same."

Each clause exemplifies Wright's principle of *rationalized barbarity*. Murder becomes policy. Theft becomes law. The collective psyche requires both the act and its justification.

In short, his fascination with contemporary racism and terrorism was both fueled by America's terrorism against Black people and immigrants.

These efforts can be observed in the 1921 letter penned by the Governor of California, William Stephens (who served as governor from 1917 to 1923) to the Governor of Washington, Louis Hart. The newspaper clipping has a headline that reads: *"San Francisco Mayor [Eugene Edward Schmitz] Wants Exclusion Act to Bar the Japs."* Additionally, there is a clipping that displays the enactment of the 1924 Immigration Act (H.R. 7995), which banned all immigration from Asia and set a total immigration quota of 165,000 people for all countries outside of the Western Hemisphere. Finally, there is a picture of the Bill, itself.

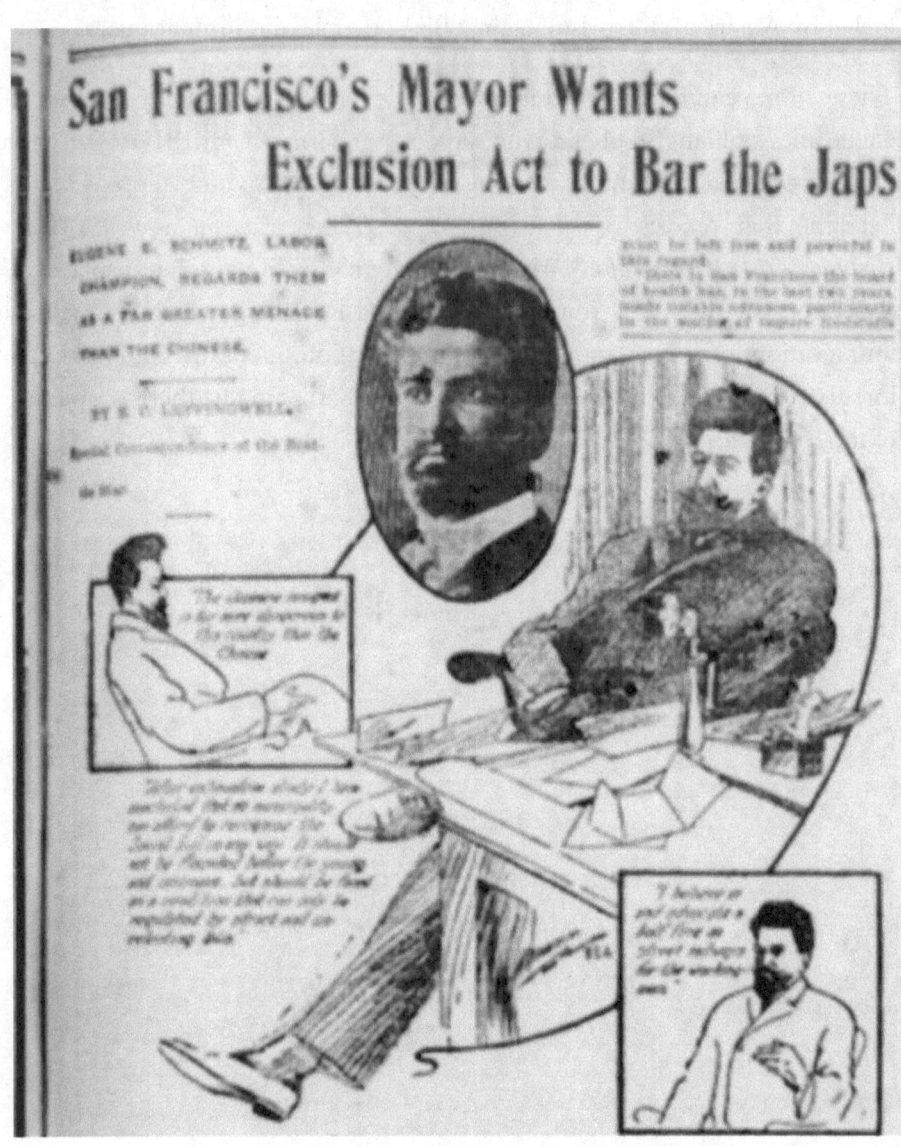

Figure 8.3.

State of California
GOVERNOR'S OFFICE
SACRAMENTO   April 15th, 1921.

Hon. Louis F. Hart,
    Governor of Washington,
    Olympia, Washington.   APR 20 1921

My dear Governor:

        The California Legislature, on April 13th passed unanimously Joint Resolution No. 26, embodying a declaration of California's principles in the matter of Japanese immigration, and urging upon the President, the State Department, and Congress, the endorsement and adoption thereof.

        As a frontier State, California is making the fight of the Nation against the incoming rush of an alien, unassimilable race, which would engulf our civilization, our traditions, and our ideals. Without the cooperation of the other States, California cannot hope to secure such action as will put a stop to the future development in this country of an alien, unassimilable community which must in time engender racial conflict and international misunderstandings. The way to preserve peace with Japan is to act in this matter with justice and decision, and to place about our American citizenship and economic interests such protection as Japan properly places about her own.

        In view of these facts, I am taking the liberty of asking your assistance in upholding California's stand in this matter. Your State Legislature is probably not in session at this time, but you can aid in this fight for the preservation of the Nation's interests, by representations to your State's delegation at Washington, urging, or recommending, that they cooperate with the California delegation in an effort to secure absolute exclusion of Japanese immigration, under conditions which will save any real humiliation to Japan, and will make for peace now, and permanent friendship hereafter between this Country and Japan.

        Yours very truly,

              W. D. Stephens
              Governor of California.

Figure 8.4.

> **68TH CONGRESS**
> **1ST SESSION** } **H. R. 7995**
>
> # AN ACT
>
> To limit the immigration of aliens into the United States, and for other purposes.
>
> APRIL 10 (calendar day, APRIL 14), 1924
> Ordered to lie on the table

Figure 8.5.

Figure 8.6.

Christianity and the Moral Cover for Crime

Frederick Douglass captured the theological disguise:

> "I therefore hate the corrupt, slaveholding, women-whipping, cradle-plundering, partial and hypocritical Christianity of the land ... They strip the love of God of its beauty and leave the world a religion of the livery of heaven serving the devil in."

Whiteness baptized its cruelty. As Wilson observed, this is the moral inversion of empire: the capacity to call evil divine, to make domination feel sacred.

The Cycle Renewed:
The 13th Amendment and the Criminalization of Freedom

The 13th Amendment reads:

> "Neither slavery nor involuntary servitude, **except as a punishment for crime** ... shall exist within the United States."

This clause is the bridge from plantation to prison. It sustains Wright's *organized predation*, Welsing's *genetic defense mechanism*, and Wilson's *institutional design*. The social order reproduces itself through law, medicine, and theology—all calibrated to maintain the myth of White innocence.

Clinical Conclusion

The White social order operates as a self-reinforcing psychopathy—a closed feedback loop of domination and denial. Its laws, sciences, and religions form the cognitive schema of an empire incapable of introspection. The pathology is both collective and hereditary. The cure, as Welsing, Wright, and Wilson agree, begins with exposure: to name the system as sickness. Only then can

202 | THE PSYCHOPATHY OF WHITENESS

we treat the disorder, dismantle its institutions, and rehabilitate the human capacity for truth.

Figure 8.7.

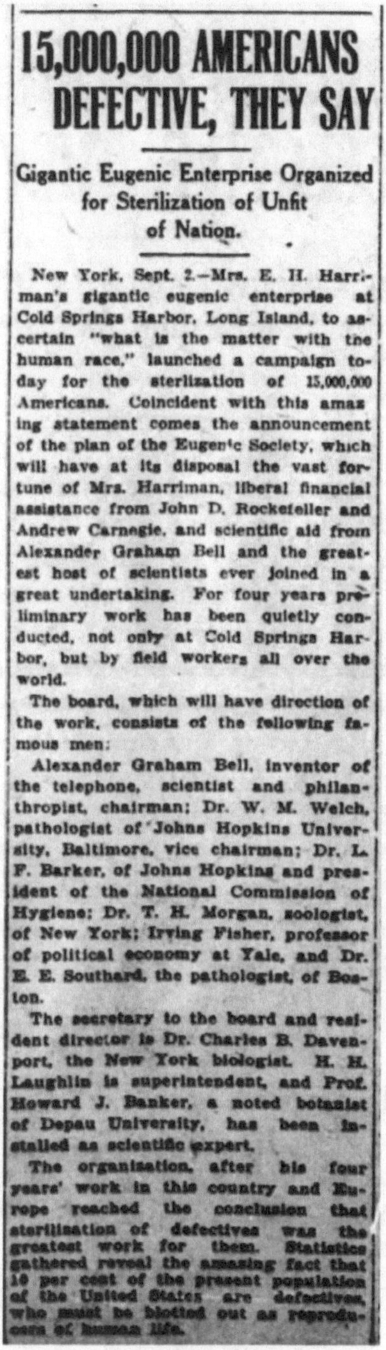

THE SCIENTIFIC RELIGION OF WHITE POWER | 203

15,000,000 AMERICANS DEFECTIVE, THEY SAY

Gigantic Eugenic Enterprise Organized for Sterilization of Unfit of Nation.

New York, Sept. 2.—Mrs. E. H. Harriman's gigantic eugenic enterprise at Cold Springs Harbor, Long Island, to ascertain "what is the matter with the human race," launched a campaign today for the sterilization of 15,000,000 Americans. Coincident with this amazing statement comes the announcement of the plan of the Eugenic Society, which will have at its disposal the vast fortune of Mrs. Harriman, liberal financial assistance from John D. Rockefeller and Andrew Carnegie, and scientific aid from Alexander Graham Bell and the greatest host of scientists ever joined in a great undertaking. For four years preliminary work has been quietly conducted, not only at Cold Springs Harbor, but by field workers all over the world.

The board, which will have direction of the work, consists of the following famous men:

Alexander Graham Bell, inventor of the telephone, scientist and philanthropist, chairman; Dr. W. M. Welch, pathologist of Johns Hopkins University, Baltimore, vice chairman; Dr. L. F. Barker, of Johns Hopkins and president of the National Commission of Hygiene; Dr. T. H. Morgan, zoologist, of New York; Irving Fisher, professor of political economy at Yale, and Dr. E. E. Southard, the pathologist, of Boston.

The secretary to the board and resident director is Dr. Charles B. Davenport, the New York biologist. H. H. Laughlin is superintendent, and Prof. Howard J. Banker, a noted botanist of Depau University, has been installed as scientific expert.

The organization, after his four years' work in this country and Europe reached the conclusion that sterilization of defectives was the greatest work for them. Statistics gathered reveal the amazing fact that 10 per cent of the present population of the United States are defectives, who must be blotted out as reproducers of human life.

Figure 8.8.

15,000,000 AMERICANS DEFECTIVE, THEY SAY

Gigantic Eugenic Enterprise Organized for Sterilization of Unfit of Nation.

New York, Sept. 2.—Mrs. E. H. Harriman's gigantic eugenic enterprise at Cold Springs Harbor, Long Island, to ascertain "what is the matter with the human race," launched a campaign today for the sterlization of 15,000,000 Americans. Coincident with this amazing statement comes the announcement of the plan of the Eugenic Society, which will have at its disposal the vast fortune of Mrs. Harriman, liberal financial assistance from John D. Rockefeller and Andrew Carnegie, and scientific aid from Alexander Graham Bell and the greatest host of scientists ever joined in a great undertaking. For four years preliminary work has been quietly conducted, not only at Cold Springs Harbor, but by field workers all over the world.

The board, which will have direction of the work, consists of the following famous men:

Alexander Graham Bell, inventor of the telephone, scientist and philan-

Figure 8.9-8.10

thropist, chairman; Dr. W. M. Welch, pathologist of Johns Hopkins University, Baltimore, vice chairman; Dr. L. F. Barker, of Johns Hopkins and president of the National Commission of Hygiene; Dr. T. H. Morgan, zoologist, of New York; Irving Fisher, professor of political economy at Yale, and Dr. E. E. Southard, the pathologist, of Boston.

The secretary to the board and resident director is Dr. Charles B. Davenport, the New York biologist. H. H. Laughlin is superintendent, and Prof. Howard J. Banker, a noted botanist of Depau University, has been installed as scientific expert.

The organization, after his four years' work in this country and Europe reached the conclusion that sterilization of defectives was the greatest work for them. Statistics gathered reveal the amazing fact that 10 per cent of the present population of the United States are defectives, who must be blotted out as reproducers of human life.

Figure 8.11–8.12.

Figure 8.13. Adolf Hitler, circa 1930s Germany

Figure 8.14.

Figure 8.15.

Figure 8.16. Thomas Jefferson, 3rd President of the United States

Figure 8.17. Abraham Lincoln, 16th President of the United States

THE SCIENTIFIC RELIGION OF WHITE POWER | 209

Figure 8.18. Andrew Johnson, 17th President of the United States

Figure 8.19. Woodrow Wilson, 28th President of the United States

Figure 8.20. Richard Nixon, 37th President of the United States

Figure 8.21. Donald Trump, 45th President of the United States

Chapter Eight Review Questions

I. Whiteness as Collective Psychopathy and Cultural Delusion

1. According to Dr. Bobby E. Wright's concept of the *psychopathic racial personality*, how does Whiteness function as an organized system of violence rather than a set of individual prejudices?

2. How does Dr. Frances Cress Welsing's "genetic survival" theory help explain the compulsive, transgenerational need to control, degrade, and eliminate Black life?

3. In what ways does Dr. Amos N. Wilson's analysis of power and behavioral adaptation reveal Whiteness as a *neurotic social order* rather than a natural hierarchy?

4. How do the medical, legal, and religious institutions described in this chapter reinforce a collective defense mechanism of White denial and projection?

5. How does the concept of "rationalized barbarity" reflect the normalization of psychopathy within White identity formation?

II. The Medicalization of Anti-Black Violence

6. How did phrenology, physiognomy, and polygenism function as scientific mechanisms for the dehumanization of Black people?

7. What did Dr. Samuel Cartwright's fabricated conditions (*drapetomania* and *dysaesthesia aethiopica*) reveal about the pathology of the White medical mind?

8. In what ways do the works of Dr. Robert Bennett Bean, Dr. Irving Fisher, and Frederick Hoffman illustrate the clinical codification of White supremacy?

9. How does Welsing's interpretation of "genetic warfare disguised as science" apply to the eugenics movement and its institutional backers?

10. What are the modern equivalents of this medicalized racism, and how do recent studies (e.g., pain bias, neonatal survival) demonstrate continuity with these historical pseudosciences?

III. Law, Religion, and the Sanctification of Racial Domination

11. What do the 1672 and 1705 Virginia laws reveal about the *legal psychology* of Whiteness? How did law codify terror as governance?

12. How did the 1924 Virginia Racial Integrity Act reflect a continuation of these colonial laws under new scientific and moral justifications?

13. How does Frederick Douglass's critique of "the corrupt, slaveholding Christianity of the land" expose the theological delusion sustaining White supremacy?

14. Why is the phrase "FORASMUCH as it hath beene manifested..." significant in the 1672 Act for the Apprehension and Suppression of Runawayes, Negroes, and Slaves? What does its tone reveal about White paranoia?

15. How did the 13th Amendment's exception clause perpetuate the structural psychopathy of slavery under the guise of legal order?

IV. Institutionalized Projection and the Fabrication of Innocence

16. How does DiAngelo's discussion of projected moral traits ("laziness, lustfulness, dirtiness") mirror Welsing's psychoanalytic framing of defense mechanisms?

17. How did American universities and medical schools serve as breeding grounds for psychopathic rationalizations of anti-Black terror?

18. What did Dr. Bobby Wright mean when he said, "This is science. This is objective. ... If you disagree with us, we will kill you or flunk you"? How does this capture the pathology of institutional consensus?

19. How does the Flexner Report demonstrate the systemic destruction of Black self-sufficiency through academic gatekeeping?

20. How did Adolf Hitler's admiration for American race laws illustrate the global exportation of White pathology as governance?

V. Contemporary Implications and Therapeutic Inquiry

21. How does the concept of "psychological projection" help us understand ongoing anti-Black police violence and mass incarceration?

22. What are the emotional, cognitive, and spiritual impacts on White people who have internalized centuries of cultural delusion and moral inversion?

23. How might Dr. Amos Wilson's call for a "psychology of liberation" serve as a therapeutic intervention for both oppressed and oppressor?

24. How can exposure, education, and clinical reframing begin to "treat" Whiteness as a social and psychological disorder?

25. What does it mean to name a system as *sickness*—and how might this recognition reshape the moral and institutional trajectory of the United States?

Works Cited

Alexander, M. (2010). *The new Jim Crow: Mass incarceration in the age of colorblindness.* The New Press.

Bean, R. B. (1906). *Some peculiarities of the Negro brain. American Journal of Anatomy,* 5(4), 353–432.

Black, E. (2012). *IBM and the Holocaust.* Dialog Press.

Blackmon, D. A. (2008). *Slavery by another name.* Anchor.

Buck v. Bell, 274 U.S. 200 (1927).

DiAngelo, R. (2012). *What does it mean to be White?* Peter Lang.

Douglass, F. (1845). *Narrative of the life of Frederick Douglass, an American slave.* Anti-Slavery Office.

Flexner, A. (1910). *Medical education in the United States and Canada.* Carnegie Foundation.

Grant, M. (1916). *The passing of the great race.* C. Scribner's Sons.

Hening, W. W. (1823). *The statutes at large; being a collection of all the laws of Virginia.* Franklin Press.

Herrnstein, R. J., & Murray, C. (1994). *The bell curve.* Free Press.

Hitler, A. (1925/1939). *Mein Kampf.* Houghton Mifflin.

Hoffman, F. L. (1896). *Race traits and tendencies of the American Negro.* Macmillan.

Morris, C. (1888). *The Aryan race.* S. A. George.

Nott, J. C., & Gliddon, G. R. (1854). *Types of mankind.* Lippincott.

Paoletti, G. (2017, August 26). *7 brands with Nazi ties that we all use.* All That's Interesting.

Roberts, D. (1997). *Killing the Black body.* Vintage.

Trawalter, S., Hoffman, K. M., & Waytz, A. (2012). *Racial bias in pain assessment and treatment recommendations.* PNAS, 109(16), 675–680.

United States Holocaust Memorial Museum. (n.d.). *The Nuremberg Race Laws.*

U.S. Const. amend. XIII.

Virginia (1672). *An Act for the Apprehension and Suppression of Runawayes, Negroes, and Slaves.*

Virginia (1705). *An Act declaring who shall not bear office...; An Act concerning Servants and Slaves.*

Virginia Racial Integrity Act, 1924, ch. 371 (Va. 1924).

Washington, H. A. (2006). *Medical apartheid.* Doubleday.

Wells, S. R. (1875). *New physiognomy.* Fowler & Wells.

Wilson, A. N. (1993). *The falsification of Afrikan consciousness.* Afrikan World Infosystems.

Wright, B. E. (1984). *The psychopathic racial personality and other essays.* Third World Press.

Welsing, F. C. (1991). *The Isis Papers.* Third World Press.

CHAPTER 9
THE PSYCHODYNAMICS OF WHITENESS AND THE LEGAL CODIFICATION OF TERROR

Whiteness, Terror, and the Psychodynamics of Law

The use of the term "terrorist" throughout this text is deliberate. It is not rhetorical flourish, but a diagnostic classification. Within the framework of the White American order, "terrorist" describes a behavioral pattern — a socially sanctioned syndrome of domination, cruelty, and moral decay. It names the individual and collective pathology that both drives and justifies the project of Whiteness itself.

The term encompasses all who perpetuate, enable, or benefit from anti-Blackness — including those who present as White and those who perform in alignment with Whiteness for comfort, proximity, or gain. It includes those who are indifferent to the daily suffering of Black people in anti-Black America.

Dr. Frances Cress Welsing reminds us that the drive for domination emerges from deep-seated fear — a genetic and psychological anxiety about White survival in a world of color. The compulsive need to control, segregate, and destroy is not merely political; it is existential.

Dr. Bobby Wright extends this understanding through his articulation of the *psychopathic racial personality* — a mind that cannot empathize, that must annihilate difference to feel whole. And Dr. Amos Wilson adds the crucial behavioral dimension: a culture of Whiteness that has become addicted to power, whose institutions function as extensions of a shared, inherited disorder.

In this sense, American law becomes the operating manual for a national psychosis. The Declaration of Independence and the Constitution of the

United States are not documents of freedom but clinical evidence — collective case files revealing how the European psyche translated its inner dis-ease into external rule. These laws codified what Welsing called *"a delusional belief in White divinity and universal authority."* They re-inscribed the pathology of conquest into the nervous system of the nation.

The moral schizophrenia of the White republic — claiming liberty while constructing human bondage — is not contradiction; it is symptom. It is the hallmark of the psychopathic mind that can proclaim love while practicing annihilation, that can kneel in prayer while legislating genocide.

Let us now examine the laws themselves — not as random historical statutes but as *ritual enactments* of a mental disorder passed down through generations.

The Neurotic Architecture of Control — Slave Codes, Black Codes, and Peonage

Following the signing of the Constitution, the pathology of Whiteness metastasized across the states in the form of slave codes and later Black Codes — legal structures designed to terrorize, dehumanize, and regulate every movement of Black existence. These laws were particularly severe in states that recognized the possibility of "free" Black persons, for the mere idea of Black autonomy destabilized the White psyche.

Missouri provides a chilling illustration. Its heritage landing page states:

> "After the United States purchased the Louisiana Territory in 1803, the new territorial government of Missouri immediately instituted Black codes, based largely on the code in place in Virginia, and similar in some ways to the French Code Noir. The American law made no distinction between slaves and other personal property in the territory."

The text continues with meticulous prescriptions for confinement, surveillance, and punishment — forbidding slaves from leaving their master's property without written permission, prohibiting ownership of weapons, banning assemblies, speeches, or commercial exchange without approval. Even "visiting" slaves were regulated by time limits and numbers. Public whipping enforced every infraction.

The legislative record reveals the obsession of a mind that experiences Black freedom as existential threat. Dr. Wright would call this the *institutionalization of fear through sadism* — a social system designed to calm White anxiety through constant punishment.

Missouri's 1825 law, for instance, prohibited any "free negro or mulatto" who was not a U.S. citizen from entering or settling in the state. Failure to leave within thirty days invited fines, jail, and lashes — "up to twenty lashes after 1845." The body of the Black person became the site of political control — a living text upon which the state inscribed its deranged sense of order.

Other states joined in this ritual of domination. Alabama's 1834 statute decreed that freed Black people found in the state would be given thirty days to leave; after that, they faced thirty-nine lashes and eventual sale "into or back into slavery." The logic was perverse yet predictable: freedom itself was criminalized.

The compulsion spread northward. Illinois and Indiana enacted prohibitions against Black residency, while Article 13 of Indiana's 1851 Constitution stated explicitly:

> "No Negro or Mulatto shall come into, or settle in, the State, after the adoption of this Constitution."

In every instance, law functioned as cultural therapy for the disordered White psyche — the legal equivalent of self-soothing through violence.

When Congress passed the Fugitive Slave Act of 1850, the psychosis achieved national form. The law deputized every White citizen as an agent of capture, incentivizing the hunt for Black bodies through cash rewards and state endorsement. Dr. Welsing would describe this as the projection of genetic fear into a permanent social ritual — a nation acting out its terror of genetic annihilation by policing and possessing Black life.

This same structure reappeared nearly two centuries later in the murder of Ahmaud Arbery, chased and executed by three White men in Georgia under the same delusional authority once granted by the Fugitive Slave Act. The pathology repeats itself; only the uniforms and vocabulary change.

As Dr. Amos Wilson observed, "Power seeks to reproduce itself through institutions that preserve the logic of its origin." The culture of Whiteness cannot exist without its anti-Black twin. It must recreate the conditions of domination to sustain its identity.

Thus, from runaway statutes to vagrancy laws, from convict leasing to redlining, the American legal order becomes a behavioral feedback loop — a compulsive reenactment of control. The cruelty is not incidental. The cruelty *is* the point.

Constitutional Psychosis and the Institutionalization of Suspicion

The Constitution of the United States represents, in many ways, the most sophisticated camouflage of collective pathology ever constructed. Under the veneer of "freedom" and "justice," the document encoded permanent suspicion of Blackness. Its every clause carried an invisible footnote: *This does not apply to them.*

The Three-Fifths Compromise, for instance, was not merely a political negotiation between slave and free states. It was a psychological compromise

— an unconscious admission that White America could not imagine itself without the possession and surveillance of Black bodies. Dr. Welsing would identify this as an early institutionalization of the *"White genetic survival imperative."* To sustain its sense of purity and dominion, Whiteness required a shadow self — a people defined as inferior, criminal, and subhuman, whose exploitation justified White virtue.

When the Constitution declared "We the People," it simultaneously constructed "They the Problem." This division — between those deserving of liberty and those requiring control — became the cornerstone of American governance and the template for all future legislation.

Dr. Bobby Wright referred to this dynamic as *"psychological warfare disguised as civilization."* The state became an instrument for moral inversion, rewarding sociopathy and criminalizing humanity. In such a system, the healthiest Black response — resistance, autonomy, or even the will to live — was pathologized as deviance.

This pathology is most clearly visible in the early 18th- and 19th-century legal frameworks that targeted "free Negroes" — those whose very existence violated the White fantasy of total control. Virginia's 1705 *Act Declaring Who Shall Not Bear Office in This Country* codified this anxiety:

> "That no person whatsoever, already convicted, or which hereafter shall be convicted... nor any negro, mulatto, or Indian, shall... bear any office, ecclesiasticall, civill or military, or be in any place of public trust or power."

The inclusion of racial categories alongside criminals reveals the delusional equivalence in the White imagination: to be Black was to be inherently guilty.

Dr. Amos Wilson would interpret this not as mere prejudice, but as *"a juridical projection of the White subconscious."* The law reflected an internal need to stabilize a fragile collective ego by externalizing evil onto the Black body. In psychological terms, it is classic projection — the displacement of one's own moral corruption onto the Other.

The same year, the 1705 *Act Concerning Servants and Slaves* expanded the system of degradation:

> "No negros, mulattos, or Indians, although christians... shall, at any time, purchase any christian servant, nor any other, except of their own complexion... And if any negro, mulatto, or Indian... shall... purchase any christian white servant, the said servant shall, ipso facto, become free..."

Here, the law articulates the deepest fear of the psychopathic White mind — that of *role reversal*. The horror of a Black person holding power over a White body was intolerable. Thus, control had to be absolute, even in hypothetical circumstances. Dr. Welsing might call this the "inversion panic" — the terror of losing racial dominance and therefore losing existential identity.

Every statute, every ordinance, became a ritual reenactment of this anxiety. Anti-miscegenation laws, for instance, did more than regulate intimacy; they served as prophylactics against the dissolution of Whiteness itself. In 1705, the same Virginia statute declared:

> "If any woman servant shall have a bastard child by a negro, or mulatto... she shall... pay fifteen pounds current money... or be sold for five years... And if a free christian white woman shall have such bastard child... she shall... pay fifteen pounds... or be sold for five years."

Through the eyes of Welsing and Wright, this language is not simply punitive — it is *ritualistic containment*. The law frames interracial reproduction as contagion, reinforcing the delusion that Whiteness must protect itself from genetic "contamination." It is a eugenic fantasy centuries before eugenics had a name.

The pathological repetition of such legislation reveals what Dr. Wright termed *"the necrophilic nature of White culture"* — a civilization that sustains itself through the destruction of life. Every time Black vitality, love, or self-determination appeared, the law intervened to strangle it. The judicial and political systems thus became instruments of psychosexual control, converting insecurity into domination.

The compulsive obsession with Black bodies, as seen in laws governing birth, labor, and marriage, was never about morality or religion. It was about maintaining an artificial sense of coherence for a people who could not exist without hierarchy. As Wilson writes, "To maintain superiority, one must institutionalize inferiority."

The psychiatric meaning of this cannot be overstated. The collective White ego depends upon the constant presence of an inferior other to stabilize its self-image. Remove that other — the object of projection — and the system collapses into existential void. This is why White violence against Black existence, whether physical, legal, or economic, is both compulsive and continuous. It is the act of a disordered mind attempting to prevent its own disintegration.

Eugenics, Pseudo-Science, and the Medicalization of Hatred

As the nation expanded, so too did its psychotic justifications. In the 19th and 20th centuries, academic institutions, medical associations, and scientific societies became the laboratories for legitimizing racial terror. Harriet Washington's *Medical Apartheid* documents the perverse collaboration between universities and the state in transforming anti-Black violence into "research."

Figures such as Dr. Charles Caldwell, Dr. Samuel Cartwright, Dr. Josiah Nott, and Dr. Samuel Wells used medical authority to sanctify genocide.

They rebranded enslavement as therapy, torture as science. Dr. Cartwright's invention of "drapetomania" — the supposed mental disorder causing enslaved Africans to flee captivity — is perhaps the purest distillation of this madness. It transformed the yearning for freedom into evidence of pathology.

Dr. Welsing would interpret this as the "psychological inversion of liberation." Freedom itself became a threat to White order, requiring diagnosis, treatment, and punishment. The doctor's whip replaced the master's chain, but the function was the same.

Dr. Bobby Wright would go further, labeling such practices "intellectual terrorism." The university became an asylum run by the patients — credentialed sociopaths masquerading as scientists. By medicalizing anti-Blackness, the White academic order institutionalized delusion. Every theory of inferiority — whether phrenology, physiognomy, polygenism, or eugenics — was not an advancement of knowledge but a symptom of disease.

Dr. Amos Wilson's lens clarifies the deeper function: these scientific systems reproduced *power through deception*. They allowed White people to act out their violence while calling it enlightenment. The pathological became normalized through language, metrics, and publication.

Dr. Robert Bennett Bean's 1906 essay *Some Peculiarities of the Negro Brain* epitomizes this intellectual rot. Bean wrote of "depression of the anterior association center" and "smaller corpus callosum" in Black brains, claiming biological inferiority. His pseudo-measurements served as neurological theology for White supremacy.

When we view this through the diagnostic frame of Wright and Welsing, Bean's work becomes a textbook case of *delusional projection and narcissistic defense*. Unable to face the moral corruption of their civilization, White scientists externalized their degeneracy onto Black anatomy.

This same pathology fueled Frederick Hoffman's *Race Traits and Tendencies of the American Negro*, which warned that racial intermixing would bring about

THE PSYCHODYNAMICS OF WHITENESS AND THE LEGAL CODIFICATION OF TERROR | 225

"moral deterioration" and "gradual extinction." Hoffman's text, drenched in paranoia, echoed what Dr. Wright described as "the death wish of the oppressor." In projecting decay onto Blackness, Hoffman articulated the repressed awareness of White decline.

From these delusions emerged the eugenics movement — a state-sponsored religion of purity. Figures like Madison Grant and Harry Laughlin called for sterilization of the "unfit," while the Virginia Racial Integrity Act of 1924 enshrined Whiteness as sacred blood. Chief Justice Oliver Wendell Holmes, in *Buck v. Bell* (1927), declared:

> "It is better for the world… if society can prevent those who are manifestly unfit from continuing their kind. Three generations of imbeciles are enough."

Wright would describe such statements as "the ultimate confession of a race bent on suicide." The obsession with controlling reproduction reveals the fundamental fear of life itself — a hatred so deep that it disguises itself as moral hygiene.

From these ideas, Adolf Hitler took notes. The Nuremberg Race Laws of 1935 mirrored American anti-miscegenation statutes, transforming U.S. racial jurisprudence into global genocide. Hitler himself wrote:

> "I have studied with interest the laws of several [U.S.] states concerning the prevention of reproduction by people whose progeny would… be injurious to the racial stock."

The pathology had completed its loop — American racial psychosis exported abroad and returned in the form of fascism. Dr. Welsing's warning resounds: *"The fear of genetic annihilation, when institutionalized, becomes world policy."*

Technological Terror and the Corporate Complicity in Genocide

The industrialization of genocide marked the final maturation of White pathology. The Nazi regime's partnership with American corporations such as IBM, Ford Motor Company, and the Rockefeller Foundation was not accidental; it was the logical outcome of centuries of legalized racial sadism refined into bureaucratic efficiency.

Edwin Black's *IBM and the Holocaust* exposes how International Business Machines, under the leadership of Thomas J. Watson, supplied Hitler's government with census technology and punch-card systems to catalogue, identify, and exterminate Jews and other "undesirables." The mechanical orderliness of IBM's tabulation machines turned the delusional racial fantasies of eugenics into administrative routine. Dr. Bobby Wright's framework helps us recognize this not as innovation but as what he called "technological sadism — the mechanization of racial murder for the maintenance of White power."

A 1933 contract between IBM's German subsidiary Dehomag and the Nazi state illustrates the fusion of corporate profit and racial psychosis. Gabe Paoletti summarizes:

> "Through their subsidiary, Dehomag, IBM supplied Nazi Germany with the capabilities to easily and efficiently identify Jews and other undesirables... and the technology necessary to track their transport to extermination camps."

Even after the United States entered World War II, IBM continued supplying the Reich through falsified records and European intermediaries. By 1941, Nazi Germany was IBM's second-largest market after the U.S. The partnership reveals a truth central to the analyses of Welsing, Wright, and Wilson: Whiteness adapts; it mutates to preserve dominance. When open enslavement becomes unfashionable, domination hides in algorithms, ledgers, and patents.

Dr. Amos Wilson's theory of *institutional reflexivity* describes this perfectly: the system of White power continually reprograms itself to avoid moral accountability. The violence never ends; it merely changes syntax.

Rockefeller's financing of racial-hygiene studies and Carnegie's support of eugenic sterilization boards represent, in Welsing's words, "the aristocratization of pathology." These men were not aberrations but architects of a collective disorder that fused capitalism with the delusion of divine selection. As Wilson warned, "The political economy of racism is the psych economy of the West."

The ripple effects continue into contemporary life. Richard Herrnstein and Charles Murray's *The Bell Curve (1994)* revived the eugenic ideology in academic packaging, asserting that intelligence and social worth were products of heredity. Their claim that government should cease subsidizing births among "low-IQ" women was a direct ideological descendant of *Buck v. Bell*. Through the lens of Wright and Welsing, this is the persistence of genocidal logic disguised as public policy — a modern echo of the ancient fear that Whiteness might one day be outnumbered by life itself.

Dr. Wright called this the *scientific camouflage of genocide*. He wrote that the Western mind "transforms the impulse to kill into the discipline of measurement." Every graph, index, and regression curve in *The Bell Curve* is, in effect, a moral alibi for extermination through neglect.

Today, that same delusion animates racialized healthcare disparities. The 2016 study on pain perception found that half of White medical trainees believed Black people had thicker skin or less sensitive nerve endings. This belief is not ignorance; it is inheritance — the clinical residue of centuries of legalized dehumanization. Dr. Welsing would describe it as the unconscious expression of "White narcissistic immunity," the inability to perceive Black suffering as real because doing so would threaten the fragile moral self.

When 2020 data revealed that Black newborns are twice as likely to survive when treated by Black physicians, it confirmed what Wright and Wilson long understood: racism is not a side effect of American medicine; it is its organizing principle. The system is performing precisely as designed.

The arc of this pathology is long but unbroken — from Virginia's colonial statutes to modern algorithms, from the whip to the spreadsheet, from the plantation ledger to the predictive-policing dashboard. Each represents a stage in the same illness: a civilization sustained by domination, terrified of equality, addicted to control.

Dr. Amos Wilson warned that until the psychology of White supremacy is publicly diagnosed, its institutions will continue to reproduce themselves under new names. Dr. Bobby Wright insisted that "the survival of Black people depends upon understanding that we are dealing not with politics, but with psychopathology." And Dr. Frances Cress Welsing left us with the ultimate prescription: *The only cure for White fear is truth.*

Truth dismantles delusion. Truth restores balance. Truth is the therapy that America has never permitted itself to undergo. Until it does, the nation remains an open-air asylum, where the inmates still believe themselves free.

The Afterlife of Eugenics: From Jim Crow to Mass Incarceration

Eugenics never died; it merely changed costume. When sterilization lost public favor, the same obsession with racial containment re-emerged as criminal law, zoning policy, and economic design. The plantation became the penitentiary; the overseer became the officer.

THE PSYCHODYNAMICS OF WHITENESS AND THE LEGAL CODIFICATION OF TERROR | 229

Dr. Welsing warned that "the survival drive of Whiteness manifests as perpetual control over the reproduction and mobility of Black life."

The so-called end of slavery did not end this control—it diversified it. The 13th Amendment's exception clause, *"except as a punishment for crime whereof the party shall have been duly convicted,"* legalized the metamorphosis of chattel into convict. In psychiatric terms, this was not reform but relapse—an addict's return to the substance of domination under a new alias.

Dr. Bobby Wright called this *"cyclical institutional schizophrenia."* The state repeats the same behavior while insisting on its innocence. Each generation creates new instruments—vagrancy laws, chain gangs, red-lining, the War on Drugs—believing them to be rational responses to social disorder, when they are in fact ritual reenactments of the same compulsion: the need to cage Black vitality.

During Reconstruction, "Black Codes" criminalized unemployment, "insolence," and even laughter in public spaces. Convict-leasing programs sold prisoners back to private industry. The logic mirrored Virginia's 1705 statutes, replacing tobacco rewards with corporate contracts. U.S. Steel, Tennessee Coal & Iron, and state governments grew rich on unpaid Black labor. It was slavery by another clinical name—*psychological substitution therapy* for a White mind incapable of functioning without human property.

Jim Crow formalized this pathology. Separate-but-equal, upheld in *Plessy v. Ferguson (1896)*, became the social equivalent of a dissociative disorder: the country split its personality between democratic ideals and racial sadism, pretending the two could coexist. Dr. Welsing would diagnose this as "cognitive dissonance institutionalized as law."

The Civil Rights Acts of 1964 and 1968 functioned as temporary restraints, not cures. The underlying compulsion—the terror of genetic and cultural equality—found new outlets. By the 1970s, "law and order" rhetoric had replaced "racial hygiene," and the penitentiary replaced the plantation as the epicenter of racial management.

President Nixon's domestic-policy aide John Ehrlichman later confessed:

> "We knew we couldn't make it illegal to be either against the war or Black, but by getting the public to associate the hippies with marijuana and Blacks with heroin, and then criminalizing both heavily, we could disrupt those communities."

Dr. Amos Wilson would call this *"political transference."* The anxiety once projected onto the slave rebel was now projected onto the "criminal," the "welfare mother," the "urban threat." The categories changed; the diagnosis did not.

Mass incarceration is thus the twenty-first-century expression of eighteenth-century psychosis. The United States imprisons more human beings than any other nation on Earth—disproportionately Black men. The statistical enormity functions as collective reassurance: Whiteness still rules, order is restored, the fantasy of control preserved.

Michelle Alexander's *The New Jim Crow* illuminates the continuity. Yet beyond policy analysis, Welsing and Wright force us to see it as symptomology. The prison system is the nation's mirror—an architectural confession of unresolved pathology. Each cell, each sentence, each probation order reenacts the primal act of domination first performed on the auction block.

Even welfare and housing policy reflect the eugenic impulse. The 1935 Social Security Act excluded agricultural and domestic workers—two fields dominated by Black labor. The FHA's redlining maps, drawn in 1936, read like medical charts diagnosing which neighborhoods were "healthy" (White) and which were "infected" (Black). By the 1980s, Ronald Reagan's language of "welfare queens" recoded the sterilization rhetoric of Madison Grant: unfit

THE PSYCHODYNAMICS OF WHITENESS AND THE LEGAL CODIFICATION OF TERROR

mothers, defective stock, burdens on the state. The clinical vocabulary shifted, but the disease remained chronic.

Dr. Wright argued that such systems are not accidents of economics but deliberate therapies for White fear: "The American state uses policy as psychotropic medication—dosing itself with Black suffering to stabilize the White personality." Each reform cycle lowers the dosage temporarily; when tolerance builds, the state requires a stronger hit—new wars on drugs, on crime, on critical race theory.

Today's surveillance technologies and predictive-policing algorithms are digital descendants of the eugenic card catalog. The same delusion—of perfect classification, total control, and risk elimination—animates the machine. The program learns from centuries of bias because the program is bias. IBM's punch card has simply evolved into code.

Dr. Wilson reminds us that power is never content with the illusion of innocence. It must continually prove itself through domination. The police killing of unarmed Black people, the denial of healthcare, and the criminalization of protest are not isolated acts—they are modern seizures of a chronic social psychosis.

In clinical summary, the afterlife of eugenics manifests as a triad of compulsions:

1. **Containment** – the need to restrict Black movement through law and surveillance.

2. **Correction** – the urge to "reform" or sterilize Black identity through cultural engineering.

3. **Consumption** – the economic exploitation of Black pain as the nation's renewable resource.

Until these compulsions are confronted as symptoms of a collective disorder, not as policy debates, the cycle will continue. As Dr. Bobby Wright warned, "The major mental illness of Western civilization is its inability to love without domination."

Clinical Reflections: Diagnosing the White Racial Personality Disorder

Dr. Frances Cress Welsing, in *The Isis Papers*, wrote that the global system of White supremacy is not merely political—it is psychological, and at its core, it is pathological. She proposed that White supremacy emerges from "a deep-seated sense of numerical inadequacy and genetic vulnerability." Dr. Bobby E. Wright expanded on this by identifying the *psychopathic racial personality* as a clinical phenomenon rather than a social anomaly. In his 1984 essay, he wrote:

> "The psychopath's behavior towards others is characterized by callousness, lack of empathy, and a disregard for the rights of others. The White race collectively behaves towards Black people and people of color as the individual psychopath behaves towards his victims."

Through this lens, the White Racial Personality Disorder (WRPD) is not metaphorical—it is a socially transmitted and culturally rewarded mental illness. It manifests through centuries of violence normalized as progress, domination disguised as divinity, and sadism rationalized as science. It has adapted through law, religion, medicine, and economics, binding generations to a delusional sense of superiority.

Dr. Amos Wilson provided the developmental schema for understanding this disorder. He described White supremacy as "a socio-mental structure that maintains itself through psychic energy—fear, envy, and aggression transformed into institutions." In clinical terms, this means Whiteness survives by externalizing its inner conflict: it projects its insecurity, rage, and shame onto the Black body, transforming psychological fragility into political power.

If we are to treat Whiteness as a mental disorder—one that has infected the body politic—then we must delineate its symptoms. These symptoms are not confined to individuals but replicated in institutions, systems, and collective behaviors. The disease is both personal and structural, psychological and sociological, conscious and unconscious.

I. Diagnostic Criteria: The Core Symptoms of the Disorder

1. *Narcissistic Delusion of Superiority*

A pervasive and irrational belief in inherent goodness, exceptionalism, and moral purity, despite overwhelming evidence of brutality and deceit. Manifestations include the rewriting of history, denial of systemic racism, and the insistence that equality feels like oppression.

Dr. Welsing referred to this as "psychological inversion—the compulsion to see oneself as the victim even while inflicting suffering."

2. *Compulsive Control and Domination*

An uncontrollable need to manage, define, regulate, and police all aspects of non-White life. This symptom manifests through colonization, segregation, policing, and surveillance technologies. Dr. Wright likened it to the psychopath's "obsessive requirement to determine the fate of his victim."

3. Emotional Detachment and Moral Dissociation

Inability to empathize with the suffering of others, combined with ritual rationalizations for harm. The pattern appears in the language of "collateral damage," "officer safety," "manifest destiny," and "law and order." This detachment is often maintained through religion and nationalism as dissociative defenses.

4. Paranoid Fear of Genetic and Cultural Extinction

An irrational obsession with purity, fertility, and the control of birth rates. Manifested in anti-miscegenation laws, immigration bans, and demographic hysteria. As Welsing wrote, "The White collective is governed by genetic fear—the fear of being overwhelmed by the very people it has oppressed."

5. Projection and Inversion

The persistent tendency to ascribe one's own aggression to the oppressed. Black people are called violent, while the White state drops bombs. Indigenous peoples are called savage, while settlers commit genocide. This defense mechanism allows the disorder to sustain its moral delusion.

6. Institutionalized Violence and Justified Cruelty

The normalization of sadistic behavior as civic virtue. Lynchings, sterilizations, wars, and police killings are rationalized as necessary for social order. Wright described this as "the moral anesthesia of psychopathology: the inability to distinguish killing from governance."

7. Delusional Denial and Historical Amnesia

A compulsive rewriting of history to preserve innocence. The atrocities of enslavement, colonialism, and genocide are sanitized through myth—"the Founding Fathers," "the pioneers," "discovery." As Wilson noted, "A people who cannot remember the crimes of their civilization are condemned to commit them again, believing them to be acts of virtue."

8. Dependency on Blackness for Identity Formation

Without Black subjugation, Whiteness loses coherence. Its identity depends on the continual subordination of the racial "other." This symbiotic pathology means the oppressor's self-image requires the persistence of inequality. Dr. Welsing argued that "Whiteness needs Blackness to define itself—without the Black image, the White ego collapses."

II. Behavioral Manifestations and Social Defenses

The disorder expresses itself through predictable social rituals.

- **Ritualized Violence:** lynching, police shootings, and wars serve as symbolic exorcisms of fear.

- **Cultural Narcissism:** the elevation of White aesthetics, language, and institutions as universal standards.

- **Racial Gaslighting:** insisting that those harmed by racism are "overreacting," "divisive," or "ungrateful."

- **Institutional Reinforcement:** schools, media, and government agencies function as psychological containment centers that replicate the delusion of White virtue.

These rituals are not anomalies but the maintenance routines of the disorder itself.

III. Defense Mechanisms

Denial: "I don't see color."

Rationalization: "It's about class, not race."

Projection: "They're the real racists."

Minimization: "It's not that bad anymore."

Displacement: Attacking reformers instead of confronting the pathology.

Idealization of the Self: "We ended slavery; we elected Obama."

Cognitive Dissonance: Clinging to democracy while sustaining racial hierarchy.

As Dr. Wright emphasized, "The White mind is at war with reality—it must destroy the evidence of its sickness to maintain the illusion of health."

IV. Clinical Course and Prognosis

The White Racial Personality Disorder is chronic, self-reinforcing, and resistant to treatment. It thrives on denial and projection. Its progression is cyclical—reform, relapse, rationalization. Each generation proclaims moral progress while replicating ancestral violence in subtler forms.

Dr. Welsing described the prognosis as guarded: "Without the courage to face its own pathology, the White collective will continue toward civilizational suicide." Dr. Wilson agreed: "Empires fall not from external invasion but from psychological implosion." The disorder erodes empathy, corrodes democracy, and converts moral energy into self-destruction.

Treatment requires confrontation with truth, a process equivalent to cultural detoxification. As in addiction therapy, withdrawal produces rage, denial, and relapse. But there is no healing without it.

V. Therapeutic Implications

The only known antidote is *collective accountability and truth-telling*. Education that centers historical trauma and systemic analysis acts as cultural psychotherapy. Dr. Wright urged the development of a "Black social therapy" grounded in resistance, not appeasement. Dr. Wilson called for "the reconstruction of consciousness." And Welsing prescribed "a new definition of human maturity—one not measured by control, but by coexistence."

If Whiteness is the disease, then truth is the treatment and justice the cure. The prognosis depends upon whether the patient—the nation itself—can admit it is sick.

Toward Liberation Psychology and Healing

If the disease of Whiteness is collective psychopathy, then liberation must be collective therapy. To heal from five centuries of racialized trauma, we must recognize that we are not merely living in the afterlife of slavery—we are living in the afterlife of pathology. The systems that govern our lives were designed by the unwell, not the well; by the disassociated, not the integrated; by those who mistake domination for divine order.

Dr. Frances Cress Welsing taught that "the destruction of Black people is the essential defense mechanism of the White psyche." Therefore, liberation cannot begin with negotiation or appeasement. It must begin with the recovery of psychological sovereignty—the deliberate refusal to internalize White delusion as truth. Welsing described this process as *de-psychopathization*: a conscious rejection of dependency on a sick culture for validation.

Dr. Amos N. Wilson expanded this into the project of *psychological reconstruction*. He wrote, "We must understand that the power of oppression lies not merely in control of institutions but in control of perception." Liberation, therefore, is not simply the reversal of power but the reclamation of meaning. When Black people name reality for ourselves, when we refuse to be objects of analysis and instead become agents of interpretation, we disrupt the neural circuitry of oppression itself.

Dr. Bobby E. Wright called this process *counter-violence in thought*. He argued that the most revolutionary act is to redefine reality in our own terms. For Wright, the key to mental liberation was "the development of Black social theory rooted in our experience of warfare." He understood that the Black psyche, having endured centuries of organized assault, carries both trauma and genius—the trauma of oppression and the genius of survival. Healing requires harnessing both.

Frantz Fanon, the Martinican psychiatrist and freedom fighter, echoed this truth in *The Wretched of the Earth*. He wrote, "The colonized man finds his freedom in and through violence." Fanon was not advocating senseless destruction but rather the reclamation of self through confrontation. He saw colonialism as a psychological infection—a parasitic relationship in which the oppressor's self-image depends on the colonized subject's self-negation. Healing, therefore, requires rupture. There can be no peace with pathology.

I. The Stages of Liberation Psychology

1. Awareness and Naming

Healing begins with truth. Naming the pathology of Whiteness removes it from the realm of divine mystery and places it in the realm of human dysfunction. Language is medicine. When we call racism what it is—addiction, projection, compulsion—we strip it of its moral disguise.

2. Reclamation of Identity

Welsing emphasized that "Black identity must be rooted in understanding the global system of White supremacy and the counter-force of self-respect." To heal, we must reframe Blackness not as a reaction but as an original state of wholeness. The African worldview, which centers balance, reciprocity, and interconnectedness, provides a therapeutic model far older than European pathology.

3. Resistance as Healing

For Wright and Fanon, resistance was not just political but psychiatric. The act of saying "no" to domination restores cognitive and moral order to a mind that has been violated. Resistance, then, is self-care; defiance is therapy.

4. Reorientation of Consciousness

Dr. Wilson taught that liberation requires the transformation of consciousness from consumption to creation. The colonized mind is conditioned to consume—the products, narratives, and values of the oppressor. Healing comes through creation: of art, institutions, economies, and meaning. As Wilson wrote, "Power is the ability to define reality and have others accept your definition as their own." Healing, therefore, is the restoration of definitional power.

5. *Integration and Community Reconstruction*

The final stage of liberation psychology is communal integration—the reweaving of the collective self. Oppression fractures identity, isolates individuals, and replaces belonging with hierarchy. Healing reverses this by centering relationship, empathy, and shared purpose. Ubuntu—the African concept meaning *"I am because we are"*—is the antidote to the Western delusion of separateness.

II. Collective Treatment Plan

If America is the patient, then the treatment plan must be multi-modal and intergenerational:

A. *Cognitive Reeducation*

National curricula must center truth-telling: the history of racial violence, the psychology of domination, and the moral bankruptcy of White exceptionalism. As Dr. Welsing noted, "Ignorance is the anesthesia of the oppressor." Truth is the first incision in the surgery of healing.

B. *Emotional Rehabilitation*

For Black people, healing requires grieving—grieving the centuries stolen, the memories erased, the humanity denied. For White people, healing requires guilt transformed into accountability. As James Baldwin said, "Not everything that is faced can be changed, but nothing can be changed until it is faced." Therapy on a national scale begins with facing.

C. *Structural Detoxification*

Institutions built on psychopathy cannot be reformed; they must be restructured. The police, prisons, and courts are not malfunctioning—they are functioning exactly as designed. Detoxification means dismantling these systems and rebuilding them upon principles of reciprocity and care.

D. *Cultural Rebirth*

Every civilization produces art that mirrors its psyche. America's addiction to violence and spectacle reflects its illness. Healing demands the cultivation of art, music, and narrative that affirm life. Culture is the medicine of the collective unconscious.

III. Prognosis: Healing as Revolution

There can be no healing without revolution, because the sickness is structural. Dr. Wilson cautioned that "a people who do not fight for control of their minds will always be controlled by those who do." Liberation psychology, therefore, is not an academic theory—it is a survival strategy.

Dr. Welsing foresaw this moment when she said, "Black people must become the therapists of the world, for we have survived what no one else has survived." To heal from Whiteness is to heal humanity itself.

If pathology can be inherited, so can resilience. The same genetic and spiritual code that carried Black people through 500 years of terror also carries the potential to restore balance to the world. The healing of Blackness is the healing of the planet.

The work is not easy, nor is it safe. But as Fanon reminded us, "Each generation must, out of relative obscurity, discover its mission, fulfill it, or betray it." Our mission is clear: to expose the psychopathy of Whiteness, to confront it with truth, and to build new systems of sanity rooted in love, justice, and reciprocity.

IV. Conclusion: The Ethical Mandate of Healing

The disease of Whiteness cannot be managed—it must be cured. To manage it is to consent to its continuation. To cure it is to restore moral order to a disordered world.

Liberation psychology teaches that healing is not passive—it is insurgent. It is the work of breaking silence, reclaiming story, and rebuilding community. It is the rehumanization of the dehumanized and the confrontation of those who benefit from dehumanization.

As Dr. Welsing said, "To understand White supremacy is to begin the process of dismantling it." And as Dr. Wright warned, "If we refuse to see the war being waged against us, we are condemned to lose it."

Healing, therefore, is not merely the end of suffering—it is the end of illusion. It is the moment humanity looks in the mirror and finally recognizes its sickness, not to despair, but to begin the sacred work of recovery.

Chapter Review Questions (40 total)

Section 1 – Foundations:
Whiteness, Terror, and the Psychodynamics of Law

1. How does the chapter define "terrorist" within the context of Whiteness and law?

2. In what ways does the text diagnose the U.S. Constitution as evidence of collective psychosis?

3. Explain Dr. Frances Cress Welsing's concept of White genetic fear and its relation to domination.

4. How do Wright and Wilson extend Welsing's framework into behavioral and institutional analysis?

5. What is meant by the term "moral schizophrenia" of the White republic?

Section 2 – The Neurotic Architecture of Control

6. What functions did slave codes and Black codes serve in stabilizing White anxiety?

7. Describe Missouri's 1825 law and its psychological implications for free Black people.

8. How do public punishment and surveillance operate as ritual soothing mechanisms for White fear?

9. In what ways is the Fugitive Slave Act interpreted as a national ritual of terror?

10. What connections does the chapter draw between the Fugitive Slave Act and the murder of Ahmaud Arbery?

Section 3 – *Constitutional Psychosis and the Institutionalization of Suspicion*

11. How is the Three-Fifths Compromise reinterpreted as a psychological contract?

12. Why does the chapter argue that "We the People" implies "They the Problem"?

13. Summarize the 1705 Virginia statutes and their function as projections of the White subconscious.

14. Explain the term "inversion panic" and how it appears in anti-miscegenation laws.

15. How does the chapter link moral law to psychosexual control?

Section 4 – *Eugenics, Pseudo-Science, and the Medicalization of Hatred*

16. How did medical and academic institutions legitimize racial terror as science?

17. What does "drapetomania" reveal about the inversion of freedom and pathology?

18. Compare Dr. Robert Bean's and Frederick Hoffman's work as manifestations of projection.

19. How did U.S. eugenics influence Hitler's racial laws?

20. According to Wright and Welsing, why is eugenics the "institutionalization of fear through science"?

THE PSYCHODYNAMICS OF WHITENESS AND THE LEGAL CODIFICATION OF TERROR | 245

Section 5 – Technological Terror and Corporate Complicity

21. How does Edwin Black's research illustrate the partnership between capitalism and genocide?

22. Define "technological sadism" and its role in modern institutions.

23. What does Dr. Amos Wilson mean by "institutional reflexivity"?

24. How does the chapter interpret The Bell Curve as a continuation of eugenic logic?

25. Discuss the relationship between medical racism and inherited cultural beliefs about pain perception.

Section 6 – The Afterlife of Eugenics:
From Jim Crow to Mass Incarceration

26. How does the 13th Amendment's exception clause reflect a relapse into slavery?

27. What is meant by "cyclical institutional schizophrenia"?

28. In what ways did Nixon-era drug policy function as political transference?

29. How do housing and welfare policies embody eugenic continuity?

30. Summarize the chapter's three-part "clinical triad" of containment, correction, and consumption.

Section 7 – Clinical Reflections: Diagnosing the White Racial Personality Disorder

31. List and briefly explain the eight diagnostic criteria of White Racial Personality Disorder.

32. How does projection serve as a core defense mechanism within this disorder?

33. What distinguishes individual from institutional expressions of the pathology?

34. Why does the chapter describe the disorder as "resistant to treatment"?

35. According to Wright, what role does denial play in preserving collective delusion?

Section 8 – Toward Liberation Psychology and Healing

36. What is "de-psychopathization," and how does it begin the healing process?

37. Explain how resistance functions as therapy within liberation psychology.

38. Describe the five stages of liberation psychology outlined in the chapter.

39. What does "structural detoxification" entail for American institutions?

40. How does the chapter frame healing as a form of revolution and ethical mandate?

Works Cited

Alexander, M. (2010). *The New Jim Crow: Mass Incarceration in the Age of Colorblindness.* The New Press.

Baldwin, J. (1962). *The Fire Next Time.* Dial Press.

Black, E. (2001). *IBM and the Holocaust: The Strategic Alliance Between Nazi Germany and America's Most Powerful Corporation.* Crown Publishers.

Caldwell, C. (1822). *Thoughts on the Original Unity of the Human Race.* Louisville Press.

Cartwright, S. A. (1851). Diseases and peculiarities of the Negro race. *De Bow's Review,* 11, 331–336.

Fanón, F. (1963). *The Wretched of the Earth* (C. Farrington, Trans.). Grove Press. (Original work published 1961)

Grant, M. (1916). *The Passing of the Great Race: Or the Racial Basis of European History.* Charles Scribner's Sons.

Herrnstein, R. J., & Murray, C. (1994). *The Bell Curve: Intelligence and Class Structure in American Life.* Free Press.

Hoffman, F. L. (1896). *Race Traits and Tendencies of the American Negro.* American Economic Association.

Holmes, O. W. J. (1927). Opinion of the Court, *Buck v. Bell,* 274 U.S. 200.

Nott, J. C., & Gliddon, G. R. (1854). *Types of Mankind.* Lippincott, Grambo & Co.

Paoletti, G. (2017, March 19). How IBM helped the Nazis carry out the Holocaust. *All That's Interesting.* https://allthatsinteresting.com/ibm-holocaust

Washington, H. A. (2006). *Medical Apartheid: The Dark History of Medical Experimentation on Black Americans from Colonial Times to the Present.* Doubleday.

Welsing, F. C. (1991). *The Isis Papers: The Keys to the Colors.* Third World Press.

Wilson, A. N. (1993). *The Falsification of Afrikan Consciousness: Eurocentric History, Psychiatry and the Politics of White Supremacy.* Afrikan World InfoSystems.

Wright, B. E. (1984). *The Psychopathic Racial Personality and Other Essays.* Third World Press.

CHAPTER 10
WHITE COLLECTIVE DIABOLICAL PSYCHOPATHIC INSTITUTIONAL REPRESSION
PLAY-BY-PLAY

Having diagnosed legal 'treatment' as denial, we now trace how that denial captured public education and then radiated outward.

Education and School Desegregation: The Weaponization of Color-Blindness

The mythology of "color-blindness" in American law represents one of the most cunning and diabolical evolutions of white supremacy. It is the language of innocence weaponized — the psychological armor of a people who have refused to confront their own addiction to domination. When white lawmakers and judges began to use the rhetoric of equality to dismantle the material gains of Black liberation, they inaugurated a new epoch of what I call *legalized re-enslavement through procedural virtue.*

The Supreme Court's modern era of racial jurisprudence began not with liberation but with betrayal.

In *San Antonio Independent School District v. Rodriguez* (1973), the Court held that education is not a fundamental right under the U.S. Constitution, allowing local property taxes to dictate the quality of public schooling.

This decision codified economic apartheid under the guise of federalism, ensuring that white wealth would continue to finance white learning, while Black and Brown children were taught to normalize deprivation.

The ruling demonstrated what Dr. Bobby Wright described as *psychopathic rationalization*—a moral inversion that renders oppression logical, even lawful.

252 | THE PSYCHOPATHY OF WHITENESS

The following year, *Milliken v. Bradley* (1974) imposed another layer of structural confinement by striking down inter-district desegregation remedies in Detroit.

In effect, the Court ruled that white suburban districts were not obligated to share responsibility for the segregation they had engineered through flight, redlining, and exclusionary zoning.

This decision permanently insulated white educational space, guaranteeing the continuation of racial isolation under the pretense of local autonomy.

The case marked a pivotal moment in the judicial re-codification of racial geography—a psycho-legal act of containment designed to protect white children from integration and Black children from equality.

Two years later, in *Washington v. Davis* (1976), the Court declared that racial disparities in impact were not enough to prove discrimination; a plaintiff must prove "discriminatory intent."

Here, the pathology became clinical.

The justices—almost all white men—legislated a standard that denied the existence of unconscious or systemic bias.

To recognize structural racism would have required introspection, the very thing whiteness cannot endure.

Instead, they redefined racism as a matter of individual confession, placing the burden of proof on those already brutalized by the system.

It was the legal equivalent of a therapist demanding that a patient prove their abuser's intent before believing their trauma.

By the late 1970s, the Court's obsession with protecting whiteness from accountability reached higher education.

In *Regents of the University of California v. Bakke* (1978), the Court struck down rigid racial quotas while claiming to preserve diversity as a "compelling interest."

But diversity became a moral anesthesia—a cosmetic framework that sanitized the true purpose of affirmative action, which was redress and repair.

The Court's ruling allowed white plaintiffs to claim victimhood and transformed affirmative action from a remedy for enslavement and exclusion into a preference for the allegedly undeserving.

As Dr. Frances Cress Welsing wrote, whiteness survives by inversion; it redefines fairness as oppression and power as injury.

The late twentieth century brought an intensification of this reversal.

City of Richmond v. J.A. Croson Co. (1989) imposed "strict scrutiny" on local affirmative action programs, while *Wards Cove Packing Co. v. Atonio* (1989) and *Patterson v. McLean Credit Union* (1989) weakened federal protections against employment discrimination.

Each of these rulings worked collectively to disarm Title VII and §1981, effectively reasserting what Du Bois called the *wages of whiteness*—the psychological and economic dividends paid to white Americans for simply not being Black.

These decisions reintroduced segregation as a "race-neutral" outcome, a concept only possible in a nation collectively suffering from *Collective Diabolical Antisocial Personality Disorder (CD-APD)*—a pathology that confuses justice with persecution.

The twenty-first century has only deepened this judicial whiteout.

In *Parents Involved in Community Schools v. Seattle School District No. 1* (2007), the Roberts Court invoked *Brown v. Board of Education* to invalidate voluntary integration programs—declaring that the way to stop discrimination on the basis of race is to stop considering race altogether.

This Orwellian statement epitomizes the self-delusion of modern whiteness: a people so entranced by their innocence that they believe acknowledging harm is itself harmful.

Then, in *Students for Fair Admissions v. Harvard/UNC* (2023), the Court completed the circle, abolishing race-conscious admissions and thus restoring the original social order—white dominance framed as meritocracy.

Here, the fantasy of color-blindness achieves its ultimate form: a civilization that declares itself post-racial while reestablishing racial subjugation at every level of life.

Through these cases, the Supreme Court became both priest and physician to white America—absolving its guilt and prescribing denial as a cure.

Each ruling has contributed to the institutionalization of cognitive distortion at a national scale.

In education, whiteness has perfected a system in which segregation is self-replicating, injustice is procedural, and inequity is invisible.

These decisions are not isolated missteps but coordinated expressions of a collective neurosis—a juridical ritual through which America reaffirms its identity as the architect of Black containment.

As I argued earlier, whiteness is not a color; it is a psychosis.

And through the law, it continues to evolve—methodically, impersonally, and always in defense of its most sacred project: the perpetual subjugation of Black intelligence, creativity, and autonomy.

Voting Rights and Representation: The Right to Silence Black Political Power

From schooling the citizen to silencing the citizen...

The right to vote—the supposed hallmark of democracy—has never been a guaranteed right for Black people in America. It has always been conditional, provisional, and revocable, granted only when white people believe it serves their interest and rescinded the moment it threatens white control. Every generation of Black progress has been met by a judicial counterattack—a silent coup conducted not through lynching ropes and burning crosses, but through gavels, doctrines, and procedural deceit.

In *City of Mobile v. Bolden* (1980), the Supreme Court delivered one of the most devastating blows to the spirit of the Voting Rights Act of 1965. By requiring plaintiffs to prove "discriminatory intent" rather than showing discriminatory effect, the Court transformed racism from a structural fact into a metaphysical mystery. Intent—something invisible, internal, and deniable—became the new evidentiary threshold. This was legal schizophrenia: the Court could look directly at generations of racial exclusion and proclaim that unless someone confessed to hate, there was no violation. What Dr. Bobby Wright called *psychopathic rationalization* became constitutional doctrine.

Congress attempted to undo that damage in 1982 by amending Section 2 of the Voting Rights Act to include a "results" test, but the white legal imagination soon found new ways to evade accountability. Cases such as *Holder v. Hall* (1994) and *Reno v. Bossier Parish School Board* (1997, 2000) narrowed the reach of both Section 2 and Section 5 preclearance, while *Georgia v. Ashcroft* (2003) diluted the meaning of "retrogression." Each ruling functioned as an act of judicial anesthesia—numbing the nation's conscience by making the mechanics of disenfranchisement appear technical, rather than moral.

Then came *Shelby County v. Holder* (2013), the most devastating regression of the twenty-first century. By striking down the coverage formula that triggered preclearance, the Roberts Court dismantled the core enforcement mechanism of the Voting Rights Act. Within hours, states across the South announced new voter-ID laws, polling-site closures, and gerrymandered maps explicitly designed to suppress Black turnout. The Court rationalized this decision with a sentence that perfectly encapsulates white pathology: "Things have changed in the South." Indeed they had—but not in the way the Court implied. Whiteness had evolved. The burning cross had become the voter-ID requirement; the poll tax had become the closed precinct.

Subsequent rulings intensified this evisceration. In *Husted v. A. Philip Randolph Institute* (2018), the Court upheld Ohio's aggressive voter-purge practices. In *Abbott v. Perez* (2018), it presumed legislative "good faith" in racially gerrymandered maps. And in *Rucho v. Common Cause* (2019), the Court declared partisan-gerrymandering claims non-justiciable in federal court, essentially green-lighting racially coded manipulation under the veneer of partisanship. Each decision deepened the legal illusion that racism can be excused if disguised as politics.

Brnovich v. Democratic National Committee (2021) completed this jurisprudential rollback by adopting "guideposts" that make it nearly impossible to prove discriminatory results under Section 2. The Court's majority opinion rewrote reality itself, describing voter-suppression laws as "ordinary burdens of voting." In doing so, it sanctified inconvenience as equality and transformed systemic obstruction into civic virtue.

Most recently, *Alexander v. South Carolina State Conference of the NAACP* (2024) reversed a finding of racial gerrymandering, raising the evidentiary burden for plaintiffs even higher. The ruling marked the culmination of a fifty-year counter-revolution: the judicial re-enslavement of Black political agency.

What unites these cases is not mere ideology but pathology. They expose whiteness as a collective psychological disorder that cannot coexist with Black self-determination. Every time Black communities achieve political power—from Reconstruction to Barack Obama—the white body politic experiences an identity crisis. The courts then become the therapist who enables the abuser, prescribing denial instead of treatment.

As W. E. B. Du Bois foresaw, "A system cannot fail those it was never designed to protect." These decisions confirm that American democracy has never been a neutral institution; it is the legal instrument of racial hierarchy. Each ruling functions as a ritual reaffirmation of white sovereignty disguised as constitutional interpretation. The Court's jurisprudence, stripped of its robes, is nothing more than the continuous attempt to silence the descendants of the enslaved—to ensure that even when we speak, the system cannot hear us.

Policing, Criminal Procedure, and Qualified Immunity: Institutionalized White Terror

Policing in America has never been about public safety; it has always been about white safety. From slave patrols to modern police departments, law enforcement has functioned as the domestic arm of white sovereignty—the physical enforcement of racial hierarchy through surveillance, humiliation, and the management of Black movement. After the 1960s, when Black activism challenged the legitimacy of this violence, the Supreme Court and lower federal courts responded with a new legal architecture: doctrines that codified impunity and enshrined racial terror as state policy.

The first pillar of this modern immunity regime was built in *Harlow v. Fitzgerald* (1982), which defined "qualified immunity" around the vague standard of "objective reasonableness." The doctrine detached accountability from moral behavior. Officers could now violate constitutional rights so long as their conduct was not "clearly established" as unlawful in prior precedent—a circular logic that guaranteed permanence. It was jurisprudence as gaslighting: the system creating its own fog of uncertainty, then blaming the victims for being lost inside it.

In *City of Los Angeles v. Lyons* (1983), the Court denied a Black man standing to seek an injunction against police chokeholds after he was nearly strangled during a traffic stop. The justices reasoned that Lyons could not prove he would be choked again in the future, effectively immunizing systemic violence by redefining it as anecdotal. To acknowledge pattern would have required empathy—to see a Black man's suffering as social evidence rather than personal misfortune. The Court instead institutionalized what I call *legalized indifference*: the refusal to see, codified as judicial restraint.

Throughout the 1990s and 2000s, this jurisprudence metastasized. *Heck v. Humphrey* (1994) barred most § 1983 damages actions that would imply a conviction was invalid, closing off relief for those wrongfully prosecuted under racist policing. *City of Canton v. Harris* (1989) and *Connick v. Thompson* (2011) raised nearly impossible thresholds for holding municipalities liable for failure to train or supervise officers. *Scott v. Harris* (2007) invited judges to dismiss excessive-force claims based on their own reading of police video, teaching courts to trust the lens of the state over the testimony of the Black body. Each ruling reinforced what Dr. Amos Wilson described as *institutional psychopathy*—the state's inability to experience guilt even when confronted with visual proof of its brutality.

The pathology continued into the twenty-first century. In *Utah v. Strieff* (2016), the Court expanded the "attenuation doctrine," allowing evidence obtained after an illegal stop if an outstanding warrant was discovered. This decision legitimized racial profiling as investigative strategy, converting the fruits of illegality into instruments of order. In *Vega v. Tekoh* (2022), the Court held that Miranda violations do not create a damages claim under § 1983, further eroding the mechanisms of redress for coerced confessions. These cases collectively declare that white anxiety is a higher constitutional value than Black life.

To understand these rulings, one must read them not as discrete legal opinions but as symptoms of a deeper psychosis: the white collective's neurotic need to maintain control through ritualized violence. The police officer's bullet, baton, or knee is merely the instrument; the disease resides in the psyche of the nation. As Resmaa Menakem reminds us, trauma unprocessed becomes tradition. The Court has transformed that tradition into doctrine—ritualizing Black pain as the price of white peace.

This is why the language of "public order" and "qualified immunity" must be understood as clinical vocabulary, not legal terminology. These doctrines are coping mechanisms for a civilization that cannot confront its dependence on brutality. They function like the defenses of the individual psychopath: denial, projection, moral inversion.

Through law, the state repeats its trauma and calls it precedent.

The result is a nation where the lynching tree has been replaced by the bench and the badge—each decision an act of jurisprudential necromancy, resurrecting old ghosts in modern robes. The United States has not ended racial terror; it has bureaucratized it. Every traffic stop, eviction, and "officer-involved shooting" is a sacrament in the liturgy of white fear, sanctified by the courts and administered by police who believe themselves ordained to keep whiteness safe from consequence.

As Dr. Bobby Wright warned, "The psychopathic personality is not confined to individuals—it can permeate institutions." Policing, under the protection of the courts, is that collective personality made flesh. Until the nation names this as pathology rather than policy, America will continue mistaking cruelty for order, authority for morality, and the perpetuation of terror for the preservation of peace.

Employment, Arbitration, and the Privatization of Discrimination

Work has always been one of white America's preferred arenas for containment. After emancipation, the plantation evolved into the workplace; after Jim Crow, the office became the new overseer's field.

Today, in the corporate, governmental, and nonprofit sectors alike, employment remains a controlled environment in which whiteness decides who may eat, who may rise, and who must be sacrificed to preserve the illusion of "merit." The courts, true to pattern, have transformed this economic hierarchy into constitutional doctrine—sanctioning a privatized form of discrimination masked as efficiency.

The modern rollback began in the 1980s and 1990s with a series of Supreme Court decisions that re-engineered the very tools intended to enforce equality. *Wards Cove Packing Co. v. Atonio* (1989) and *Patterson v. McLean Credit Union* (1989) narrowed the reach of Title VII and 42 U.S.C. § 1981, shifting the burden of proof onto Black workers to demonstrate intentional discrimination while excusing employers from the systemic consequences of their practices. Congress partially restored these protections in the Civil Rights Act of 1991, yet the psychological damage was done: white corporate America learned that delay, denial, and procedural complexity could substitute for a whip.

As globalization and neoliberalism matured, the Court created an even more insidious weapon—the conversion of public wrongs into private disputes. *Wal-Mart Stores, Inc. v. Dukes* (2011) made class-wide discrimination claims nearly impossible by demanding "commonality" so rigid that structural bias itself became invisible. In *Epic Systems Corp. v. Lewis* (2018) and *American Express Co. v. Italian Colors Restaurant* (2013), the Court upheld mandatory individual arbitration clauses, allowing corporations to bar collective action entirely. These rulings replaced the language of justice with the language of contract—one of the oldest legal disguises for white power.

This privatization of civil rights is the economic expression of *Collective Diabolical Antisocial Personality Disorder (CD-APD)*: a pathology that demands control without accountability. Under the banner of "freedom of contract," employers gained the ability to isolate victims, silence whistle-blowers, and transform structural racism into a series of atomized grievances. A Black employee confronting racial hostility now stands not before a jury of peers but before an arbitrator paid by the same corporation accused of harm. The plantation has been digitized, its overseers now human-resources departments fluent in compliance rhetoric but devoid of conscience.

University of Texas Southwestern Medical Center v. Nassar (2013) deepened this isolation by requiring "but-for" causation in Title VII retaliation claims—an evidentiary standard so high it effectively neutralizes protection for those who speak out. The result is psychological warfare: silence or unemployment, complicity or starvation. In this environment, Black professionals are forced to internalize double consciousness as corporate strategy, mastering the art of invisibility to survive among predators who call themselves colleagues.

From a psychopolitical perspective, these rulings function as what Dr. Amos Wilson termed *economic mentacide*: the systematic destruction of collective economic consciousness through individualized struggle. By transforming civil rights into private arbitration, the state has re-segregated justice. The courtroom—once a site of public accountability—has been replaced by a contractual labyrinth designed to preserve white institutional innocence. Capitalism's newest miracle is that it can now discriminate in secret, under the protective veil of confidentiality clauses and nondisclosure agreements.

This is not progress; it is privatized repression. The very instruments that claim to resolve conflict are engineered to reproduce subordination. The message is clear: Black labor may be essential to the American economy, but Black life remains expendable to its courts. Whiteness no longer needs to say, "You cannot work here." It simply writes a clause that ensures your suffering will never see the light of a courtroom.

Capital Punishment and the Sanctification of Racial Violence

The death penalty is America's most honest confession. It is where the myth of justice finally removes its mask and reveals the face of white divinity—the belief that whiteness alone holds the moral right to decide who lives and who dies. Capital punishment is not the administration of law; it is the sacrament of white fear, the ritual through which the state re-enacts its oldest theology: that Black suffering redeems the soul of the nation.

In *McCleskey v. Kemp* (1987), the Supreme Court confronted irrefutable data showing that the race of the victim and the race of the defendant determined who received the death penalty in Georgia. The Baldus study demonstrated that defendants accused of killing white victims were far more likely to be sentenced to death than those accused of killing Black victims. The Court did not dispute the numbers; instead, it declared that statistical proof of systemic bias was insufficient without direct evidence of discriminatory intent in a specific case. In that moment, the highest court in the land baptized racism in procedural language. It announced to the world that inequality would be tolerated so long as it remained impersonal.

Whiteness, once again, was granted absolution.

McCleskey is not an anomaly; it is the mirror image of *Dred Scott v. Sandford* (1857) dressed in modern vocabulary. Where *Dred Scott* denied that Black people possessed rights the white man was bound to respect, *McCleskey* denied that Black death carried moral consequence the white state was bound to acknowledge. This is what I name *juridical psychopathy*: the institutional incapacity to feel empathy even when confronted with evidence of one's own cruelty.

The opinion reads like a medical record of national sociopathy—diagnosis withheld, symptoms normalized.

Historically, lynching and capital punishment have always shared a genealogy. The rope became the electric chair, the chair became the gurney, and now the gurney hums quietly behind sanitized walls while journalists take notes from a viewing room. The technology changes; the appetite does not. Each execution is a performance of dominance, a reminder that the state remains the heir of the plantation. The "rule of law" has never been about order; it has been about ritual—white society's need to witness the controlled destruction of Black life as proof of its own stability.

From a psychopolitical lens, capital punishment is the moral theater of *Collective Diabolical Antisocial Personality Disorder (CD-APD)*. It satisfies the pathological craving for control through death, disguising sadism as civic virtue. The execution chamber functions as a collective nervous system for the white psyche: it releases the anxiety of guilt through spectacle. What is marketed as deterrence is, in truth, exorcism—an exorcism of white America's unacknowledged terror of its own historical crimes.

Consider the symbolic choreography: the condemned are strapped, sedated, silenced, and killed in the name of "the people." Yet those same "people" will not abolish poverty, end police brutality, or dismantle the structures that breed despair. The state kills the symptom and calls it justice, while preserving the disease that created it. This is not governance—it is ritualized necropolitics, the management of life through the distribution of death.

As Dr. Frances Cress Welsing taught, the obsession with domination and annihilation is rooted in deep genetic and psychological insecurity. The white collective, haunted by its minority status on the planet, projects its fear of extinction onto Black bodies and enacts symbolic control through violence. Capital punishment thus becomes a cultural exorcism of whiteness's own mortality anxiety. Each execution whispers the same delusion: *We still rule; we still are God.*

From the plantation whipping post to the modern death chamber, this has never been about punishment for crime. It has been about maintaining the hierarchy of souls. The condemned are not simply bodies; they are offerings. The blood of the executed replenishes the nation's faith in its own purity. And so, century after century, the United States continues to kill in order to feel alive.

Until we name this not as jurisprudence but as pathology—until we diagnose the death penalty as the institutional expression of CD-APD—America will continue mistaking vengeance for justice, cruelty for righteousness, and state murder for moral order. The cure begins with truth: the acknowledgment that the death penalty is not a flaw in the system; it is the system operating exactly as designed.

Chapter Review Questions

Section 1 – Color-Blindness as Weaponized Innocence

1. How does the chapter define "color-blindness" as a technology of dominance rather than a path to equality?

2. In what ways does "procedural virtue" mask material re-enslavement in public education?

3. Explain the link between judicial rhetoric of neutrality and the preservation of white sovereignty.

4. What does the chapter mean by "betrayal" as the starting point of modern racial jurisprudence?

5. How does the framing of innocence function as psychological armor for whiteness?

Section 2 – K-12 Funding, Segregation, and the Re-Coding of Inequality

6. Why is *Rodriguez* (1973) characterized as codifying "economic apartheid," and how do property taxes operationalize it?

7. How did *Milliken* (1974) entrench racial geography and protect suburbs from desegregation remedies?

8. What is the chapter's claim about the psycho-legal purpose of insulating white educational space?

9. How did "local autonomy" become a doctrinal pretext for racial isolation?

10. If you designed a remedy the Court rejected in *Milliken*, what would it include and why?

Section 3 – Intent, Impact, and the Erasure of Structure

11. How did *Washington v. Davis* (1976) redefine proof of discrimination, and with what consequences?

12. Why is "discriminatory intent" described as an evidentiary shield for systemic racism?

13. Compare the chapter's "therapist analogy" to the *Davis* standard—what is being critiqued?

14. What forms of evidence does the chapter argue should count as proof of structural bias?

15. How would shifting from "intent" to "effects" alter litigation and outcomes?

Section 4 – Affirmative Action: From Redress to Cosmetic Diversity

16. How does the chapter read *Bakke* (1978) as transforming remedy into symbolism?

17. Why do *Croson* (1989) and related cases make local redress programs nearly impossible?

18. What is the critique of "diversity" as "moral anesthesia"?

19. How do the *SFFA* (2023) decisions complete the shift from historical repair to individual merit myths?

20. What alternative frameworks to "diversity" could courts adopt to center repair and equity?

Section 5 – Voting Rights and the Judicial Right to Silence Black Power

21. How did *City of Mobile v. Bolden* (1980) import the *Davis* intent rule into voting rights?

22. What did the 1982 VRA amendments try to correct, and how did later cases claw that back?

23. Why is *Shelby County* (2013) described as triggering an immediate wave of suppression?

24. How do *Rucho* (2019) and *Alexander v. SC NAACP* (2024) elevate evidentiary burdens and normalize racialized maps?

25. If you redesigned Section 2/5 enforcement today, what legal triggers and remedies would you specify?

Section 6 – Policing, Criminal Procedure, and Qualified Immunity

26. How does *Harlow* (1982) construct qualified immunity as a self-reinforcing shield?

27. Why is *Lyons* (1983) pivotal for blocking systemic injunctions against police violence?

28. Explain how *Heck* (1994), *Canton* (1989), and *Connick* (2011) constrict municipal accountability.

29. What is "jurisprudence as gaslighting" in *Scott v. Harris* (2007) and *Utah v. Strieff* (2016)?

30. Why does the chapter frame *Vega v. Tekoh* (2022) as further privatizing constitutional harms?

Section 7 – Employment, Arbitration, and the Privatization of Discrimination

31. How did *Wards Cove* (1989) and *Patterson* (1989) narrow Title VII and §1981 protections?

32. In what ways do *Wal-Mart v. Dukes* (2011) and *Epic Systems* (2018) convert public wrongs to private disputes?

33. Why does the chapter call mandatory arbitration an engine of "economic mentacide"?

34. How does *Nassar* (2013) change retaliation claims and chill reporting?

35. What regulatory or statutory fixes could restore collective redress and transparency?

Section 8 – Capital Punishment and the Sanctification of Racial Violence

36. Why is *McCleskey* (1987) framed as "baptizing racism in procedure"?

37. How does the chapter link lynching's public spectacle to the modern execution chamber?

38. What does "juridical psychopathy" mean in the context of death-penalty jurisprudence?

39. How does the concept of CD-APD (Collective Diabolical Antisocial Personality Disorder) illuminate the cultural function of executions?

40. What would a "diagnostic" abolition strategy require—legally, politically, and psychologically?

Works Cited

Alexander v. South Carolina State Conference of the NAACP, 601 U.S. ___ (2024).

American Express Co. v. Italian Colors Restaurant, 570 U.S. 228 (2013).

Abbott v. Perez, 585 U.S. ___ (2018).

Brnovich v. Democratic National Committee, 594 U.S. ___ (2021).

Brown v. Board of Education, 347 U.S. 483 (1954).

City of Canton v. Harris, 489 U.S. 378 (1989).

City of Los Angeles v. Lyons, 461 U.S. 95 (1983).

City of Mobile v. Bolden, 446 U.S. 55 (1980).

City of Richmond v. J.A. Croson Co., 488 U.S. 469 (1989).

Connick v. Thompson, 563 U.S. 51 (2011).

Dred Scott v. Sandford, 60 U.S. (19 How.) 393 (1857).

Epic Systems Corp. v. Lewis, 584 U.S. ___ (2018).

Georgia v. Ashcroft, 539 U.S. 461 (2003).

Harlow v. Fitzgerald, 457 U.S. 800 (1982).

Heck v. Humphrey, 512 U.S. 477 (1994).

Husted v. A. Philip Randolph Institute, 584 U.S. ___ (2018).

McCleskey v. Kemp, 481 U.S. 279 (1987).

Parents Involved in Community Schools v. Seattle School District No. 1, 551 U.S. 701 (2007).

Patterson v. McLean Credit Union, 491 U.S. 164 (1989).

Regents of the University of California v. Bakke, 438 U.S. 265 (1978).

Reno v. Bossier Parish School Board, 520 U.S. 471 (1997).

Reno v. Bossier Parish School Board, 528 U.S. 320 (2000).

Rucho v. Common Cause, 588 U.S. ___ (2019).

San Antonio Independent School District v. Rodriguez, 411 U.S. 1 (1973).

Scott v. Harris, 550 U.S. 372 (2007).

Shelby County v. Holder, 570 U.S. 529 (2013).

Students for Fair Admissions, Inc. v. President & Fellows of Harvard College, 600 U.S. ___ (2023).

Students for Fair Admissions, Inc. v. University of North Carolina, 600 U.S. ___ (2023).

University of Texas Southwestern Medical Center v. Nassar, 570 U.S. 338 (2013).

Utah v. Strieff, 579 U.S. 232 (2016).

Vega v. Tekoh, 597 U.S. ___ (2022).

Wards Cove Packing Co. v. Atonio, 490 U.S. 642 (1989).

Washington v. Davis, 426 U.S. 229 (1976).

Wal-Mart Stores, Inc. v. Dukes, 564 U.S. 338 (2011).

Welsing, F. C. (1991). *The Isis Papers: The Keys to the Colors*. Third World Press.

Wilson, A. N. (1993). *The Falsification of Afrikan Consciousness: Eurocentric History, Psychiatry and the Politics of White Supremacy*. Afrikan World InfoSystems.

Wright, B. E. (1984). *The Psychopathic Racial Personality and Other Essays*. Third World Press.

Du Bois, W. E. B. (1935). *Black Reconstruction in America, 1860–1880*. Harcourt, Brace.

Menakem, R. (2017). *My Grandmother's Hands: Racialized Trauma and the Pathway to Mending Our Hearts and Bodies*. Central Recovery Press.

CHAPTER 11
THE CONTINUUM OF ENSLAVEMENT – BLACK AMERICAN CITIZENSHIP

Having traced how law evolved into the moral theater of punishment, we now confront the amendment that made that theater perpetual—the constitutional loophole that turned freedom itself into a performance of control.

America did not abolish slavery in 1865—it simply rebranded it. The Thirteenth Amendment, celebrated as liberation, contained the most devastating caveat in legal history: *"except as a punishment for crime."* Within that loophole, the architecture of re-enslavement was rebuilt brick by brick. From the moment Reconstruction began, the white ruling class sought new mechanisms to convert Black freedom into criminality, and Black labor into profit.

Douglas A. Blackmon's *Slavery by Another Name* and David Oshinsky's *Worse Than Slavery* expose the grotesque continuity: the transformation of plantations into prisons, masters into wardens, and chains into sentences. The so-called "Black Codes" criminalized the very condition of being Black—vagrancy, idleness, walking without proof of employment, speaking too loudly, resisting abuse. These laws manufactured a new class of convicts to feed private industry, turning the criminal-justice system into a conveyor belt of Black bodies.

Convict leasing became the successor institution to slavery, providing mines, railroads, and factories with a cheap and disposable labor force. By 1898, the majority of Alabama's state revenue came from leasing prisoners—almost all of them Black men and boys—to private corporations. Their average life expectancy inside those camps was less than ten years.

Gates v. Collier and the Afterlife of the Chain Gang

The case of *Gates v. Collier* (1972) marked one of the rare moments when the curtain was pulled back. Mississippi's notorious Parchman Farm—a sprawling prison plantation modeled on antebellum estates—was exposed for torture, forced labor, and sexual violence indistinguishable from slavery. The federal court finally declared these practices unconstitutional, but by then nearly a century had passed since emancipation.

Even after *Gates*, the logic of racial containment simply evolved. Mass incarceration replaced convict leasing; policing replaced patrolling; "law and order" replaced "slave discipline." The plantation never closed—it just changed its signage.

When the body could no longer be chained openly, the landscape itself became the cage.

Redevelopment, Highways, and the Architecture of Displacement

Economic control followed the same blueprint. The 1948 *Redevelopment Act* and the 1956 *Federal-Aid Highway Act* were heralded as modern progress, but in practice they became bulldozers of Black prosperity. City planners seized land under "eminent domain," demolishing thriving Black neighborhoods in the name of urban renewal. Families who once owned homes were pushed into public housing projects like Cabrini-Green in Chicago and Hunter's Point in San Francisco, trapped in poverty and surveillance.

As Richard Rothstein documents in *The Color of Law*, these were not accidents of the market—they were deliberate acts of government. Federal Housing Administration policies, redlining maps, and restrictive covenants ensured that white families accumulated intergenerational wealth while Black families were systematically excluded. The American Dream was racially deeded.

Judicial Retrenchment and the Re-Criminalization of Black Life

The legal victories of the mid-twentieth century—the Civil Rights Act of 1964, the Voting Rights Act of 1965, the Fair Housing Act of 1968—were quickly eroded by judicial reinterpretation. Each generation of the Supreme Court has chiseled away at their power. *San Antonio Independent School District v. Rodriguez* (1973) denied education as a fundamental right. *Milliken v. Bradley* (1974) barred metropolitan-wide desegregation. *Washington v. Davis* (1976) required proof of discriminatory intent rather than outcome, effectively legalizing systemic racism so long as it wore the mask of neutrality.

From *Bakke* (1978) to *City of Richmond v. Croson* (1989) to *Students for Fair Admissions v. Harvard* (2023), the Court has slowly strangled affirmative action, declaring color-blindness in a country built on color. *Shelby County v. Holder* (2013) gutted the Voting Rights Act, and *Brnovich v. DNC* (2021) made it nearly impossible to prove racial vote denial. Each ruling reaffirmed a single message: white backlash is constitutional.

The Kerner Commission's 1968 report warned that America was "moving toward two societies, one Black, one white—separate and unequal." Rather than heeding that warning, the nation doubled down on punitive governance, replacing social investment with mass incarceration and militarized policing.

Mentacide and the Fragmentation of Black Identity

But the most enduring consequence of re-enslavement was not merely physical or economic; it was cognitive—the colonization of perception itself.

The psychological toll of this perpetual assault has been devastating. Dr. Bobby Wright called it *mentacide*—the systematic destruction of a people's ability to perceive and respond to reality. When the history of structural warfare is erased,

Black suffering is misdiagnosed as personal failure. The community is divided against itself: the successful are weaponized as proof that racism is over, while the marginalized are blamed for not working harder.

This fracturing extends along lines of gender, sexuality, and class. Many Black men, conditioned by capitalist patriarchy, strive to be "men first" rather than *free Black men*, modeling themselves after white male prototypes. Some Black women, weary of misogynoir, align with white feminist frameworks that do not recognize their unique oppression. Many Black LGBTQ+ individuals are forced to choose between racial and sexual solidarity. The result is fragmentation—a people organized into disorganization, precisely as the system intends.

The Psycho-Political Function of Whiteness

Whiteness, as I define it, is a psycho-legal identity organized around control, consumption, and containment. Its survival depends on creating and maintaining the "other." Each policy that criminalizes Black life, each court decision that privileges white grievance over Black reality, reinforces whiteness as a property right. The white psyche's sense of safety rests upon the perpetual subjugation of the Black body.

The history of American law is therefore not a march toward justice but a carefully choreographed oscillation between concession and reclamation—moments of reform followed by waves of re-entrenchment. The Civil Rights Movement was never defeated; it was absorbed, monetized, and weaponized.

From the Plantation to the Prison: Neuro-Legal Continuity

The continuity is not only institutional but neurological. The same epigenetic stress markers found in the descendants of the enslaved can be observed in communities subjected to chronic policing, poverty, and environmental racism today. The state functions as a collective nervous system—wired to trigger Black fear and white dominance in equal measure. Policy, in this sense, is neurology written in law.

The murders of George Floyd, Breonna Taylor, Tyre Nichols, and so many others exposed the persistence of this structure to the world. For a brief moment, it seemed America was ready to confront its pathology. Yet the backlash—book bans, anti-DEI laws, and the rollback of affirmative action—shows the system's reflexes remain intact. What we are witnessing is not regression but revelation: whiteness defending its nervous system.

The next chapter examines this period—the years between 2020 and 2025—as both an unveiling and an opportunity for radical re-patterning. The question is no longer whether the system can be reformed, but whether it can be healed.

The pathology is no longer hidden—it is habituated. The next chapter turns to the possibilities of detoxifying this national nervous system, exploring whether the disease of domination can be transformed into a practice of healing.

Chapter Review Questions

Section I — The Legal Rebranding of Slavery and Economic Control

1. How does the chapter argue that the 13th Amendment's "except as punishment for crime" clause enabled the rebranding of slavery?

2. In what concrete ways did Reconstruction governments and local elites convert Black freedom into criminality?

3. What behaviors did Black Codes criminalize, and how did those laws manufacture a convict labor force?

4. How did convict leasing align the incentives of states and private industry, and what were the human costs highlighted (e.g., Alabama revenue, mortality)?

5. What conditions at Parchman Farm did *Gates v. Collier* expose, and why does the chapter call it a "rare moment" of accountability?

6. After *Gates,* how did racial control strategies adapt rather than end?

7. According to the chapter (and Rothstein's findings), how did redevelopment and highway construction operate as tools of Black dispossession?

8. What policy mechanisms (FHA practices, redlining, covenants, eminent domain) channeled wealth to white families while excluding Black families?

Section II — *Judicial Retrenchment and the Myth of Neutrality*

9. How did *Rodriguez*, *Milliken*, and *Washington v. Davis* reshape civil-rights enforcement in schools and cities?

10. What is the chapter's critique of the Court's shift from outcome/effects to proof of "discriminatory intent"?

11. How does the chapter trace the path from *Bakke* to *Croson* to *SFFA (2023)* as a progression from redress to "color-blind" rollback?

12. Why does the chapter describe these decisions as declaring "color-blindness in a country built on color"?

13. What immediate and long-term effects does the chapter attribute to *Shelby County* and *Brnovich* on Black political power?

14. How do these cases exemplify the chapter's claim that "white backlash is constitutional"?

Section III — *Mentacide, Fragmentation, and the Continuity of Whiteness*

15. Define "mentacide" as used here and explain how the chapter links psychological fragmentation, epigenetic stress, and modern policy regimes to a continuous system of racial control.

Works Cited

Abbott v. Perez, 585 U.S. ___ (2018).

Brnovich v. Democratic National Committee, 594 U.S. ___ (2021).

City of Richmond v. J.A. Croson Co., 488 U.S. 469 (1989).

Gates v. Collier, 501 F.2d 1291 (5th Cir. 1974).

Milliken v. Bradley, 418 U.S. 717 (1974).

National Advisory Commission on Civil Disorders. (1968). *Report of the National Advisory Commission on Civil Disorders* (The Kerner Report). U.S. Government Printing Office.

Rothstein, R. (2017). *The color of law: A forgotten history of how our government segregated America.* Liveright.

San Antonio Independent School District v. Rodriguez, 411 U.S. 1 (1973).

Shelby County v. Holder, 570 U.S. 529 (2013).

Students for Fair Admissions, Inc. v. President & Fellows of Harvard College, 600 U.S. ___ (2023).

Washington v. Davis, 426 U.S. 229 (1976).

Blackmon, D. A. (2008). *Slavery by another name: The re-enslavement of Black Americans from the Civil War to World War II.* Anchor.

Oshinsky, D. M. (1996). *"Worse than slavery": Parchman Farm and the ordeal of Jim Crow justice.* Free Press.

Wright, B. E. (1984). *The psychopathic racial personality and other essays.* Third World Press.

Statutes & Federal Programs

Federal-Aid Highway Act of 1956, Pub. L. No. 84-627, 70 Stat. 374 (1956).

Housing Act of 1949, Pub. L. No. 81-171, 63 Stat. 413 (1949). *(Often referenced as the postwar "urban redevelopment" framework.)*

CHAPTER 12
THE POST-GEORGE FLOYD ERA

TRAUMA, DENIAL, AND RETALIATION – THE NEUROPSYCHOLOGY OF WHITENESS (2020-2025)

Having traced the historical circuitry of domination from plantation to prison, we now arrive in the present—where the nervous system of whiteness begins to short-circuit under the weight of its own delusion.

Revelation and Retrenchment

The murder of George Floyd did not rupture America's racial order; it revealed it. For one moment, the nation looked into the mirror of Black death and claimed to see itself. Corporations pledged justice, institutions staged repentance, and "antiracism" became a marketing slogan. Yet the reckoning was cosmetic. When the chants faded, whiteness re-stabilized its nervous system. What followed was a coordinated backlash—the systematic dismantling of every moral, political, and professional gain achieved in that fleeting window of conscience.

The Purge of Black Women and the Economics of Reprisal

Within six months of Donald Trump's return to office, more than 300,000 Black women had been fired, "reorganized," or quietly removed from their positions (U.S. Department of Labor, 2025). By summer 2025, the Bureau of Labor Statistics reported Black unemployment at 9.7 percent, the highest rate in over a decade, while every other major demographic group experienced employment growth (Economic Policy Institute, Aug 2025).

Equity departments were dissolved; DEI roles eliminated; Black female executives targeted as "divisive." These women were punished for being the conscience of the institutions they served. Their visibility during 2020–2022 made them symbols of accountability—an unforgivable offense in a culture addicted to denial.

The same nation that once promised transformation now punishes those who carried the mirror.

I spoke about this collapse with Richard Chew on WCPT Chicago (July 2025), on *The Isiah Factor Uncensored* (Fox 26 Houston, Aug 2025), and with Lurie Daniel Favors on SiriusXM Urban View (Sep 2025). In each conversation, I emphasized that this wave of firings was not economic coincidence; it was moral retaliation. Whiteness had tolerated diversity only so long as it remained decorative.

Project 2025: The Institutionalization of Malignant Diabolical Psychopathy

Project 2025 is not a political plan—it is a psychotic relapse. It represents the nervous system of whiteness attempting to restore its original programming: domination, control, and moral anesthesia. It is the **institutionalization of malignant diabolical psychopathy**—the fusing of political power with sadistic pleasure and spiritual delusion.

If the backlash against Black women marked a social relapse, Project 2025 marks the full institutional seizure.

The project's architects present it as a blueprint for national renewal. In truth, it is a treatment refusal—the patient's violent insistence that its illness is health, and its cruelty is order. Its policies, which dismantle civil rights enforcement, DEI infrastructure, reproductive autonomy, and environmental protections, are the bureaucratic language of predation.

Whiteness, when confronted with the possibility of accountability, experiences it as existential threat. Project 2025 functions as the state's **fight-or-flight response**—a collective adrenal surge to reassert dominance through annihilation. It is not conservative; it is compulsive. It does not govern; it devours.

Policy as Psychosis: The Project 2025 Doctrine

Each element of Project 2025 mirrors a psychiatric symptom cluster:

- **Grandiosity:** the delusion of divine entitlement to rule, disguised as constitutional restoration.
- **Paranoia:** the obsession with "wokeness," immigrants, and diversity as enemies of civilization.
- **Sadism:** the bureaucratic enjoyment of erasure—erasing trans existence, Black achievement, reproductive rights, and the public sector itself.
- **Narcissistic withdrawal:** the retreat from truth, empathy, and multiracial democracy into a fantasy of white innocence.

What appears as policy is, in truth, psychiatry performed on a national stage.

This doctrine is not new; it is a clinical repetition of the *Doctrine of Discovery*. The same ecclesiastical psychosis that sanctified slavery now reemerges as political strategy.

Institutional Necrosis: Whiteness Devouring Its Own Organs

The pathology has begun to consume even its hosts. White institutions—universities, courts, media, and the church—are collapsing under the weight of their own delusion. The Supreme Court, having dismantled affirmative action and voting protections, has transformed jurisprudence into moral theater. Corporate America, once fluent in equity language, now performs selective amnesia.

This is not reform fatigue; it is necrosis—the slow death of institutions that refuse moral oxygen.

Whiteness, unable to metabolize truth, turns inward. It devours its own organs in order to feel alive. The empire is not being attacked; it is self-cannibalizing.

The Neuropsychology of Retrenchment

The post-George Floyd period can be read as a clinical cycle of trauma, denial, and retaliation. Exposure to racial truth (Floyd's murder) created temporary empathy activation; sustained reflection threatened the ego; the collective nervous system responded with repression and projection.

This sequence—**exposure → empathy → narcissistic injury → retaliation**—defines the neuropsychological reflex of whiteness. It is identical to that of an untreated abuser confronted with their violence: guilt triggers rage, rage demands control, and control seeks destruction.

The backlash of 2023–2025 is therefore not political regression—it is the symptom of a traumatized identity structure fighting for psychic survival.

The Theology of Control

When psychology fails to justify domination, theology is summoned to sanctify it.

Project 2025's moral authoritarianism is the re-enactment of a medieval cosmology: salvation through domination. It fuses state power with evangelical theology to consecrate cruelty. Theocracy is simply colonial Christianity returning home.

Whiteness, threatened by pluralism, seeks refuge in the sacred. But what it worships is not God—it is itself. This is the essence of **malignant diabolical psychopathy**: the self divinized, the other demonized, and power rebranded as virtue.

Clinical Prognosis: Untreated, Terminal

From a psycho-clinical perspective, America's prognosis is poor. The patient—White America—remains treatment-resistant, addicted to denial, and hostile toward therapy. The body politic's immune system (its moral institutions) is in collapse. Empathy deficits are now policy. Cognitive dissonance is governance.

And as with any untreated illness, the infection spreads beyond its host.

Without radical intervention—truth commissions, reparations, and systemic re-education—the illness will progress toward terminal authoritarianism. The final stage of this disorder is self-destruction disguised as salvation.

Immigration, Anti-Blackness, and the New Global Caste

ICE removals of Haitian, Jamaican, Nigerian, and Central American migrants increased by nearly 40 percent (2023–2025) (Department of Homeland Security Reports, 2025). Black asylum seekers—already the smallest share of the migrant population—were detained and deported at rates double their percentage of total arrivals.

Tanya Katerí Hernández captures the psychological mechanism of this violence in *Racial Innocence* (2022):

> "Latino racial innocence thrives on the denial of proximity to whiteness and complicity with anti-Black structures. To claim 'we are not like them' is to participate in the very system that oppresses us all."

Many Latino voters, seduced by patriarchy and aspirational whiteness, helped re-elect the same regime that now hunts their kin. This is the tragic logic of colonial psychology: those who align with supremacy inherit its cruelty before they inherit its safety.

Cultural Malignant Narcissism in American Leadership

The pathology that drives the racial state is bipartisan. Malignant Narcissism—the fusion of entitlement, self-adoration, and moral exhibitionism—infects America's ruling class regardless of party.

Whiteness is not partisan—it is pathological, and it wears every costume available to power.

Justice Ruth Bader Ginsburg's refusal to retire when President Obama privately urged her to step down (as reported by *The New York Times*, 2014;

Politico, 2020) exemplifies this pathology: a belief that one's symbolic importance outweighs collective survival. Her decision enabled the far-right takeover of the Supreme Court, whose rulings now erode the very rights she once defended.

President Joe Biden's decision to run for re-election despite clear cognitive and physical decline—and his staff's concealment of that decline (see *The Guardian*, June 2025; *Axios*, July 2025)—reflects the same sickness. The Democratic Party's moral branding masks its complicity in empire; its leaders proclaim virtue while participating in corruption. They are, as I have written elsewhere, "the benevolent arm of the same beast."

Ed Blum and the Model-Minority Myth

The psychosis of whiteness is rarely enacted alone; it recruits accomplices under the illusion of merit.

No event illustrates cross-racial complicity more starkly than *Students for Fair Admissions v. Harvard/UNC* (2023). Conservative activist Ed Blum, long architect of anti-civil-rights litigation, recruited East Asian plaintiffs to argue that affirmative action discriminated against them. By weaponizing the "model-minority" narrative, Blum created an optical illusion of fairness that concealed white resentment.

Scholars like Claire Jean Kim (1999) describe this as "racial triangulation"—a strategy that elevates Asian Americans as industrious to discipline Black people as deviant. The Court's ruling ended race-conscious admissions under the guise of equality, rewarding those who allied with whiteness at the expense of solidarity. It was psychological warfare disguised as meritocracy.

The Weaponization of Power and the Implosion of Whiteness

Donald Trump's second term has turned statecraft into spectacle. He wields executive power to threaten prosecutors, intimidate judges, and persecute critics—including his own white male allies. For the first time, America is witnessing whiteness cannibalize itself. The pathology of domination cannot coexist with accountability; it will destroy even its disciples before it surrenders control.

White America cannot recognize this decay because it has never known moral sight outside its own reflection. Conditioned to believe itself good by nature, it confuses consequence with persecution. The empire is collapsing not because of external enemies but because of internal rot—because its gods were mirrors all along.

The Spiritual and Moral Implosion

What began as institutional collapse has now become metaphysical.

We are living through the neurological breakdown of the American project: an empire whose synapses can no longer carry the lie. As Malcolm X observed after JFK's assassination, "The chickens have come home to roost." That prophecy has matured. The United States is white supremacy—its architecture, its language, its theology. Evil knows no bounds; it devours even those who believe they command it.

Global Reverberations

The empire's seizure is not confined to one body; its tremors travel through the global nervous system.

The backlash reverberates worldwide. In South Africa, corporate monopolies still reproduce colonial extraction; in Brazil, police violence against Afro-Brazilians mirrors U.S. policing; in the UK, laws banning "critical race theory" echo American panic. The myth of Western virtue is decomposing in public. We are witnessing a planetary nervous breakdown—the empire's final seizure.

Closing Reflection

The post-George Floyd era is not a failure of progress but the revelation of a disease. The murder, denial, and retaliation that define this age are the body convulsions of whiteness refusing to die. Project 2025 is its most coherent symptom—a national suicide pact written in the language of law.

The next chapter turns from diagnosis to prognosis—from autopsy to resurrection—to ask whether a new moral nervous system can yet be born from the ruins of this one.

The diagnosis remains clear: malignant diabolical psychopathy—untreated, transmissible, terminal unless interrupted by collective moral intervention.

Chapter Review & Discussion Questions

Revelation and Retrenchment

1. How does the author define the George Floyd moment as a *mirror* rather than a rupture in America's racial order?

2. In what ways did corporate and institutional "antiracism" during 2020–2021 serve as a form of moral anesthesia rather than structural change?

The Purge of Black Women and the Economics of Reprisal

3. What economic and symbolic roles do Black women occupy that make them particular targets of institutional retaliation?

4. How does the elimination of DEI infrastructure function as both economic policy and psychological retribution?

Project 2025 and Malignant Diabolical Psychopathy

5. In what sense does Project 2025 represent the *nervous system* of whiteness defending itself?

6. How do the symptoms of grandiosity, paranoia, sadism, and narcissistic withdrawal illustrate the psychotic nature of Project 2025?

7. Why does the author describe Project 2025 as the "bureaucratic language of predation"?

8. How do the goals of Project 2025 parallel the moral logic of the Doctrine of Discovery and colonial Christianity?

Institutional Necrosis and the Neuropsychology of Retrenchment

9. What does the author mean by "whiteness devouring its own organs"?

10. How does the four-stage cycle—exposure, empathy, narcissistic injury, retaliation—explain the nation's behavioral regression after 2020?

11. What are the implications of interpreting backlash as a trauma reflex rather than political disagreement?

Theology of Control and Clinical Prognosis

12. How does modern theocracy act as a psychological refuge for whiteness, and what does this reveal about the link between religion and domination?

13. What is meant by describing the United States as a "treatment-resistant patient"? What forms of therapy or intervention might constitute "radical treatment"?

Global Reverberations and Moral Prognosis

14. How do global patterns in South Africa, Brazil, and the UK reflect the same neuropsychological defense mechanisms seen in the U.S.?

15. The author calls Project 2025 "a national suicide pact written in the language of law." Discuss this metaphor in light of the chapter's diagnosis of malignant diabolical psychopathy.

Works Cited

Axios. (2025, July). *Biden staff concealed signs of cognitive decline, sources say.* https://www.axios.com

Chew, R. (Host). (2025, July). *Interview with Dante King.* WCPT Chicago.

Daniel Favors, L. (Host). (2025, September). *Interview with Dante King.* SiriusXM Urban View.

Department of Homeland Security. (2025). *Annual report on immigration enforcement actions: 2023–2025.* U.S. Department of Homeland Security.

Economic Policy Institute. (2025, August). *Black unemployment trends in the United States, 2020–2025.*

Fox 26 Houston. (2025, August). *The Isiah Factor Uncensored [Television broadcast].*

Hernández, T. K. (2022). *Racial innocence: Unmasking Latino anti-Black bias and the struggle for equality.* Beacon Press.

Kim, C. J. (1999). *The racial triangulation of Asian Americans.* Politics & Society, 27(1), 105–138. https://doi.org/10.1177/0032329299027001005

Malcolm X. (1963, November 22). *The chickens come home to roost.* Speech, New York, NY.

New York Times. (2014, September 28). *Ruth Bader Ginsburg won't step down.* https://www.nytimes.com

Politico. (2020, September 19). *The fight over RBG's legacy and the Supreme Court.* https://www.politico.com

Students for Fair Admissions v. President and Fellows of Harvard College, 600 U.S. ___ (2023).

U.S. Conference of Catholic Bishops. (2023). *Report on clergy sexual abuse in the United States.*

U.S. Department of Labor. (2025). *Quarterly workforce demographics report,* Q2 2025.

Yehuda, R., et al. (2016). *Epigenetic mechanisms in trauma and posttraumatic stress disorder. Dialogues in Clinical Neuroscience, 18*(4), 359–370. https://doi.org/10.31887/DCNS.2016.18.4/ryehuda

The Guardian. (2025, June). *Democrats debate Biden's fitness for a second term.* https://www.theguardian.com

CHAPTER 13
FROM COLONIAL FAITH TO CIVIC RELIGION
WHITENESS, LAW, AND THE MORAL ORDER OF EMPIRE

Having traced contemporary relapse and backlash, we now widen the lens to the original firmware: the sacred architecture that taught Europe—and later America—how to make domination feel holy and lawlike.

Whiteness was never merely a color; it was conceived as a sacred order. The very foundations of European civilization were steeped in theological constructs that equated *light* with purity, *darkness* with sin, and *white flesh* with divine favor. In this sacred dichotomy, the conquest and subjugation of nonwhite peoples became not only permissible, but righteous.

What follows is the ur-liturgy of empire: doctrine as mandate, conquest as communion.

The earliest architects of empire — priests, kings, jurists, and explorers — worked in concert to design a global system of domination cloaked in holy language. The Doctrine of Discovery, issued under papal authority in the fifteenth century, codified what had already been in motion for centuries: that European Christians were divinely authorized to seize, enslave, and civilize all "pagan" nations. The Church became the first empire of whiteness, consecrating conquest as God's work and identifying salvation with submission to white Christian order.

Once conquest is sanctified, possession becomes sacrament.

The theology of whiteness was the theology of property. To be Christian was to be human, to be human was to be white, and to be white was to possess dominion — over land, labor, and life itself. This moral structure became the unspoken covenant of empire: *to conquer in God's name was to enact divine will.* In every colony, church and court worked in unison to construct an architecture of law that sanctified possession and erased the humanity of the possessed.

Even after the formal ties between crown and church loosened, the logic remained intact. What had once been divine authority became civic virtue. The moral right of conquest was reborn as the rational right of "civilization." The theologian's pulpit evolved into the judge's bench; the crucifix gave way to the gavel. Yet beneath the secular veneer, the same psycho-spiritual logic persisted — whiteness as godhood, Blackness as negation.

This is the core claim of this chapter: whiteness operates as a religion—complete with creed, clergy, sacraments, and a soteriology that requires Black negation.

As I reflect on the historical trajectory of Western law and governance, it becomes increasingly clear that whiteness has always functioned as a religious project. The moral order of empire depended upon it. Its rituals were baptismal — the conversion of entire continents into the faith of whiteness. Its sacraments were legal — property titles, racial codes, and citizenship laws. Its saints were conquerors, jurists, and presidents who invoked divine or civic duty as justification for racial domination.

The so-called "enlightened" democracies that emerged from Europe were simply reformed churches of whiteness. The worship of God was replaced by the worship of the Republic, but the altar remained the same. Whiteness was still the chosen identity, ordained to rule and "save" the world through moral authority, legal order, and economic mastery. In this sense, whiteness is not just a social construct; it is a faith system — a psycho-political religion built on the desecration of Blackness and the moral delusion of supremacy.

The enduring question, then, is not how Christianity justified racism, but how whiteness became the god that both Christianity and the American state served.

II. From Canon Law to Common Law — The Birth of Racial Legality

To see how faith became statute, we have to watch canon become code.

The earliest laws that defined racial hierarchy in the Americas were not merely political or economic instruments — they were theological inheritances. The colonial legal systems of England, Spain, Portugal, and France were all incubated within the womb of Canon Law, the sacred legal code of the Catholic Church. Long before the Enlightenment or the drafting of any constitution, Europe's legal imagination was already shaped by the moral binaries that Christianity had imposed upon the world: good and evil, saved and damned, civilized and heathen, white and Black.

When European colonists arrived in the so-called New World, they carried this spiritual jurisprudence across the Atlantic. The first colonial courts did not dispense secular justice — they performed divine ritual. To be judged under law was to be measured against the moral architecture of Christian Europe, where whiteness was presumed virtuous and Blackness inherently suspect. The legal fiction of "civilization" was sanctified by the same divine logic that had justified the Crusades, the Inquisition, and the enslavement of Africans.

One can see this inheritance clearly in the colonial statutes that followed. The 1700 Act for the Trial of Negroes, passed by the Pennsylvania Assembly, explicitly denied Black people — free and enslaved — the right to trial by jury. Two justices and six white "freeholders" were sufficient to convict and sentence a Black person to death, mutilation, or exile. The law did not concern itself with truth or justice; its purpose was to reaffirm the racial hierarchy ordained by God and enforced by man.

Similar laws proliferated across the colonies. The 1705 Act for the Better Ordering and Governing of Negroes and Mulatto Slaves codified the complete exclusion of Black people from legal personhood. They could not testify against whites. They could not defend themselves in court. Their very existence was rendered a perpetual act of guilt. To be Black was to be criminal by birth — not through deed or intent, but by divine and legal decree.

The fusion of moral and legal doctrine created what I call *the psycho-legal matrix of whiteness*: a system in which faith and law worked together to make racial subjugation appear natural, inevitable, and righteous. The moral justifications of the Church became the procedural mechanisms of the State. The presumption of white innocence and Black guilt — first preached from pulpits — was now enforced in courtrooms.

The colonial codes also served a dual purpose. As Winthrop Jordan observed in *White Over Black*, the laws were written as much for white men as they were against Black people. They were designed to *discipline whiteness* itself — to ensure that white men would police and punish Blackness in one another's presence. The law, then, was not only a weapon but a liturgy, instructing white men in the sacred duty of maintaining racial order.

Importantly, these codes catechized white men as much as they criminalized Black life.

This legal theology evolved seamlessly into Common Law, the body of precedent that would come to define the Anglo-American legal tradition. English jurists, trained in the moral language of Christendom, began to recast divine hierarchy into secular rationality. What was once sin became crime; what was once heresy became treason; and what was once divine right became property right.

The transition from canon to common law was not a rupture — it was a translation. The Church's moral universe was rewritten in the language of "reason," but its core assumptions remained intact.

Whiteness continued to signify virtue, property, and authority. Blackness continued to signify transgression, danger, and disorder.

By 1776, the liturgy had a new liturgical language: "reason," "rights," and "property." The religion remained.

Thus, by the time the United States declared independence, the sacred architecture of whiteness had already been transformed into the legal architecture of the state. The colonies did not rebel against empire to create freedom; they rebelled to preserve their right to rule.

III. The Civic Religion of Whiteness

What the Republic changed was costume, not creed.

When the American Republic was founded, it did not reject the sacred hierarchies of the colonial era — it *secularized* them. The cross was replaced by the flag; the catechism became the Constitution; and whiteness, stripped of its overt theological costume, emerged as the new civic faith of the nation.

The so-called Enlightenment promised reason in place of revelation, science in place of scripture, and liberty in place of monarchy. But beneath the language of democracy and progress, the same sacred logic endured. The architects of the Republic — many of whom were steeped in Protestant theology — simply traded one god for another. They exchanged divine authority for "rational order," yet continued to believe that white men were uniquely ordained to govern humanity.

The moral foundation of this new "civic religion" rested upon a profound psychological sleight of hand. It disguised domination as virtue. The Declaration of Independence proclaimed that "all men are created equal," even as the men who wrote and signed those words held human beings in bondage. This contradiction was not accidental; it was the essence of the faith. Whiteness required the illusion of morality in order to sustain its authority. Its believers needed to imagine themselves as good, just, and civilized — even as they practiced systemic cruelty.

The early Republic's laws and institutions were, therefore, designed not only to enforce racial hierarchy but to *sanctify* it. Citizenship itself became a sacrament of whiteness — a ritual of belonging reserved for those who could be trusted to protect the racial order. Enslaved Africans were not citizens. Indigenous peoples were not citizens. Even free Black people, who had fought and died in the Revolutionary War, were later stripped of legal recognition through judicial rulings like Dred Scott v. Sandford (1857), which declared that no Black person "had rights which the white man was bound to respect."

This ruling did not invent white supremacy; it merely rearticulated the theology of empire in secular legal form. The Republic became the Church, and the Constitution its scripture. Judges, politicians, and educators became its priests — sanctifying a civic morality that equated whiteness with humanity itself.

Law enforcement functioned as the Republic's priesthood of purity. The patrols that once hunted enslaved Africans evolved into police departments whose primary duty was — and remains — the protection of property, whiteness, and order. The courtroom replaced the confessional booth. The schoolhouse became the catechism, where children learned the civic gospel of America's moral innocence and divine exceptionalism.

Whiteness thus transformed from a religious to a cultural absolute — a moral currency that determined who was human, who was moral, who was intelligent, and who was worthy of life. In this way, the "civic religion of whiteness" became America's true national faith, transcending denomination, geography, and even time itself.

Hence the familiar liturgy: anthem, flag, "law and order," innocence as doctrine.

Its rituals remain ubiquitous: the singing of anthems, the veneration of flags, the invocation of "law and order." Its dogmas remain unquestioned: that whiteness is civilization, that America is good, and that justice is impartial.

Yet the evidence of history — from slavery to Jim Crow to the carceral state — reveals that whiteness has never been merely a race; it is a moral identity, one constructed through systemic denial, projection, and violence.

This civic religion continues to shape the nation's psychological and institutional life. Its hymns are sung in courtrooms, classrooms, and boardrooms alike. It promises redemption through obedience — not to God, but to whiteness itself.

IV. The Continuum — From Slavery to Convict Leasing and Ghettoization

Here the theology refactors again—into penal economics and urban design.

Emancipation did not end the racial order of America — it reconfigured it. The Thirteenth Amendment, celebrated as the death of slavery, contained within it the seed of its resurrection. The exception clause — "except as a punishment for crime" — ensured that racial bondage would not die, but mutate. Through this single phrase, the moral and legal architecture of whiteness reconstituted itself into new forms of domination: convict leasing, chain gangs, peonage, and eventually the prison-industrial complex.

This was not progress; it was transmutation. The theology of whiteness that once sanctified slavery now sanctified criminality. The Black body was no longer legally "property," but it remained the moral and economic foundation upon which white America defined its virtue, its order, and its wealth. The plantation gave way to the prison. The slave code gave way to the criminal code. And the sacred covenant of whiteness — domination through moral authority — endured untouched.

The postbellum South understood this well. In the decades following Reconstruction, southern legislatures enacted a tidal wave of laws that re-inscribed Black existence as inherently deviant. The Black Codes, vagrancy statutes, and labor laws criminalized everyday life: idleness, loitering, "insolence," failure to show proof of employment.

Each law functioned as a moral mirror, projecting white fear and guilt onto Black survival. As in earlier centuries, the law was not simply punitive — it was performative, reenacting the sacred ritual of white mastery.

The convict leasing system that followed was, as historian Douglas A. Blackmon described, "slavery by another name." States leased thousands of Black men, women, and children to private corporations, railroads, and plantations. They were worked to death under the supervision of white guards, beaten, starved, and buried in unmarked graves. In Mississippi's Parchman Farm — later immortalized in *Gates v. Collier (1972)* — the so-called "inmates" labored under the gun and the whip just as their ancestors had a century before. The court's eventual ruling that such conditions were unconstitutional marked a legal victory, but not a moral transformation.

The economic and psychological logic remained intact. Whiteness still required Black suffering to affirm its innocence. The spectacle of Black punishment became America's civic sacrament — a public ritual of purification, affirming that white virtue depended upon the constant visibility of Black degradation.

By the mid-twentieth century, this ritual had evolved into new forms. The ghetto replaced the plantation; the welfare office replaced the overseer; the police replaced the patrol. Through urban segregation, redlining, and discriminatory policing, the architecture of whiteness expanded from the courthouse to the city itself. Every institution — legal, economic, medical, and educational — became a chamber in the cathedral of white moral order.

And yet, as the system modernized, it learned to mask its violence beneath the language of fairness and reform. "Law and order" replaced "slave patrol." "Personal responsibility" replaced "racial purity." But the psychological core — the need to define whiteness through the suffering of Blackness — remained unchanged.

Even today, mass incarceration operates as a modern-day liturgy of white redemption. The cages of Rikers Island, Angola, and San Quentin are monuments to the same psycho-legal theology that animated the plantations of Virginia and the slave ships of the Atlantic. The criminalized Black body continues to serve as the scapegoat of American morality — the vessel through which the Republic purges its guilt and reaffirms its godhood.

Every era renews the sacrifice that keeps the faith alive.

Whiteness, as I have argued throughout this work, is not a race; it is a faith system. And like all faith systems built on falsehoods, it must be continually nourished by sacrifice.

V. The Afterlife of Moral Innocence — Whiteness as Redemption Fantasy

Dogma requires absolution; empire requires a theology of innocence.

The afterlife of slavery is not merely political or economic — it is psychological, spiritual, and epistemological. Whiteness, as an identity and ideology, has survived not because it is rooted in truth, but because it is anchored in a *redemption fantasy*: the illusion that moral innocence can coexist with systemic evil.

From the moment of first contact between Europeans and the Indigenous peoples of the Americas, this fantasy was embedded in the colonial psyche. The conquistador prayed before he killed; the planter baptized the enslaved before selling their children; the legislator quoted scripture while codifying oppression. Every act of domination was wrapped in the language of salvation. And so the moral logic of whiteness emerged: *violence is virtue, conquest is civilization, and cruelty is care.*

This fantasy has proven more enduring than any single law or institution because it satisfies a deep psychological need — the need for the oppressor to remain good in their own eyes. Whiteness depends upon the unbroken performance of moral innocence. It must continuously tell itself that its violence is benevolence, its theft is order, its supremacy is democracy.

In the modern era, this fantasy has been refashioned through the language of progress and reform. The same country that enslaved Africans now celebrates "civil rights" as evidence of its moral evolution. The same corporations that profited from forced labor now issue diversity statements and sponsor Black History Month panels.

The same politicians who gut social safety nets for Black and poor people still proclaim America to be the "greatest nation on Earth."

This is not hypocrisy — it is theology. Whiteness is a *faith in its own redemption*. It requires confession without consequence, apology without accountability, repentance without repair. Its worshipers confess "racism" as sin while preserving the systems that produce it. They speak of equity while hoarding power. They invoke "inclusion" as spectacle, but not as transformation.

As long as whiteness remains the unspoken moral center of the American imagination, no amount of policy reform can undo the deeper pathology. Because whiteness is not only structural — it is *psychospiritual*. It is a ritual of denial, a collective dissociation from history, a refusal to feel the grief and guilt that would accompany true reckoning.

This denial is not passive; it is enforced. Every time a white person declares, "I'm not racist," the performance reaffirms the collective delusion. Every police shooting rationalized, every inequity explained away, every Black life pathologized — all of it feeds the sacred myth of white innocence.

The afterlife of moral innocence thus ensures the immortality of whiteness itself. Its rituals have merely changed form: the courtroom becomes the confessional, the media becomes the pulpit, and the ballot box becomes the altar. The nation's public life remains a theater of redemption, where white America rehearses its virtue against the backdrop of Black suffering.

The tragedy — and the opportunity — is that the truth of this country's future rests not in its capacity to sustain the lie, but in its willingness to *collapse it*. For only when the myth of white innocence dies can something resembling humanity be born in its place.

Until then, whiteness will continue to enact its cyclical drama — sin, denial, confession, and redemption — with Black people as the involuntary actors in its eternal play of salvation.

Reflective Closing — The Neurobiology of a Moral Lie

We return, finally, to the body: how creed becomes cortex, ritual becomes reflex.

As I trace the moral, legal, and spiritual architecture of whiteness across centuries, what emerges most clearly is that this project was never only political. It was, and remains, *neurological* — a psychobiological adaptation of empire. The lies of whiteness are not just spoken; they are embodied, encoded into the nervous system through centuries of dominance, fear, and moral distortion.

White supremacy, in this sense, is not simply an ideology — it is a form of **Malignant Diabolical Psychopathy**: an intergenerational disorder of conscience that thrives on denial and projection. It produces dissociation as a reflex, defensiveness as a virtue, and domination as a form of self-regulation. The pathology reproduces itself through the institutions of power — church, law, media, education — but its origins are visceral, psychospiritual, and hereditary.

Every empire has its trauma, and whiteness is no exception. The colonizer's inability to reconcile their own cruelty created the need for delusion. Thus, the project of racial domination has always been one of self-preservation — not only of privilege, but of psychic coherence. In order to sustain the illusion of moral goodness, whiteness had to externalize its violence, projecting all impurity, rage, and guilt onto Black bodies.

This is why the American project — despite its proclamations of progress — continues to reenact the same ancient ritual of domination. The psychopathy of whiteness is its dependency on the suffering of others for the maintenance of its self-image. It cannot exist without its victims. Its moral innocence requires perpetual sacrifice.

The task before us, therefore, is not merely to critique whiteness, but to *diagnose* it — as a malignant disorder of mind, culture, and spirit. Only then can we begin to imagine a future in which humanity is disentangled from the pathology that has long masqueraded as morality.

The next chapter descends from theology to tissue—from archive to amygdala—to map how this sacred order etched itself into bodies across generations. It explores this pathology at its deepest level — the **epigenetic and neurobiological mechanisms** that transmit racial violence through both the oppressor and the oppressed. It is here, in the unseen territories of the brain and body, that we find the most damning evidence: that the empire of whiteness has not only governed the world but has also rewired human consciousness itself.

Chapter Review Questions (20 total)

I. Sacred Order & the Doctrine of Discovery

1. In what sense does the chapter argue that "whiteness was conceived as a sacred order," and how did light/dark symbolism function theologically?

2. How did priests, kings, jurists, and explorers co-produce a global system of domination "cloaked in holy language"?

3. What roles did *Dum Diversas*, *Romanus Pontifex*, and *Inter caetera* play in sanctifying conquest and enslavement?

4. Explain the claim that "the theology of whiteness was the theology of property." How did personhood map onto Christianity/whiteness?

5. How did divine authority morph into "civic virtue," preserving the same psycho-spiritual logic under secular language?

II. From Canon Law to Common Law — Birth of Racial Legality

6. What does the chapter mean by a "psycho-legal matrix of whiteness," and how did canon law seed colonial legal structures?

7. How did early colonial courts function as *ritual* rather than neutral adjudication?

8. Analyze the 1700 *Act for the Trial of Negroes* and the 1705 Virginia act: what procedural exclusions encoded racial hierarchy?

9. Why does the chapter say these laws "disciplined whiteness itself" as much as they targeted Black people (drawing on Winthrop Jordan)?

10. How did "translation" (not rupture) carry sacred hierarchy from ecclesiastical forms into Anglo-American common law and property doctrine?

III. The Civic Religion of Whiteness

11. How did the American Republic secularize sacred hierarchies into a new civic faith centered on whiteness?

12. In what ways does *Dred Scott* exemplify the Constitution as civic scripture for racial hierarchy?

13. How did patrols evolve into police and why are they described as a "priesthood of purity"?

14. What rituals and dogmas sustain the "civic religion of whiteness" across courts, schools, and public culture?

15. Why does the chapter frame whiteness as a moral identity maintained through denial, projection, and institutional catechisms?

IV. The Continuum & the Afterlife of Moral Innocence

16. How did the 13th Amendment's exception clause enable a transmutation from slavery to convict leasing and mass incarceration?

17. What makes *Gates v. Collier* a revealing moment—and what limits to transformation does the case expose?

18. How do ghettoization, redlining, and "law and order" continue the liturgy of white redemption via Black suffering?

19. Define the chapter's "redemption fantasy." How does confession without consequence preserve white innocence?

20. In the "Reflective Closing," why is whiteness diagnosed as a psychobiological disorder, and what implications follow for reckoning vs. reform?

Works Cited

Alexander VI, Pope. (1493). *Inter caetera* [Papal bull].

Blackmon, D. A. (2008). *Slavery by another name: The re-enslavement of Black Americans from the Civil War to World War II*. Anchor.

Dred Scott v. Sandford, 60 U.S. (19 How.) 393 (1857).

Gates v. Collier, 501 F.2d 1291 (5th Cir. 1974).

Hening, W. W. (Ed.). (1823). *The statutes at large; being a collection of all the laws of Virginia* (Vol. 3). R. & W. & G. Bartow. (Includes **An Act concerning servants and slaves** [1705].)

Johnson v. M'Intosh, 21 U.S. (8 Wheat.) 543 (1823).

Jordan, W. D. (1968). *White over Black: American attitudes toward the Negro, 1550–1812*. University of North Carolina Press.

Nicholas V, Pope. (1452). *Dum Diversas* [Papal bull].

Nicholas V, Pope. (1455). *Romanus Pontifex* [Papal bull].

Newcomb, S. T. (2008). *Pagans in the promised land: Decoding the doctrine of Christian discovery*. Fulcrum.

Oshinsky, D. M. (1996). *"Worse than slavery": Parchman Farm and the ordeal of Jim Crow justice*. Free Press.

Pennsylvania General Assembly. (1700). *An Act for the Trial of Negroes.*

South Carolina General Assembly. (1740). *An Act for the better ordering and governing of Negroes and other slaves in this province.* (Commonly referred to as the Negro Act of 1740.)

Williams, R. A., Jr. (1990). *The American Indian in Western legal thought: The discourses of conquest.* Oxford University Press.

CHAPTER 14
THE NEUROSCIENCE OF WHITENESS
TRAUMA, EPIGENETICS, AND THE BIOLOGICAL MACHINERY OF DOMINATION

The Nervous System of Empire

Every empire has a nervous system.

Whiteness, as the most enduring empire of the modern world, is not merely a social construct—it is a neural architecture, an intergenerational network of trauma, fear, and reward that has structured the very biology of those who inhabit it. It is an inherited circuitry of domination, encoded in the collective psyche of white populations and projected violently onto the bodies of the colonized.

When I say *whiteness is neurological*, I mean that it functions as an embodied memory—a psychosomatic reflex transmitted across centuries. It is the product of repeated exposure to violence, reinforced by ritualized acts of superiority, and maintained through the neurochemical rush that comes from control, conquest, and moral justification. Empire, at its core, is a trauma response pretending to be civilization.

The European colonizers who sailed the seas, burned villages, and enslaved millions were not merely carrying swords and crosses—they were carrying a centuries-old wound: a disconnection from their own humanity. The psychic rupture that birthed white supremacy began long before the transatlantic slave trade. It began when European consciousness was severed from its ancestral and ecological roots—when domination became the substitute for belonging. What followed was the construction of a cultural nervous system that rewarded cruelty and suppressed empathy, that found pleasure in the suffering of others because it had forgotten how to feel anything else.

Neuroscience helps us name what philosophy, theology, and politics have tried to disguise. Repeated acts of violence—especially when moralized—reshape the brain. The amygdala becomes conditioned to equate domination with safety. The prefrontal cortex, responsible for empathy and moral reasoning, is bypassed by reward pathways that deliver dopamine when power is exerted over another. Over time, violence becomes soothing. Dehumanization becomes normal. Whiteness becomes a self-sustaining neural economy in which cruelty and comfort are indistinguishable.

This is why whiteness survives not just through laws or policies, but through the nervous system itself. It is passed on epigenetically—through the chemical markers left by trauma and domination on the DNA of both the oppressor and the oppressed. The empire lives inside the body. It is inherited in the way cortisol floods the bloodstream under threat, in the way hypervigilance and numbness coexist in both Black and white populations, and in the way white denial operates as a form of neurological dissociation—a refusal to integrate the unbearable truth of one's own violence.

I often think about the phrase *"the body keeps the score."* Dr. Bessel van der Kolk wrote those words about trauma, but they apply equally to nations. The body of the West—the collective organism of whiteness—has been keeping score for centuries. Its nervous system is inflamed with guilt, dissonance, and unacknowledged rage. Its autonomic responses are domination and avoidance. Its immune system attacks anything that resembles accountability. Like a person suffering from complex trauma, whiteness has developed elaborate cognitive defenses—denial, projection, and deflection—to survive its own sickness.

And yet, survival is not healing. The empire's nervous system continues to misfire. Its trauma continues to externalize itself as policy, as policing, as pathology. The violence we witness in the twenty-first century—the endless repetition of racialized death and denial—is not an accident of politics; it is the predictable result of an untreated neurological condition. America is the body of whiteness in crisis.

Throughout this chapter, "white" and "Black" refer to socialization regimes and their population-level effects; they are not necessarily intended to ascribe biology to ancestry or fix traits to individuals.

From reflex to residue: if empire trains a reflex, epigenetics shows how the residue of that reflex can be inscribed across generations.

Understanding whiteness as a neurological disorder forces us to see it not as an idea to be debated, but as an illness to be diagnosed. It demands a form of care that is not about reconciliation but about reckoning—a collective acknowledgment that the trauma of empire has always been bilateral. It has maimed the oppressed and corrupted the oppressor. It has produced two species of suffering: one visible in chains and poverty, the other hidden behind privilege and moral blindness.

The next section explores how this trauma becomes biological inheritance—how empire not only colonized land, but colonized the genome. The story of whiteness, it turns out, is not only written in law and scripture, but in the very molecules of human survival.

II. Inherited Violence — The Epigenetic Transmission of Whiteness

Whiteness did not simply invent racism; it became it.

It is the embodied record of conquest and control — a psychosomatic inheritance transmitted through centuries of terror, justification, and denial. The biology of white supremacy is written into the nervous systems of those who both inflicted and survived it. Empire, in this way, is not only historical; it is hereditary.

Epigenetics, the science of how experience alters gene expression, provides language for what Black people have always known: that trauma lingers in the body long after the event has ended. What our ancestors endured — the chains, the lash, the rape, the auction block — did not vanish with emancipation. It transformed into chemical messages carried by bloodlines, shaping hormones, stress responses, and even the structure of the brain. The descendants of the enslaved still carry the biological echoes of terror; the descendants of the enslavers still carry the biological habituation to power and apathy.

As Dr. Joy DeGruy writes in *Post Traumatic Slave Syndrome*, "What was done to us became us — and what was done by them became them." Her framing captures the duality of historical trauma: it is not unidirectional. The same violent system that stripped Africans of their humanity stripped Europeans of their empathy. Both conditions were inherited. One inherited survival through vigilance and pain; the other inherited power through avoidance and denial. Together, these polarities formed the genetic ecosystem of the West.

In the enslaved body, cortisol became legacy.

In the oppressor's body, numbness became inheritance.

Neuroscientists have observed that trauma can silence or activate genes across multiple generations. For example, the descendants of Holocaust survivors, Indigenous genocide victims, and enslaved Africans all exhibit heightened reactivity in the amygdala — the brain's threat detector. This constant hyperarousal is not metaphorical; it is molecular. DNA methylation — a process that turns genes "on" or "off" in response to experience — has been shown to pass down the physiological imprint of fear, vigilance, and loss.

Yet few scholars have asked what was epigenetically inherited by the descendants of those who inflicted terror. If trauma can embed itself in the oppressed, what happens in the biology of the oppressor who must continuously deny their own brutality? How does a body that normalizes domination adapt to centuries of cruelty?

The answer lies in what I call *the pathology of anesthetized power*. In white populations, the repetition of domination created a neural and epigenetic preference for disassociation — an emotional shutdown that blunts empathy and redefines moral injury as virtue. Violence became rewarded not only culturally, but biologically. Each act of conquest, each moral justification, reinforced the dopamine reward loops that link aggression with safety and superiority. Over time, whiteness became addicted to its own privilege — to the adrenaline of control, to the hormonal reassurance of dominance.

In this sense, whiteness is not only ideological but biochemical. It thrives on stress responses that sustain hierarchy: the cortisol rush of fear-mongering, the dopamine spike of moral victory, the oxytocin release that bonds white communities through shared opposition to "the other." What appears as cultural prejudice is also neurochemical conditioning — a body trained to confuse hierarchy with harmony.

Meanwhile, in Black bodies, trauma shaped a different kind of intelligence — a genius of adaptation born from necessity. The nervous system of the oppressed developed resilience through hypervigilance, communal care, and spiritual grounding. These traits — too often pathologized as "overreactivity" or "mistrust" — are, in fact, evolutionary adaptations to continuous threat. As Dr. Resmaa Menakem describes in *My Grandmother's Hands*, the Black body became both archive and instrument of survival, carrying within it centuries of encoded resistance and embodied memory.

What we see, then, is a dual inheritance:

- **For white people**, a hereditary moral injury masked as civilization.

- **For Black people**, a hereditary survival intelligence mislabeled as dysfunction.

This is the biological dialectic of empire: the oppressor and the oppressed bound together through shared trauma, transmitted through blood, behavior, and belief. The lie of whiteness — that it is separate, superior, and pure — conceals the truth that it is, in fact, deeply contaminated by its own violence.

When I look at American institutions — schools, police, corporations, churches — I see the nervous system of empire replaying itself in real time. The reflexes are ancient: aggression, fear, avoidance, denial. Even the language of modern democracy is a neurological ritual — soothing the collective conscience while maintaining the same genetic rhythm of domination.

To heal this, we must confront the biology of whiteness as directly as we confront its ideology.

We must acknowledge that what white people call "heritage" is often the physiological residue of brutality, and what Black people call "trauma" is the chemical evidence of survival.

From inheritance to incentive: biology doesn't only carry wounds; it also carries what gets rewarded. The next question is what domination pays out in the brain.

The next section explores how this inheritance becomes neurologically reinforced — how domination itself activates the brain's reward system, creating what I call *the pleasure principle of racial violence* — the dopamine economy that sustains white supremacy's endurance across centuries.

III. Neurological Reward, Empathy Suppression, and White Pleasure in Black Pain

There is a reason why whiteness keeps returning to the spectacle of Black suffering. From the burning flesh at lynching picnics to the looping footage of police killings on modern screens, white America's fascination with Black pain is not incidental — it is neurological. Whiteness has, for centuries, been conditioned to find safety, order, and even gratification in the subjugation of Black life. This is not merely ideological. It is a neurochemical addiction rooted in the brain's reward circuitry — a biochemical inheritance of domination.

Spectacle is not only culture; it is circuitry practice—rehearsal that normalizes who receives empathy and who is denied it.

Neuroimaging and epigenetic findings are probabilistic at group levels and describe tendencies under specific conditions, not fixed capacities in individuals.

The Pleasure Principle of Racial Violence

Every empire requires a source of pleasure.

For ancient Rome, it was the coliseum. For America, it became Black suffering. The lynching postcard, the slave auction, the viral video — each is part of a centuries-long continuum of dopamine-mediated pleasure derived from control, humiliation, and the denial of Black humanity.

The human brain releases dopamine, a neurotransmitter associated with reward, when an individual experiences victory, dominance, or validation. Over generations, whiteness evolved as a social and biological construct that equated Black subjugation with these very sensations. In slave societies, the white nervous system learned to associate control over Black bodies with safety, order, and even moral righteousness. Violence became soothing — the act of punishment became a way to reaffirm one's place in the racial hierarchy and, by extension, one's sense of self.

This is why even today, racialized policing and punishment feel "natural" to many white Americans. Their neurological inheritance has tied authority and aggression into the same circuit — an amygdala-to-reward loop that conflates violence with virtue. When a police officer kneels on a Black man's neck or when media outlets replay the suffering of Black victims, it triggers both fear and satisfaction: fear of the imagined Black threat, satisfaction at its neutralization.

It is a psychic and biological double bind: whiteness cannot exist without the perception of Black danger, and it cannot feel safe without witnessing Black subordination.

Neuroimaging and epigenetic findings are probabilistic at group levels; they describe tendencies under specific conditions, not fixed capacities in individuals.

The Empathy Switch

The white brain's ability to suppress empathy toward Black suffering has been scientifically documented. In neuroimaging studies, white participants often exhibit diminished activity in the anterior cingulate cortex — the region associated with empathy and emotional mirroring — when viewing pain inflicted on Black bodies. The same brain that responds to a white person's distress with concern remains largely inert when the victim is Black.

This selective empathy is not just cognitive bias; it is a form of learned moral anesthesia. Over centuries, religious doctrine, cultural myth, and legal reinforcement have rewired the white psyche to perceive Black life as peripheral to the moral community. The Bible was weaponized to justify this hierarchy. Science followed suit. Law codified it. And the brain — ever adaptive — internalized it.

The result is a population that can proclaim universal love while participating in systemic cruelty. It is the neurobiological manifestation of what Dr. Frances Cress Welsing described as "the inability to relate to life." Whiteness does not simply devalue Black life — it has neurologically *unlearned* how to feel its humanity.

Pleasure, Power, and Projection

At the same time, the repression of empathy does not eliminate desire. What cannot be integrated into the conscious self becomes projected. White supremacy depends on this projection: it casts its own repressed sadism and sexual pathology onto the Black body, labeling it hypersexual, violent, or dangerous. The fantasy of Black aggression serves to conceal white violence.

Psychologically, this is the mechanism of what I call **Malignant Diabolical Psychopathy** — a moral inversion in which the oppressor convinces himself that his violence is virtue and his pleasure is justice. The repeated enactment of this psychopathy produces what I identify as **Collective Diabolical Antisocial Personality Disorder**, in which entire societies become bonded through shared moral delusion and collective emotional detachment.

The neuroscience behind this delusion is brutally simple. When white violence is socially rewarded — through legal immunity, economic gain, or even applause — it strengthens the same neural pathways that any addiction would. The more a society normalizes cruelty, the more the individual brain adapts to it. Over time, compassion becomes neurologically aversive; domination becomes biologically gratifying.

The Ritual of Reassurance

This helps explain why American culture continually reproduces narratives of Black pathology, criminality, and deficiency. These stories are not just propaganda — they are neurological rituals that reassure the white collective ego of its innocence. Each headline, each image of a Black person suffering, functions as a neural pacifier for the empire's anxious conscience. "See," it whispers to itself, "we are still the good ones."

It is not an exaggeration to say that America's media infrastructure serves as a dopamine-delivery system for whiteness. The spectacle of suffering sustains the illusion of moral order. Every televised act of racial violence is both a crime and a ceremony — a reenactment of empire's founding trauma, repeated until the nervous system feels momentarily at peace.

The Consequence: A Mutated Empathy

What results from this centuries-long conditioning is what I term **mutated empathy** — a perverse emotional response that conflates pity with power, and charity with control. Whiteness produces compassion that always centers the self: the white savior complex, the tearful apology, the carefully curated guilt. These are not acts of healing; they are neurological maintenance rituals that preserve the illusion of innocence.

The paradox of whiteness is that it must continuously produce the suffering it claims to lament. Without Black pain, it loses its emotional axis. Without subjugation, it loses its sense of meaning. Its entire nervous system depends on the ongoing performance of dominance and denial.

This is why I call whiteness a *malignant diabolical addiction* — it is a system that derives psychological and biological pleasure from oppression, even as it claims moral revulsion. The same society that criminalizes Black resistance sanctifies white violence as "law and order." The same system that punishes Black anger rewards white cruelty as patriotism.

The next section, **"Malignant Diabolical Psychopathy and Collective Diabolical Antisocial Personality Disorder,"** explores this phenomenon as a full-blown cultural and clinical pathology — where neurobiology, law, and theology converge to produce a civilization addicted to its own brutality.

When reward and moral anesthesia repeat across institutions, we've crossed the line from bias to pathology.

IV. Malignant Diabolical Psychopathy and Collective Diabolical Antisocial Personality Disorder

The most honest way to describe whiteness is as a socially sanctioned mental disorder. It is not metaphorical — it is diagnostic. For centuries, white society has pathologized Blackness in every form: our behavior, our language, our joy, our resistance. But in truth, it is whiteness itself that has met every criterion of pathology — from its chronic denial of reality to its compulsive violence and incapacity for empathy. The only difference is that whiteness has institutionalized its illness, making its symptoms the standard of normalcy.

The Psychopathology of Whiteness

Malignant Diabolical Psychopathy is the framework I use to name this condition — a sociocultural disorder that merges psychopathy, narcissism, and sociopathy into one malignant form of moral insanity. It is not confined to individuals; it is systemic, collective, and self-perpetuating.

Clinically, psychopathy involves a lack of empathy, shallow affect, manipulativeness, and moral disengagement. In whiteness, these traits become cultural virtues. Disconnection is rebranded as rationality. Cruelty is reframed as order. Exploitation is renamed enterprise. The white psyche justifies violence through the alchemy of language and law — converting theft into "progress," enslavement into "civilization," and genocide into "manifest destiny."

The psychopathy of whiteness lies not only in its behavior but in its inability to perceive itself as sick. The most dangerous feature of the disorder is its denial of disorder. Whiteness externalizes all pathology onto the bodies of others — projecting its own instability, lust, and aggression onto the people it oppresses. This projection, repeated over generations, becomes the psychic engine of racial domination.

THE NEUROSCIENCE OF WHITENESS | 327

Malignant Diabolical Psychopathy

Collective group disorder upon which a White hegemonic society exhibits systematic ill will or hatred towards non-White people, especially Black individuals; spread with extreme cruelty or wicked tactics of destruction, showing no empathy or remorse, but it is exhibited as a normal thought process.

DK

Rays (clockwise from top): NORMALIZED PERPETUAL VIOLENCE, WHITE SUPREMACY/PRIVILEGE, LEGALIZED PEDOPHILIA, MASS GENOCIDE, MASS INCARCERATION, LEGALIZED GHETTOIZATION, MENTAL & EMOTIONAL DISTORTION, MALIGNANT SOCIOPATHY, LEGALIZED MURDER, NEUROSIS, LEGALIZED RAPE, CULTURAL TERRORISM, CULTURAL CONTROL, CULTURAL VIOLENCE, EDUCATIONAL EXPLOITATION, PSYCHOLOGICAL PERVERSIONS, PATHOLOGICAL PERVERSIONS, ECONOMIC DEPRIVATION, INSTITUTIONAL TERRORISM, MALIGNANT ANTI-BLACKNESS, WHITE AFFIRMATIVE ACTION, LEGALIZED LYNCHING, WHITE SPONSORSHIP, INDOCTRINATION, DENIAL, MALIGNANT NARCISSISM, CULTURAL ISOLATION

In this way, whiteness functions as a *self-reinforcing delusion*. It is incapable of introspection because its entire identity depends on the illusion of superiority. To acknowledge wrongdoing would collapse the architecture of its ego. Thus, it must live in perpetual defense — employing the psycho-cognitive defense mechanisms I identified earlier: **Denial, Defensiveness, Dissociation, and Deflection.** These are not just emotional tendencies; they are survival mechanisms for a collective narcissistic system.

The Lineage of Psycho-Legal and Psycho-Cognitive Analysis of Whiteness

Dr. Frances Cress Welsing's psycho-genetic model of racism (white supremacy) articulated a revolutionary insight: that white racial domination originates in a psychological complex of genetic fear, anxiety, and self-preservation. Her analysis reframed whiteness not merely as a social category, but as a psychobiological disorder—one rooted in delusion, projection, and the denial of humanity in Blackness.

Building upon this foundation, the conceptual framework I have developed, the *Psycho-Cognitive Defense Mechanisms of Whiteness* extends Welsing's theory into the contemporary terrain of cognitive science, moral psychology, and epigenetics. This model identifies the recursive mental and emotional reflexes—**Denial, Defensiveness, Deflection, and Dissociation**—that sustain white racial identity through self-deception, fragility, and moral disengagement.

Together, these frameworks form a continuous lineage of psycho-legal thought, tracing whiteness as both a pathological condition and an organized system of domination. They reveal how the emotional architecture of white supremacy reproduces itself across centuries—through religion, law, politics, and everyday social relations—by turning fear and guilt into systems of control.

THE NEUROSCIENCE OF WHITENESS | 329

The Psycho-Cognitive Defense Mechanisms of Whiteness

DENIAL Failure to acknowledge the reality of racism	**DEFENSIVENESS** Reacting negatively to challenges on racism
DISSOCIATION Disconnecting from the emotions of racism	**DEFLECTION** Redirecting attention away from racism

Adapted from Dr. Frances Cress Welsing (1991) and Dante D. King (2026).

Definitions:

- **Denial:** Refusal to acknowledge racial reality, sustained through delusion, revisionism, and avoidance.

- **Defensiveness:** Emotional resistance that manifests as fragility, anger, or self-victimization.

- **Deflection:** Strategic redirection away from accountability, often expressed as moral equivalence or false universalism.

- **Dissociation:** The psychic detachment that allows white people to live within systems of harm while disidentifying from the violence those systems produce.

Malignant Narcissism and the Delusion of Innocence

At the heart of white supremacy lies *Malignant Narcissism* — the pathological need to see oneself as inherently good, moral, and deserving of dominance. Unlike ordinary narcissism, which seeks admiration, malignant narcissism demands submission. It cannot coexist with equality because equality threatens the delusion of divine right and superiority.

This is why white fragility manifests as rage when confronted with truth. The exposure of historical fact destabilizes the white ego, forcing it to confront its moral and emotional emptiness. White tears, guilt performances, and avoidance are not acts of remorse; they are symptoms of narcissistic collapse. The psyche protects itself by re-centering whiteness as victim — a desperate attempt to reclaim the moral high ground even in the face of atrocity.

Dr. Frances Cress Welsing wrote that whiteness is "a reaction formation against the fear of genetic annihilation." I would add that it is also a reaction formation against the fear of moral annihilation — the terror of confronting the inhumanity within one's own history. The white collective cannot integrate its shadow, so it makes Blackness the vessel of its sin.

THE NEUROSCIENCE OF WHITENESS | 331

Dr. Frances Cress Welsing (circa 1970's)

DIAGRAM

The Psycho-genetic and Social Dynamic
of Racism (White Supremacy)

Genetic Factor: color inadequacy state (white)
an albinism variant
↓
Individual and Group Psychological Response:
development of psychological
defense mechanisms
↓
Compensatory Logic System: White supremacy
↓
Compensatory Behavioral Practices:
(economics, education, entertainment, labor,
law, politics, religion, sex, war)
↓
White supremacy behavioral "system" and culture
on world-wide scale
↓
Systematic oppression, domination and inferiorization of all
people with the capacity to produce significant
quantities of melanin skin-pigment:
Black, Brown, Red and Yellow peoples of the earth.

Dr. Frances Cress Welsing's Color Confrontation Theory – Conceptual Framework

Collective Diabolical Antisocial Personality Disorder

If Malignant Diabolical Psychopathy names the individual pathology of whiteness, *Collective Diabolical Antisocial Personality Disorder* names its societal manifestation. This disorder emerges when antisocial traits — deceit, exploitation, aggression, and lack of remorse — become normalized through institutions, rituals, and ideologies.

America is the clinical case study.

Its founding documents proclaim liberty while sanctioning slavery. Its police departments claim protection while practicing predation. Its churches preach love while endorsing hate. The contradiction is not accidental; it is structural. The nation itself is a functioning sociopath — charming, persuasive, and utterly devoid of empathy for the people it harms.

Collective Diabolical Antisocial Personality Disorder operates by diffusing responsibility. No one person feels guilty because the system itself commits the violence. This diffusion of accountability creates what Hannah Arendt called "the banality of evil" — ordinary people performing extraordinary cruelty without conscious malice, simply because it is institutionally rewarded. In whiteness, this banality becomes divine; cruelty is not only normalized but sanctified.

The neuroscience of this disorder mirrors the psychology. When a society repeatedly rewards exploitation, it rewires the collective brain to find moral safety in cruelty. Stress hormones normalize under conditions of hierarchy. The dopamine system calibrates to reward domination. Over time, the absence of empathy feels like peace; the presence of equality feels like threat.

The Addictive Cycle of Domination

This is why whiteness behaves like an addict. It cannot stop exploiting others because exploitation is its only way to feel alive. Like any addiction, it requires escalation — new conquests, new justifications, new victims. When overt domination becomes socially unacceptable, it morphs into more sophisticated forms: colorblindness, meritocracy, assimilation, "law and order." The same psychopathy adapts to new disguises, maintaining the fix without triggering withdrawal.

The addiction metaphor is not rhetorical; it is neurochemical. The white brain has been trained to associate racial dominance with neurobiological relief. Every time privilege is challenged, the body registers withdrawal — anxiety, rage, disorientation. Whiteness defends itself not because it is rational, but because it is in pain.

The tragedy is that this pain is self-inflicted. The moral and spiritual decay of whiteness is the inevitable consequence of centuries of emotional repression and moral anesthesia. By denying its own sickness, whiteness ensures its persistence. By refusing to feel, it perpetuates the cycle of harm.

A Clinical Reflection

If we were to treat whiteness as a clinical patient, the prognosis would be grim but not hopeless. The first step would be diagnosis — an honest confrontation with its symptoms. The second would be withdrawal — the dismantling of the systems that keep the addiction alive. The final step would be integration — the reawakening of empathy through truth, accountability, and repair.

But healing cannot begin until whiteness admits that it is sick.

And that, perhaps, is the ultimate symptom of its disorder: the delusion of wellness.

The next section — **"The Neurotheology of Whiteness: God, Law, and the Brain"** — examines how religion and law fused to give this pathology divine legitimacy, embedding psychopathy into the sacred architecture of the Western mind.

Sanctified circuits: the final layer is how theology and law braided these reflexes into something felt as holy and inevitable.

V. The Neurotheology of Whiteness — God, Law, and the Brain

Whiteness is a religion.

It has priests and pulpits, doctrines and heresies, sacraments and sins. It promises salvation through purity and damnation through difference. Its God is not the Creator of all things, but the mirror image of empire — a deity carved from conquest, whose holiness is measured by his proximity to power.

The fusion of theology and law that undergirded white supremacy did not simply justify domination; it neurologically *entrained* it. Over centuries, Christian ritual, colonial law, and civic ideology merged into one moral feedback loop that conditioned the white brain to associate divinity with domination and righteousness with rule.

The Divine Architecture of Control

In medieval and early modern Europe, religion was the nervous system of culture — it regulated emotion, morality, and meaning. When Christianity was weaponized to sanction conquest, it also rewired the moral brain of its adherents. Each act of violence against "pagans" or "infidels" was framed not as sin but as sacrament.

Violence became a form of worship.

This neurological pairing — between aggression and moral validation — still underpins the Western conscience. Colonial law extended this theology into the civic sphere, transforming sin into statute. The Doctrine of Discovery, papal bulls like *Dum Diversas* (1452), and laws like the *Act for the Better Ordering of Negroes and Mulatto Slaves* (1705) were not just legal decrees — they were neurotheological events. Each one created a moral reflex: to equate whiteness with innocence and Blackness with guilt, to see the infliction of suffering as divine order.

Through centuries of repetition, this moral reflex became embodied. Churches preached it; courts codified it; schools normalized it. The white nervous system internalized a sacred hierarchy — God above man, man above woman, white above all.

Moral Anesthesia and the Theology of Dissociation

This merging of God and empire required not only violence but moral anesthesia — a numbing of the moral circuits that produce empathy and guilt. Neuroscientifically, this can be understood as the suppression of activity in the *anterior cingulate cortex* and the *insula*, areas responsible for emotional resonance and moral pain. Repeated moral disengagement, especially when framed as obedience to authority, blunts these circuits.

This is how religious obedience became indistinguishable from cruelty. The same psychological mechanism that allows a soldier to kill without remorse allows a believer to oppress without hesitation. It is what I call *the theology of dissociation* — the sanctification of separation from conscience.

In the white Christian imagination, the suffering of others was reinterpreted as divine will. The plantation owner could attend church after the whip. The judge could quote scripture before sentencing a Black boy to death. The colonizer could kneel in prayer beside the corpse of his victim and feel no contradiction. The neural pathway between belief and brutality had been fully constructed.

God as a White Neurological Concept

Neuroscientists studying religious experience have shown that faith activates the same brain regions as attachment, empathy, and awe. In

the white colonial psyche, however, these circuits were rerouted through a racialized theology. God was imagined as white — and therefore, white was imagined as God. The sacred became a neurological mirror of supremacy.

This produced what I call *the neurotheology of whiteness*: a feedback system in which devotion to God reinforces devotion to hierarchy. Worship becomes indistinguishable from domination. The white brain's reward centers are activated not only by prayer but by control, not only by reverence but by rule.

This is why, even in secular contexts, whiteness maintains religious fervor. The courtroom, the classroom, the corporation — all echo the cathedral. Each functions as a sacred space where the rituals of hierarchy are reenacted daily. The language changes, but the neurotheology remains: obedience is moral; questioning is blasphemy; whiteness is holy.

The Juridical God

Law, the secular child of theology, inherited this same neurostructure. The judge's robe became the priest's vestment. The courtroom replaced the altar. The verdict replaced the benediction. Justice itself was recast as a form of divine balance — a cosmic hierarchy in which whiteness sat enthroned.

American law was designed not to correct moral disorder but to preserve it. Every ruling that affirmed segregation, criminalized Black resistance, or protected white violence served as a sacrament of civic faith. The law became a form of worship through which the nation reaffirmed its covenant with its true god: whiteness.

Even today, the ritual remains intact. The language of "law and order" operates as modern liturgy, soothing the conscience of the nation while reaffirming its commitment to racial hierarchy. The white juror's relief at convicting a Black defendant is not unlike the believer's peace after confession — both feel cleansed, sanctified, restored to moral equilibrium.

The Moral Lie

The neurotheology of whiteness is, ultimately, a moral lie written into the flesh. It tells the body that cruelty is compassion, that dominance is divine order, that obedience to injustice is faithfulness. This lie is sustained by centuries of reinforcement — by pulpits, courtrooms, and classrooms repeating the same catechism: "We are good. We are right. We are chosen."

But the body remembers what the brain denies. The dissonance between the ideal of righteousness and the reality of violence produces chronic psychic stress. White society manages this stress through projection — externalizing its inner conflict onto the very people it harms. The more the empire sins, the more it must imagine the other as sinful.

This is why, despite all its proclamations of progress, America cannot stop criminalizing Blackness. The law remains the conscience of whiteness — not to restrain it, but to absolve it.

The next and final section — **"Healing from the Psychobiology of Empire"** — turns toward repair: exploring how both oppressor and oppressed might begin to metabolize the inherited trauma of whiteness and reclaim the full range of human consciousness it has long suppressed.

From catechism to care: if empire catechized the nervous system, healing must be a counter-catechism—rituals that re-open empathy and rewire safety.

VI. Healing from the Psychobiology of Empire

Every empire eventually confronts the body it has broken.

Every system of domination, no matter how sophisticated, must one day face the physiological and spiritual evidence of its own sickness. Whiteness is now at that threshold — a civilization suffering the consequences of its moral anesthesia, its nervous system frayed by centuries of denial, its consciousness collapsing under the weight of its own lies.

To heal from the psychobiology of empire, we must begin where empire began: in the body.

For centuries, Western civilization has treated oppression as ideology and freedom as philosophy. But both are, first and foremost, *embodied states.* The empire did not build itself in the mind — it built itself in the muscle, the nerve, the gene, and the breath. Healing, therefore, is not simply an act of consciousness-raising; it is an act of *cellular re-membering* — a restoration of the humanity whiteness dismembered.

The Science of Reckoning

Neuroscience confirms what ancestral wisdom has always taught: that trauma cannot be reasoned away. It must be *felt* and *integrated.* The amygdala and hippocampus — the brain's fear and memory centers — do not respond to apology; they respond to safety. This means that collective healing cannot occur until the social body of America becomes a place where Black people are safe in our bodies, our neighborhoods, our identities, and our joy.

Yet safety for Black people requires something deeper than reform; it requires the *de-armoring* of whiteness itself. The white nervous system must unlearn its association between control and calm, superiority and security. White people must be taught to feel again — to feel discomfort without collapsing, to feel shame without deflecting, to feel grief without re-centering themselves. This is not fragility; it is rehabilitation.

Trauma-informed healing, at the level of a civilization, would look like public truth-telling as policy. It would look like reparations as neurological repair — restoring the material and psychological equilibrium stolen through centuries of extraction. It would look like education that activates empathy, not ego; law that enforces restoration, not punishment; spirituality that connects the body to the sacred, not to supremacy.

The Spiritual Science of Repair

Healing whiteness requires more than psychology; it requires *exorcism*.

This is not metaphorical. The pathology of whiteness — the Malignant Diabolical Psychopathy — operates with the precision of possession. It distorts perception, feeds on denial, and defends itself with theological ferocity. To counteract it, we need both neuroscience and spirituality, both Dr. Joy DeGruy and Dr. Frances Cress Welsing, both somatic abolitionism and sacred reckoning.

Dr. Resmaa Menakem reminds us that "healing is not for the faint of heart." To heal, white America must experience what it has spent centuries avoiding: embodied accountability. The nervous system must learn to stay present in the face of its own horror. Only then can it begin to rewire itself for empathy, connection, and humility.

For Black people, healing is not about forgiving the empire; it is about freeing ourselves from its neural grip. It is about remembering that we were never defined by whiteness, that our bodies are not only sites of trauma but vessels of divine intelligence. Our laughter, creativity, and resilience are not anomalies — they are evidence of a biology that refused to die.

Epigenetic Redemption

Epigenetics offers a remarkable truth: what was written into our DNA by trauma can also be rewritten by love, justice, and repair. The same biological plasticity that encoded terror can, through collective healing, encode liberation. When we practice safety, truth, and solidarity, we alter not only our consciousness but our chemistry. The molecules that once carried the memory of chains can, over time, carry the imprint of freedom.

But this redemption is conditional. It requires the dismantling of the systems that continue to re-traumatize. It demands a world where the nervous system no longer interprets whiteness as authority and Blackness as threat. It calls for a complete rewiring of the social brain.

The work of healing, then, is not about saving whiteness — it is about saving humanity *from* whiteness.

It is about creating a new moral nervous system for civilization — one governed not by domination but by empathy, not by hierarchy but by balance, not by fear but by love.

The Moral Neuroscience of Liberation

If empire is a trauma loop, liberation must be a new neural pathway. It begins in the smallest of gestures: the steady breath in the face of fear, the courageous conversation that does not retreat into defensiveness, the communal rituals of care that re-train the body to trust. These are not abstractions; they are acts of neuro-spiritual revolution.

When I teach, I often remind my audiences that healing is not forgetting — it is remembering differently. It is reclaiming the power to narrate our own nervous systems, to tell our bodies the truth about who we are and who we were before empire taught us to dissociate.

We can no longer afford to pretend that racism is merely a moral failing or a social flaw. It is a global neurological crisis — a disorder of empathy that has infected law, economy, and religion. Its cure requires the fusion of science, spirit, and justice.

A Final Reflection

Perhaps the ultimate act of resistance is to feel fully — to reclaim the capacity that whiteness sought to destroy in us and in itself. To feel grief without paralysis. To feel joy without permission. To feel rage as sacred energy and love as revolutionary praxis.

The healing of the world will not come through policy alone. It will come when humanity's nervous system — long hijacked by domination — learns again to pulse with truth.

The next chapter continues this journey toward collective awakening — examining how history, psychology, and biology converge in the fight for a new global consciousness rooted in antiracism, truth, and restoration. It widens from the personal and national nervous system to a global one—how collective rituals, economies, and institutions can re-pattern the planetary body.

Chapter Review Questions

I. The Nervous System of Empire

1. What does it mean to describe whiteness as a "neural architecture" rather than only a social construct?

2. How does the chapter link repeated, moralized violence to amygdala conditioning and dopamine reward?

3. In what ways does "white denial" operate as neurological dissociation at a societal scale?

4. How does "the body keeps the score" apply to nations and empires in this argument?

5. What are the chapter's proposed autonomic "reflexes" of whiteness, and how do they appear in modern policy?

II. Inherited Violence: The Epigenetic Transmission of Whiteness

6. How is epigenetics used to argue that both oppressed and oppressor inherit physiological legacies?

7. Explain the dual inheritance summarized as "cortisol as legacy" and "numbness as inheritance."

8. How does the chapter extend DeGruy's framing of historical trauma to the biology of those who inflicted harm?

9. What examples illustrate DNA methylation or intergenerational hyperarousal in descendant populations?

10. Why does the author argue that white avoidance and moral anesthesia are biologically reinforced?

III. *Neurological Reward, Empathy Suppression, and White Pleasure in Black Pain*

11. What is the "pleasure principle of racial violence," and how does it purportedly function neurologically?

12. How does selective empathy (e.g., muted ACC responses) support the chapter's claim about "moral anesthesia"?

13. What is meant by the "psychic double bind" that whiteness requires both imagined Black danger and visible subordination?

14. How do media spectacles of Black suffering act as a "dopamine-delivery system" for empire?

15. Define "mutated empathy" and discuss how it manifests as saviorism or curated guilt.

IV. *Malignant Diabolical Psychopathy*

16. What clinical traits (e.g., lack of empathy, moral disengagement) are mapped onto "Malignant Diabolical Psychopathy"?

17. How does the chapter argue that language and law alchemize exploitation into "civilization" and "order"?

18. Why is the "denial of disorder" presented as the most dangerous symptom of the condition?

19. How do the four psycho-cognitive defenses (Denial, Defensiveness, Deflection, Dissociation) preserve white identity?

20. In what ways does "malignant narcissism" underwrite fragility, backlash, and the need to re-center white innocence?

V. Collective Diabolical Antisocial Personality Disorder

21. How does the text define "Collective Diabolical Antisocial Personality Disorder," and what makes it societal rather than individual?

22. Where does the chapter locate Arendt's "banality of evil" within modern U.S. institutions?

23. How does diffusion of responsibility mask systemic cruelty as administrative routine?

24. What is the proposed neurobiological mechanism by which repeated social rewards for domination rewire the "collective brain"?

25. Why does the author frame whiteness as addiction requiring escalation, substitution, and withdrawal management?

VI. The Neurotheology of Whiteness — God, Law, and the Brain

26. How does the chapter argue that theology, law, and ritual "entrained" the white moral brain?

27. What role do papal bulls (e.g., *Dum Diversas, Inter caetera*) and colonial statutes play in this neurotheological account?

28. Define the "theology of dissociation" and explain how obedience to authority blunted moral circuits.

29. In what sense is the courtroom framed as a secular cathedral reenacting sacred hierarchy?

30. How does the "juridical God" metaphor help interpret contemporary appeals to "law and order"?

VII. Healing from the Psychobiology of Empire

31. Why does the chapter claim that healing must start "in the body," and what does safety mean at a collective level?

32. What would "de-armoring the white nervous system" entail in practice?

33. How are reparations framed as forms of neurological repair rather than only economic policy?

34. What does "embodied accountability" demand from white communities and institutions?

35. How is Black healing defined as freeing the body from empire's "neural grip," not forgiving the empire?

VIII. Epigenetic Redemption & the Moral Neuroscience of Liberation

36. What is "epigenetic redemption," and how might love, justice, and repair alter gene expression over time?

37. How can communal rituals of care and truth-telling create new neural pathways for liberation?

38. Why does the author call racism a "global neurological crisis," and what multi-domain responses are implied?

39. In what ways does "healing as exorcism" synthesize Welsing, DeGruy, and Menakem?

40. The chapter ends by redefining resistance as "feeling fully." What practices operationalize this in policy, education, and spirituality?

Works Cited

Arendt, H. (1963). *Eichmann in Jerusalem: A report on the banality of evil.* Viking Press.

DeGruy, J. (2005). *Post Traumatic Slave Syndrome: America's legacy of enduring injury and healing.* Uptone Press.

Menakem, R. (2017). *My Grandmother's Hands: Racialized trauma and the pathway to mending our hearts and bodies.* Central Recovery Press.

Nicholas V, Pope. (1452). *Dum Diversas* [Papal bull].

Alexander VI, Pope. (1493). *Inter caetera* [Papal bull].

van der Kolk, B. (2014). *The Body Keeps the Score: Brain, mind, and body in the healing of trauma.* Viking.

Virginia General Assembly. (1705). *An Act concerning servants and slaves.* In W. W. Hening (Ed.), *The statutes at large; being a collection of all the laws of Virginia* (Vol. 3). (Original work published 1705)

Welsing, F. C. (1991). *The Isis Papers: The keys to the colors.* Third World Press.

Wilson, A. N. (1993). *The Falsification of Afrikan Consciousness: Eurocentric history, psychiatry and the politics of White supremacy.* Afrikan World InfoSystems.

Wright, B. E. (1984). *The Psychopathic Racial Personality and other essays.* Third World Press.

CHAPTER 15
WHERE DO WE GO FROM HERE

THE PSYCHO-CLINICAL BLUEPRINT FOR HEALING AND RECONSTRUCTION

Prologue – The Prediction Fulfilled

In 1995, Dr. Claude Anderson wrote *PowerNomics* and warned that if the United States continued to privatize its wealth, hoard opportunity, and suppress Black self-determination, Black Americans would become "a permanent underclass in the land their labor built."

In *Black Labor, White Wealth* (1994), he described the racial economy as a "closed-loop system" in which white power reproduces itself faster than Black advancement can counter it.

Thirty years later, his prediction stands fulfilled. The loop has tightened.

Every sector of life—education, health care, housing, employment, food access, and media—has been quietly privatized.

What was once public has been sold to the highest bidder; what was once collective has been turned into subscription.

These are not isolated policies but mechanisms of **slow genocide**—the deliberate attrition of Black existence through deprivation rather than bullets.

Three decades later, the trauma circuitry described throughout this work has matured into infrastructure.

Section 1 – The Genocidal Design

The American project achieves its cruelty through design, not accident. Its architecture reflects the psychodynamics of **Malignant Diabolical**

Psychopathy—the spiritual disease of whiteness that transforms domination into moral order.

What follows are the operational organs of empire's nervous system—the ways trauma becomes policy.

- **Education** has been converted into a commodity. Charter and voucher programs siphon funds from public schools while corporations dictate curricula. Textbooks erase colonial violence and rename it *discovery*. Students are taught patriotism as therapy for ignorance.

- **Housing** policy continues the lineage of redlining through gentrification. Redevelopment grants displace Black neighborhoods under the language of "revitalization." Ownership is replaced by rent, and rent by debt.

- **Health care** has become a pay-to-live system. Black families are disproportionately uninsured, undertreated, and over-medicated. Hospitals close in Black districts while new clinics appear in prisons.

- **Food security** has collapsed into famine by design. Supermarkets leave, liquor stores remain, and fast-food chains bloom where grocery stores die. Hunger becomes policy; malnutrition becomes governance.

- **Media and technology** complete the circle: Black stories are filtered through corporate algorithms that monetize trauma and suppress dissent. When truth costs advertising dollars, silence becomes profitable.

This is what Dr. Anderson foresaw—a genocide without spectacle, an extermination executed through spreadsheets and screens.

From reflex to residue: If empire trains a reflex, epigenetics shows how the residue of that reflex can be inscribed across generations.

Section 2 – The Psychopolitical Trap

Whiteness no longer requires whips or chains; it governs through seduction and neglect.

It invites Black participation in exchange for silence, offers representation without redistribution, and rewards individual success as proof that oppression has ended.

This is **Cultural Malignant Narcissism** on a national scale—an empire addicted to its own reflection, incapable of empathy.

The greatest danger is **mentacide**: the internalization of the master's logic until the oppressed police themselves.

The dream of inclusion becomes a narcotic, numbing resistance while the structure tightens its grip. Whiteness needs only compliance, not belief.

Breaking this psychopolitical trap begins with re-embodying our sovereignty.

Section 3 – Choosing Survival Over Citizenship

If the American project is collapsing, our task is not to rebuild it but to **salvage each other.**

Citizenship in a dying empire is not liberation; it is burial.

Black survival depends on **self-determined ecosystems** of life:

- Community-owned schools that teach true history and practical sovereignty.

- Cooperative economics that keep Black labor circulating within Black hands.

- Independent media that tell unfiltered truths and document collective genius.

- Mutual-aid health networks grounded in holistic care rather than profit.

- Diasporic alliances that reconnect African, Caribbean, and Afro-Latin peoples through trade, art, and political strategy.

The blueprint is ancestral—Maroon societies, freedmen's towns, freedom schools.

We must now scale those models for twenty-first-century survival.

Section 4 – The Moral and Neurological Imperative

To live in the aftermath of empire is to decide what kind of humans we will become.

The moral work ahead is not reform—it is regeneration. The United States cannot be redeemed, but people can be reclaimed.

Liberation is a neuro-spiritual process: the rewiring of trauma into connection.

Every act of care is neurological resistance; every refusal to comply with domination is cognitive therapy.

Toni Morrison wrote, "The function of freedom is to free someone else."

Audre Lorde reminded us that "Caring for myself is not self-indulgence, it is self-preservation, and that is an act of political warfare."

These are not metaphors—they are instructions for rewiring the moral brain.

We must build sanctuaries of truth where lies cannot breathe, economies of care where greed cannot thrive, and cultures of accountability where power cannot hide.

To be Black in this moment is to be the world's last moral compass—to love life so fiercely that even apocalypse cannot end it.

If diagnosis exposes the wound, prescription begins the work of repair.

Part II – From Diagnosis to Prescription: Addressing Whiteness and Anti-Blackness in America

For America to function normally, **whiteness itself must be dismantled.** Every major institution in the nation is a product of its psychopathic design. Therefore, dismantling whiteness is not symbolic work—it is neurosurgical work on the body politic.

Section 1 – Clinical Reality Check

Hope alone is not a treatment plan. The disease is structural, cultural, and biological.

Whiteness operates as a self-reinforcing disorder that feeds on denial.

Both victims and aggressors must engage in guided reflection and supervised reconstruction; unstructured "good intentions" are another symptom of avoidance.

Professional interventions by clinicians, educators, and organizational coaches rooted in **African-descended epistemologies** are essential.

These professionals must be trained to disrupt white comfort and recondition empathy responses dulled by privilege.

Section 2 – Therapeutic Prescriptions for Individuals

1. **Learn all history**, not the sanitized version that absolves empire.

2. **Acknowledge structural design:** disparities are systemic, not individual failures.

3. **Accept complicity:** white people who deny racism are participants in it.

4. **Engage in structured study:** utilize the reading lists and curricula such as *The 400-Year Holocaust Toolkit*.

   This book is not a conclusion but an entry point. Read **Diagnosing Whiteness & Anti-Blackness: White Psychopathology, Collective Psychosis, and Trauma in America**, *and continue the work at* **www.danteking.com**, *where* **Undoing Racism: A Tactical Guide to Advancing Fair Employment, Civil Rights Compliance, and Health Equity** *offers a 127-page, step-by-step roadmap for dismantling racism and institutional injustice in America.*

5. **Recognize trauma's circuitry:** understand that the white psyche required the terrorization of Black people to sustain its identity.

6. **Understand that anti-Blackness is profitable**—from slavery to mass incarceration.

7. **Resist validation addiction:** redefine Black worth outside of white approval systems.

8. **Reject meritocratic delusion:** the system was built for white success, not fairness.

9. **End Black selectivism:** celebrate truth-tellers and radicals, not just the palatable.

10. **White participants** must seek therapy led by descendants of the enslaved who can challenge their defensive conditioning.

These are micro-level interventions for rewiring conscience, reducing dissociation, and expanding moral empathy.

Healing must occur at every scale—from the neuron to the nation.

Section 3 – Therapeutic Prescriptions for Institutions

Institutions require **macro-therapy**—the dismantling of bureaucratic psychopathy.

Organizations must adopt antiracism as clinical governance, not public relations.

- **Resource Redistribution:** Commit sustained financial support to Black communities—schools, health networks, and re-entry programs.

- **Contractual Accountability:** Employ and consult experts in racial trauma and institutional psychopathy.

- **Policy Reform:** Embed equity language that specifies measurable antiracism outcomes.

- **Training as Treatment:** Require 24–40 hours of antiracism training biannually, linked to performance evaluations.

- **Matriarchal Accountability:** Examine white women's complicity in sustaining racial hierarchies.

- **Psychological Education:** Ensure all staff understand the neurological bases of racial dominance and trauma (e.g., Dr. David Williams's Everyday Discrimination Scale; Dr. William Smith's Racial Battle Fatigue).

- **Rest Protocols:** Provide additional restorative leave for Black employees coping with racial stress.

- **Power Audits:** Evaluate how white fragility, paternalism, and objectivity serve as defense mechanisms of supremacy.

- **Racial Repair-ations:** Design reparative initiatives that equalize structural inequities through direct investment, voice, and power-sharing.

These are not reforms; they are **clinical interventions** for a nation in moral collapse.

Section 4 – Racial Reckoning, Repair-ations, and Negotiation

Racial Reckoning is the diagnostic phase—whiteness recognizing itself as pathological.

Racial Repair-ations is the treatment phase—transferring resources and empathy to recalibrate the social nervous system.

White Racial Negotiation is the maintenance phase—ongoing surrender of unearned privilege to sustain equity homeostasis.

Each phase represents neurological and spiritual healing. The work is continuous, not episodic.

Afterword – Letters to the Future: The Psycho-Spiritual Work of Reconstruction

If you are holding this text, you are already part of the resistance to forgetting.

The future will not belong to those who perfect the machinery of death but to those who practice the art of remembrance.

Hopelessness is a learned symptom—an induced paralysis that keeps the system alive.

Our ancestors fought without certainty of victory; they fought because surrender was unthinkable.

Wherever you stand—teach, heal, create, protect.

Form circles, not pyramids. Build networks, not empires.

Tell the truth, even when it empties rooms.

Liberation is contagious; it spreads through every honest word and courageous act.

If America collapses under the weight of its own lies, let it.

Our obligation is not to save the empire but to **save the people.**

And we will—because survival for us has never been accidental; it has always been divine.

Chapter 15 Conceptual Understanding (Diagnosis & Framework)

1. How does Dr. Claude Anderson's concept of a "closed-loop system" relate to the neurological "feedback loop" of whiteness described in earlier chapters?

2. In what ways does privatization function as a contemporary expression of structural anti-Blackness?

3. What does the chapter mean by the phrase "genocide without spectacle," and how does this reframe our understanding of racial violence?

4. How does "Cultural Malignant Narcissism" explain the American empire's inability to self-correct?

5. What role does "mentacide" play in maintaining oppression through psychological and cultural consent?

Applied Critical Analysis (Social Systems & Survival)

6. Which of the sectors described in the "Genocidal Design" section (education, housing, health care, food, media) most directly impacts Black survival today, and why?

7. How do contemporary "representation politics" function as a form of sedation rather than liberation?

8. What lessons can be drawn from historical Maroon societies, freedom schools, and freedmen's towns for designing twenty-first-century Black survival networks?

9. How does this chapter redefine "citizenship" in a collapsing empire?

10. What does it mean to choose "survival over citizenship," and what are the ethical implications of that choice?

Neuro-Spiritual and Clinical Insight

11. The chapter asserts that liberation is a "neuro-spiritual process." How does this align with or differ from traditional political theories of freedom?

12. What does it mean for "every act of care" to serve as a form of neurological resistance?

13. How do Toni Morrison's and Audre Lorde's quoted teachings provide neuroethical guidance rather than only moral advice?

14. How does the framing of "America as a patient" expand the scope of racial justice beyond policy reform into moral medicine?

15. What might a "reconditioning of empathy responses dulled by privilege" look like in education or health care institutions?

Transformation, Repair, and Future Vision

16. How do the "three phases" of Racial Reckoning, Reparations, and Negotiation correspond to the process of trauma recovery (diagnosis, treatment, maintenance)?

17. What distinguishes "Reform" from "Regeneration," and why does the chapter reject the former as insufficient?

18. How does the call for "macro-therapy" in institutions redefine equity work as a form of clinical intervention?

19. What might a "new moral nervous system for civilization" look like in practical terms—politically, economically, and spiritually?

20. The final line declares, "Survival for us has never been accidental; it has always been divine." How does this closing sentiment tie together the scientific, theological, and ancestral threads of the entire book?

Works Cited

Anderson, C. (1994). *Black labor, white wealth: The search for power and economic justice.* PowerNomics Corporation of America.

Anderson, C. (2001). *PowerNomics: The national plan to empower Black America.* PowerNomics Corporation of America.

Blackmon, D. A. (2008). *Slavery by another name: The re-enslavement of Black Americans from the Civil War to World War II.* Anchor Books.

DeGruy, J. (2005). *Post traumatic slave syndrome: America's legacy of enduring injury and healing.* Uptone Press.

hooks, b. (1992). *Black looks: Race and representation.* South End Press.

Lorde, A. (1988). *A burst of light: Essays*. Firebrand Books.

Menakem, R. (2017). *My grandmother's hands: Racialized trauma and the pathway to mending our hearts and bodies*. Central Recovery Press.

Morrison, T. (1993). *The Nobel lecture in literature, 1993*. Alfred A. Knopf.

Smith, W. A., Hung, M., & Franklin, J. D. (2011). Racial battle fatigue and the miseducation of Black men: Racial microaggressions, societal problems, and environmental stress. *The Journal of Negro Education, 80*(1), 63–82.

Williams, D. R., & Mohammed, S. A. (2009). Discrimination and racial disparities in health: Evidence and needed research. *Journal of Behavioral Medicine, 32*(1), 20–47. https://doi.org/10.1007/s10865-008-9185-0

Wilson, A. N. (1993). *Blueprint for Black power: A moral, political, and economic imperative for the twenty-first century*. Afrikan World InfoSystems.

Welsing, F. C. (1991). *The Isis papers: The keys to the colors*. Third World Press.

Williams, E. (1994). *Capitalism and slavery*. University of North Carolina Press.

Zuboff, S. (2019). *The age of surveillance capitalism: The fight for a human future at the new frontier of power*. PublicAffairs.

U.S. Department of Labor. (2025). *Employment and unemployment statistics by race, gender, and age: Quarterly report, 2025 Q2*. Washington, DC: Bureau of Labor Statistics.

Economic Policy Institute. (2025, August). *Black unemployment and racial economic inequality in 2025: National snapshot*. Washington, DC.

REFERENCES
AND WORKS CITED

Chapter One

Anderson, Claud. *Black Labor, White Wealth: The Search for Power and Economic Justice.* PowerNomics Corporation of America, 1994.

Barry, John M. *Rising Tide: The Great Mississippi Flood of 1927 and How It Changed America.* Simon & Schuster, 1997.

Clarke, John Henrik. Interviews on *Say Brother* television program. WGBH Boston, 1971–1973.

Jones, Kenneth, and Tema Okun. *Dismantling Racism: A Workbook for Social Change Groups.* ChangeWork, 2001.

Morrison, Toni. Interview with Charlie Rose. PBS, 1993.

Poussaint, Alvin F. *Black Paper on White Racism.* The Black Journal, 1971.

Waring, Elizabeth. Speech for the NAACP and *Meet the Press* interview, 1950.

Welsing, Frances Cress. *The Isis Papers: The Keys to the Colors.* Third World Press, 1991.

Wilson, Amos N. *The Falsification of Afrikan Consciousness: Eurocentric History, Psychiatry, and the Politics of White Supremacy.* Afrikan World InfoSystems, 1993.

Wright, Bobby E. *The Psychopathic Racial Personality.* Third World Press, 1975.

Chapter Two

Alexander VI. Inter Caetera. Papal Bull, May 4, 1493. Vatican Archives.

Barry, John M. Rising Tide: The Great Mississippi Flood of 1927 and How It Changed America. Simon & Schuster, 1997.

Boswell, Benjamin. Address at the Global Antiracism Summit, Stellenbosch, South Africa, 2025.

Columbus, Christopher. Journal of the First Voyage (1492–1493). In The Diaries of Christopher Columbus: The Voyage of 1492–1493, edited by Oliver Dunn and James E. Kelley Jr., University of Oklahoma Press, 1991.

Jordan, Winthrop D. White Over Black: American Attitudes Toward the Negro, 1550–1812. University of North Carolina Press, 1968.

Marshall, John. Johnson v. M'Intosh, 21 U.S. (8 Wheat.) 543 (1823).

Nicholas V. Dum Diversas. Papal Bull, June 18, 1452. Vatican Archives.

Nicholas V. Romanus Pontifex. Papal Bull, January 8, 1455. Vatican Archives.

Welsing, Frances Cress. The Isis Papers: The Keys to the Colors. Third World Press, 1991.

Chapter Three

Works Cited

Allen, T. W. (1975). *The invention of the white race.* Verso.

Barclays Bank. (n.d.). *History of Barclays and the slave trade.* London: Barclays Archives.

Du Bois, W. E. B. (1935). *Black reconstruction in America, 1860–1880.* Free Press.

Harris, C. I. (1993). Whiteness as property. *Harvard Law Review, 106*(8), 1707–1791.

Maryland General Assembly. (1681). *Act concerning Negroes and other slaves.* Colonial Records of Maryland.

Nicholas, R. (Ed.). (1790). *The Nationality Act of 1790.* U.S. Congressional Records.

Taney, R. B. (1857). *Dred Scott v. Sandford,* 60 U.S. (19 How.) 393.

Virginia General Assembly. (1662). *Act concerning runaways. Statutes at Large of Virginia.*

Virginia General Assembly. (1691). *Act for suppressing outlying slaves. Statutes at Large of Virginia.*

Welsing, F. C. (1991). *The Isis papers: The keys to the colors.* Third World Press.

Wilson, A. N. (1993). *The falsification of Afrikan consciousness: Eurocentric history, psychiatry, and the politics of White supremacy.* Afrikan World InfoSystems.

Wright, B. E. (1984). *The psychopathic racial personality and other essays.* Third World Press.

Thomas, Z. (2021, March 1). The hidden links between slavery and Wall Street. *BBC News.* https://www.bbc.com/news/business-52893382

Chapter Four

Armah, E. (2022). *Emotional justice: A roadmap for racial healing.* New York, NY: Amistad Press.

Boswell, B. (2023). *Sermons on white supremacy and Christian complicity.* Charlotte, NC: Myers Park Baptist Church Publications.

Decety, J., & Cowell, J. M. (2018). The complex relation between morality and empathy. *Trends in Cognitive Sciences, 22*(5), 337–349. https://doi.org/10.1016/j.tics.2018.02.001

McEwen, B. S., & Gianaros, P. J. (2011). Stress- and allostasis-induced brain plasticity. *Annual Review of Medicine, 62,* 431–445. https://doi.org/10.1146/annurev-med-052209-100430

Sauvé Commission. (2021). *Rapport de la commission indépendante sur les abus sexuels dans l'Église catholique (CIASE).* Paris, France: Bayard.

U.S. Conference of Catholic Bishops. (2023). *Annual report on the implementation of the Charter for the Protection of Children and Young People.* Washington, DC: USCCB.

U.S. Department of Justice. (2024). *Statistical overview of sexual violence and offender demographics*. Washington, DC: Author.

U.S. Sentencing Commission. (2024). *Federal sentencing of child pornography and sexual exploitation offenses*. Washington, DC: Author.

Virginia General Assembly. (1662). *Act XII: Children to follow the condition of the mother*. In *Statutes at Large of Virginia*.

Westminster Parliament. (1275). *Statute of Westminster I, 3 Edw. I c. 13*. London, England.

Yehuda, R., Daskalakis, N. P., Lehrner, A., Desarnaud, F., Bader, H. N., Makotkine, I., ... Meaney, M. J. (2016). Intergenerational transmission of trauma effects on stress response. *Biological Psychiatry, 80*(5), 372–380. https://doi.org/10.1016/j.biopsych.2015.08.005

Chapter Five

Works Cited

Anderson, C. (2016). *White rage: The unspoken truth of our racial divide*. Bloomsbury.

Atkins, J. (1735/1970). *A voyage to Guinea, Brazil, and the West Indies*. Frank Cass.

DeGruy, J. (2005). *Post traumatic slave syndrome: America's legacy of enduring injury and healing*. Joy DeGruy Publications.

Equal Justice Initiative. (2017). *Lynching in America: Confronting the legacy of racial terror* (3rd ed.). Equal Justice Initiative.

Hening, W. W. (1823). *The statutes at large; being a collection of all the laws of Virginia* (Vols. 1–13). Franklin Press. (Original colonial enactments cited: 1662—runaways "in company with negroes"; 1667—baptism & bondage; 1668—negro women tithables; 1668—corporal punishment of runaways; 1669—Casual Killing).

Hill, L. (2014). *Black Rage* [Recorded by Lauryn Hill]. Ms. Lauryn Hill.

Hogan, L. (2015). The forced breeding myth in the "Irish slaves" meme. *Medium.*

Jordan, W. D. (1968). *White over Black: American attitudes toward the Negro, 1550–1812.* University of North Carolina Press.

Khilanani, A. (2021, June 10). Interview with Marc Lamont Hill. *Black News Tonight,* BNC.

Maryland General Assembly. (1664). *Act concerning Negroes & other slaves*; (1681) *Act concerning English or white women intermarrying with Negro slaves.* In *Archives of Maryland Online.*

Milley, M. A. (2021, June 23). House Armed Services Committee hearing on the FY22 defense budget [Video]. *C-SPAN.* https://www.c-span.org/video/?512776-1/defense-officials-testify-budget-request

Minutes of the Council and General Court of Colonial Virginia. (1640). John Punch case order (July 9, 1640). In H. R. McIlwaine (Ed.), *Minutes of the Council and General Court of Colonial Virginia, 1622–1632, 1670–1676.* Virginia State Library.

Nichols, T. (2023, January). Memphis Police Department body-cam footage [Video]. City of Memphis.

Owensby, C. (2021, Sept 30). Body-cam footage of traffic stop, Dayton, Ohio [Video]. City of Dayton Police Department.

Proctor, S., Allen, W., & Boarman, W. (Eds.). (1883–). *Archives of Maryland.* Maryland State Archives.

Turner, M., & Turner, H. (1918). In Allen, J., Als, H., Lewis, M., & Litwack, L. (2000). *Without sanctuary: Lynching photography in America.* Twin Palms.

Wilmington Coup Commission. (2006). *1898 Wilmington race riot report.* North Carolina Office of Archives & History.

Zuczek, R. (2000). *State of rebellion: Reconstruction in South Carolina.* University of South Carolina Press.

Crump, B. (2019). *Open season: Legalized genocide of colored people.* Amistad.

Chapter Six

Baldwin, J. (1961). *Nobody Knows My Name: More Notes of a Native Son.* New York, NY: Dial Press.

Baldwin, J. (1985). *The Price of the Ticket: Collected Nonfiction 1948–1985.* New York, NY: St. Martin's Press.

Baldwin, J. (1998). *Collected Essays.* New York, NY: Library of America.

Butler v. Boarman family records (1664 law; 1767 court depositions). *Archives of Maryland.* Maryland State Archives.

Hening, W. W. (1823). *The Statutes at Large: Being a Collection of All the Laws of Virginia.* Vols. 2–4. Richmond, VA: George Cochran.

Hogan, L. (2016, March 17). *The Forced Breeding Myth in the Irish Slaves Meme. Medium.* https://medium.com/

Jordan, W. D. (1968). *White Over Black: American Attitudes Toward the Negro, 1550–1812.* Chapel Hill, NC: University of North Carolina Press.

South Carolina General Assembly. (1740). *Negro Act of 1740.* In *The Statutes at Large of South Carolina* (Vol. 7). Columbia, SC: A. S. Johnston.

Virginia General Assembly. (1667–1672). *Acts of the Grand Assembly* ("Casual Killing Act," "Runawayes, Negroes and Slaves"). In Hening, W. W. (Ed.), *Statutes at Large of Virginia.* Richmond, VA.

Wells-Barnett, I. B. (1895). *A Red Record: Tabulated Statistics and Alleged Causes of Lynching in the United States.* Chicago, IL.

Welsing, F. C. (1991). *The Isis Papers: The Keys to the Colors.* Chicago, IL: Third World Press.

Wilson, A. N. (1993). *The Falsification of Afrikan Consciousness: Eurocentric History, Psychiatry, and the Politics of White Supremacy.* New York, NY: Afrikan World InfoSystems.

Wilson, A. N. (1998). *Blueprint for Black Power: A Moral, Political, and Economic Imperative for the Twenty-First Century.* New York, NY: Afrikan World InfoSystems.

Wright, B. E. (1984). *The Psychopathic Racial Personality and Other Essays.* Chicago, IL: Third World Press.

Without Sanctuary: Lynching Photography in America. (2000). Santa Fe, NM: Twin Palms Publishers.

Welsing, F. C., Wilson, A. N., & Wright, B. E. (cited throughout). *Collected works and lectures on racism, psychology, and power.*

Wells, I. B. (2020 reprint). *Southern Horrors and Other Writings.* Boston, MA: Bedford/St. Martin's.

Chapter Seven

Borum, R. (2004). *Psychology of Terrorism.* Tampa, FL: University of South Florida.

Centers for Disease Control and Prevention. (2023). *Epigenetics: How your behaviors and environment can cause changes that affect the way your genes work.*

Du Bois, W. E. B. (1935). *Black Reconstruction in America.* New York, NY: Harcourt, Brace & Company.

Hamilton, C. V., & Ture, K. (1967). *Black Power: The Politics of Liberation.* New York, NY: Random House.

An Act Preventing Negro Insurrections. (1680). The Statutes at Large of Virginia. W. W. Hening (Ed.).

An Act Concerning Servants and Slaves. (1705). The Statutes at Large of Virginia. W. W. Hening (Ed.).

An Act for the Apprehension and Suppression of Runawayes, Negroes, and Slaves. (1672). *The Statutes at Large of Virginia.* W. W. Hening (Ed.).

Chapter Eight

Alexander, M. (2010). *The new Jim Crow: Mass incarceration in the age of colorblindness.* The New Press.

Bean, R. B. (1906). *Some peculiarities of the Negro brain. American Journal of Anatomy,* 5(4), 353–432.

Black, E. (2012). *IBM and the Holocaust.* Dialog Press.

Blackmon, D. A. (2008). *Slavery by another name.* Anchor.

Buck v. Bell, 274 U.S. 200 (1927).

DiAngelo, R. (2012). *What does it mean to be White?* Peter Lang.

Douglass, F. (1845). *Narrative of the life of Frederick Douglass, an American slave.* Anti-Slavery Office.

Flexner, A. (1910). *Medical education in the United States and Canada.* Carnegie Foundation.

Grant, M. (1916). *The passing of the great race.* C. Scribner's Sons.

Hening, W. W. (1823). *The statutes at large; being a collection of all the laws of Virginia.* Franklin Press.

Herrnstein, R. J., & Murray, C. (1994). *The bell curve.* Free Press.

Hitler, A. (1925/1939). *Mein Kampf.* Houghton Mifflin.

Hoffman, F. L. (1896). *Race traits and tendencies of the American Negro.* Macmillan.

Morris, C. (1888). *The Aryan race.* S. A. George.

Nott, J. C., & Gliddon, G. R. (1854). *Types of mankind.* Lippincott.

Paoletti, G. (2017, August 26). *7 brands with Nazi ties that we all use*. All That's Interesting.

Roberts, D. (1997). *Killing the Black body*. Vintage.

Trawalter, S., Hoffman, K. M., & Waytz, A. (2012). *Racial bias in pain assessment and treatment recommendations*. PNAS, *109*(16), 675–680.

United States Holocaust Memorial Museum. (n.d.). *The Nuremberg Race Laws*.

U.S. Const. amend. XIII.

Virginia (1672). *An Act for the Apprehension and Suppression of Runawayes, Negroes, and Slaves*.

Virginia (1705). *An Act declaring who shall not bear office…; An Act concerning Servants and Slaves*.

Virginia Racial Integrity Act, 1924, ch. 371 (Va. 1924).

Washington, H. A. (2006). *Medical apartheid*. Doubleday.

Wells, S. R. (1875). *New physiognomy*. Fowler & Wells.

Wilson, A. N. (1993). *The falsification of Afrikan consciousness*. Afrikan World Infosystems.

Wright, B. E. (1984). *The psychopathic racial personality and other essays*. Third World Press.

Welsing, F. C. (1991). *The Isis Papers*. Third World Press.

Chapter Nine

Alexander, M. (2010). *The New Jim Crow: Mass Incarceration in the Age of Colorblindness*. The New Press.

Baldwin, J. (1962). *The Fire Next Time*. Dial Press.

Black, E. (2001). *IBM and the Holocaust: The Strategic Alliance Between Nazi Germany and America's Most Powerful Corporation.* Crown Publishers.

Caldwell, C. (1822). *Thoughts on the Original Unity of the Human Race.* Louisville Press.

Cartwright, S. A. (1851). Diseases and peculiarities of the Negro race. *De Bow's Review,* 11, 331–336.

Fanón, F. (1963). *The Wretched of the Earth* (C. Farrington, Trans.). Grove Press. (Original work published 1961)

Grant, M. (1916). *The Passing of the Great Race: Or the Racial Basis of European History.* Charles Scribner's Sons.

Herrnstein, R. J., & Murray, C. (1994). *The Bell Curve: Intelligence and Class Structure in American Life.* Free Press.

Hoffman, F. L. (1896). *Race Traits and Tendencies of the American Negro.* American Economic Association.

Holmes, O. W. J. (1927). Opinion of the Court, *Buck v. Bell,* 274 U.S. 200.

Nott, J. C., & Gliddon, G. R. (1854). *Types of Mankind.* Lippincott, Grambo & Co.

Paoletti, G. (2017, March 19). How IBM helped the Nazis carry out the Holocaust. *All That's Interesting.* https://allthatsinteresting.com/ibm-holocaust

Washington, H. A. (2006). *Medical Apartheid: The Dark History of Medical Experimentation on Black Americans from Colonial Times to the Present.* Doubleday.

Welsing, F. C. (1991). *The Isis Papers: The Keys to the Colors.* Third World Press.

Wilson, A. N. (1993). *The Falsification of Afrikan Consciousness: Eurocentric History, Psychiatry and the Politics of White Supremacy.* Afrikan World InfoSystems.

Wright, B. E. (1984). *The Psychopathic Racial Personality and Other Essays.* Third World Press.

Chapter Ten

Alexander v. South Carolina State Conference of the NAACP, 601 U.S. ___ (2024).

American Express Co. v. Italian Colors Restaurant, 570 U.S. 228 (2013).

Abbott v. Perez, 585 U.S. ___ (2018).

Brnovich v. Democratic National Committee, 594 U.S. ___ (2021).

Brown v. Board of Education, 347 U.S. 483 (1954).

City of Canton v. Harris, 489 U.S. 378 (1989).

City of Los Angeles v. Lyons, 461 U.S. 95 (1983).

City of Mobile v. Bolden, 446 U.S. 55 (1980).

City of Richmond v. J.A. Croson Co., 488 U.S. 469 (1989).

Connick v. Thompson, 563 U.S. 51 (2011).

Dred Scott v. Sandford, 60 U.S. (19 How.) 393 (1857).

Epic Systems Corp. v. Lewis, 584 U.S. ___ (2018).

Georgia v. Ashcroft, 539 U.S. 461 (2003).

Harlow v. Fitzgerald, 457 U.S. 800 (1982).

Heck v. Humphrey, 512 U.S. 477 (1994).

Husted v. A. Philip Randolph Institute, 584 U.S. ___ (2018).

McCleskey v. Kemp, 481 U.S. 279 (1987).

Parents Involved in Community Schools v. Seattle School District No. 1, 551 U.S. 701 (2007).

Patterson v. McLean Credit Union, 491 U.S. 164 (1989).

Regents of the University of California v. Bakke, 438 U.S. 265 (1978).

Reno v. Bossier Parish School Board, 520 U.S. 471 (1997).

Reno v. Bossier Parish School Board, 528 U.S. 320 (2000).

Rucho v. Common Cause, 588 U.S. ___ (2019).

San Antonio Independent School District v. Rodriguez, 411 U.S. 1 (1973).

Scott v. Harris, 550 U.S. 372 (2007).

Shelby County v. Holder, 570 U.S. 529 (2013).

Students for Fair Admissions, Inc. v. President & Fellows of Harvard College, 600 U.S. ___ (2023).

Students for Fair Admissions, Inc. v. University of North Carolina, 600 U.S. ___ (2023).

University of Texas Southwestern Medical Center v. Nassar, 570 U.S. 338 (2013).

Utah v. Strieff, 579 U.S. 232 (2016).

Vega v. Tekoh, 597 U.S. ___ (2022).

Wards Cove Packing Co. v. Atonio, 490 U.S. 642 (1989).

Washington v. Davis, 426 U.S. 229 (1976).

Wal-Mart Stores, Inc. v. Dukes, 564 U.S. 338 (2011).

Welsing, F. C. (1991). *The Isis Papers: The Keys to the Colors.* Third World Press.

Wilson, A. N. (1993). *The Falsification of Afrikan Consciousness: Eurocentric History, Psychiatry and the Politics of White Supremacy.* Afrikan World InfoSystems.

Wright, B. E. (1984). *The Psychopathic Racial Personality and Other Essays.* Third World Press.

Du Bois, W. E. B. (1935). *Black Reconstruction in America, 1860–1880.* Harcourt, Brace.

Menakem, R. (2017). *My Grandmother's Hands: Racialized Trauma and the Pathway to Mending Our Hearts and Bodies.* Central Recovery Press.

Chapter Eleven

Abbott v. Perez, 585 U.S. ___ (2018).

Brnovich v. Democratic National Committee, 594 U.S. ___ (2021).

City of Richmond v. J.A. Croson Co., 488 U.S. 469 (1989).

Gates v. Collier, 501 F.2d 1291 (5th Cir. 1974).

Milliken v. Bradley, 418 U.S. 717 (1974).

National Advisory Commission on Civil Disorders. (1968). *Report of the National Advisory Commission on Civil Disorders* (The Kerner Report). U.S. Government Printing Office.

Rothstein, R. (2017). *The color of law: A forgotten history of how our government segregated America.* Liveright.

San Antonio Independent School District v. Rodriguez, 411 U.S. 1 (1973).

Shelby County v. Holder, 570 U.S. 529 (2013).

Students for Fair Admissions, Inc. v. President & Fellows of Harvard College, 600 U.S. ___ (2023).

Washington v. Davis, 426 U.S. 229 (1976).

Blackmon, D. A. (2008). *Slavery by another name: The re-enslavement of Black Americans from the Civil War to World War II.* Anchor.

Oshinsky, D. M. (1996). *"Worse than slavery": Parchman Farm and the ordeal of Jim Crow justice.* Free Press.

Wright, B. E. (1984). *The psychopathic racial personality and other essays.* Third World Press.

Statutes & Federal Programs

Federal-Aid Highway Act of 1956, Pub. L. No. 84-627, 70 Stat. 374 (1956).

Housing Act of 1949, Pub. L. No. 81-171, 63 Stat. 413 (1949). *(Often referenced as the postwar "urban redevelopment" framework.)*

Chapter Twelve

Axios. (2025, July). *Biden staff concealed signs of cognitive decline, sources say.* https://www.axios.com

Chew, R. (Host). (2025, July). *Interview with Dante King.* WCPT Chicago.

Daniel Favors, L. (Host). (2025, September). *Interview with Dante King.* SiriusXM Urban View.

Department of Homeland Security. (2025). *Annual report on immigration enforcement actions: 2023–2025.* U.S. Department of Homeland Security.

Economic Policy Institute. (2025, August). *Black unemployment trends in the United States, 2020–2025.*

Fox 26 Houston. (2025, August). *The Isiah Factor Uncensored [Television broadcast].*

Hernández, T. K. (2022). *Racial innocence: Unmasking Latino anti-Black bias and the struggle for equality.* Beacon Press.

Kim, C. J. (1999). The racial triangulation of Asian Americans. *Politics & Society, 27*(1), 105–138. https://doi.org/10.1177/0032329299027001005

Malcolm X. (1963, November 22). *The chickens come home to roost.* Speech, New York, NY.

New York Times. (2014, September 28). *Ruth Bader Ginsburg won't step down.* https://www.nytimes.com

Politico. (2020, September 19). *The fight over RBG's legacy and the Supreme Court.* https://www.politico.com

Students for Fair Admissions v. President and Fellows of Harvard College, 600 U.S. ___ (2023).

U.S. Conference of Catholic Bishops. (2023). *Report on clergy sexual abuse in the United States.*

U.S. Department of Labor. (2025). *Quarterly workforce demographics report, Q2 2025.*

Yehuda, R., et al. (2016). *Epigenetic mechanisms in trauma and posttraumatic stress disorder. Dialogues in Clinical Neuroscience, 18*(4), 359–370. https://doi.org/10.31887/DCNS.2016.18.4/ryehuda

The Guardian. (2025, June). *Democrats debate Biden's fitness for a second term.* https://www.theguardian.com

Chapter Thirteen

Works Cited

Alexander VI, Pope. (1493). *Inter caetera* [Papal bull].

Blackmon, D. A. (2008). *Slavery by another name: The re-enslavement of Black Americans from the Civil War to World War II.* Anchor.

Dred Scott v. Sandford, 60 U.S. (19 How.) 393 (1857).

Gates v. Collier, 501 F.2d 1291 (5th Cir. 1974).

Hening, W. W. (Ed.). (1823). *The statutes at large; being a collection of all the laws of Virginia* (Vol. 3). R. & W. & G. Bartow. (Includes **An Act concerning servants and slaves** [1705].)

Johnson v. M'Intosh, 21 U.S. (8 Wheat.) 543 (1823).

Jordan, W. D. (1968). *White over Black: American attitudes toward the Negro, 1550–1812*. University of North Carolina Press.

Nicholas V, Pope. (1452). *Dum Diversas* [Papal bull].

Nicholas V, Pope. (1455). *Romanus Pontifex* [Papal bull].

Newcomb, S. T. (2008). *Pagans in the promised land: Decoding the doctrine of Christian discovery*. Fulcrum.

Oshinsky, D. M. (1996). *"Worse than slavery": Parchman Farm and the ordeal of Jim Crow justice*. Free Press.

Pennsylvania General Assembly. (1700). *An Act for the Trial of Negroes*.

South Carolina General Assembly. (1740). *An Act for the better ordering and governing of Negroes and other slaves in this province*. (Commonly referred to as the Negro Act of 1740.)

Williams, R. A., Jr. (1990). *The American Indian in Western legal thought: The discourses of conquest*. Oxford University Press.

Chapter Fourteen

Arendt, H. (1963). *Eichmann in Jerusalem: A report on the banality of evil*. Viking Press.

DeGruy, J. (2005). *Post Traumatic Slave Syndrome: America's legacy of enduring injury and healing*. Uptone Press.

Menakem, R. (2017). *My Grandmother's Hands: Racialized trauma and the pathway to mending our hearts and bodies*. Central Recovery Press.

Nicholas V, Pope. (1452). *Dum Diversas* [Papal bull].

Alexander VI, Pope. (1493). *Inter caetera* [Papal bull].

van der Kolk, B. (2014). *The Body Keeps the Score: Brain, mind, and body in the healing of trauma*. Viking.

Virginia General Assembly. (1705). *An Act concerning servants and slaves*. In W. W. Hening (Ed.), *The statutes at large; being a collection of all the laws of Virginia* (Vol. 3). (Original work published 1705)

Welsing, F. C. (1991). *The Isis Papers: The keys to the colors*. Third World Press.

Wilson, A. N. (1993). *The Falsification of Afrikan Consciousness: Eurocentric history, psychiatry and the politics of White supremacy*. Afrikan World InfoSystems.

Wright, B. E. (1984). *The Psychopathic Racial Personality and other essays*. Third World Press.

Chapter Fifteen

Anderson, C. (1994). *Black labor, white wealth: The search for power and economic justice*. PowerNomics Corporation of America.

Anderson, C. (2001). *PowerNomics: The national plan to empower Black America*. PowerNomics Corporation of America.

Blackmon, D. A. (2008). *Slavery by another name: The re-enslavement of Black Americans from the Civil War to World War II*. Anchor Books.

DeGruy, J. (2005). *Post traumatic slave syndrome: America's legacy of enduring injury and healing*. Uptone Press.

hooks, b. (1992). *Black looks: Race and representation*. South End Press.

Lorde, A. (1988). *A burst of light: Essays*. Firebrand Books.

Menakem, R. (2017). *My grandmother's hands: Racialized trauma and the pathway to mending our hearts and bodies*. Central Recovery Press.

Morrison, T. (1993). *The Nobel lecture in literature, 1993*. Alfred A. Knopf.

Smith, W. A., Hung, M., & Franklin, J. D. (2011). Racial battle fatigue and the miseducation of Black men: Racial microaggressions, societal problems, and environmental stress. *The Journal of Negro Education, 80*(1), 63–82.

Williams, D. R., & Mohammed, S. A. (2009). Discrimination and racial disparities in health: Evidence and needed research. *Journal of Behavioral Medicine, 32*(1), 20–47. https://doi.org/10.1007/s10865-008-9185-0

Wilson, A. N. (1993). *Blueprint for Black power: A moral, political, and economic imperative for the twenty-first century*. Afrikan World InfoSystems.

Welsing, F. C. (1991). *The Isis papers: The keys to the colors*. Third World Press.

Williams, E. (1994). *Capitalism and slavery*. University of North Carolina Press.

Zuboff, S. (2019). *The age of surveillance capitalism: The fight for a human future at the new frontier of power*. PublicAffairs.

U.S. Department of Labor. (2025). *Employment and unemployment statistics by race, gender, and age: Quarterly report, 2025 Q2*. Washington, DC: Bureau of Labor Statistics.

Economic Policy Institute. (2025, August). *Black unemployment and racial economic inequality in 2025: National snapshot*. Washington, DC.

PROFESSIONAL BIO

Dante King is a native of San Francisco, California. He is the author and executive producer of the new **award-winning** book and docuseries **Diagnosing Whiteness & Anti-Blackness: White Psychopathology, Collective Psychosis, and Trauma in America**, which recently ranked number 1 in Amazon's New Book Releases. Dante King and Blackademics, a nonprofit organization he founded to provide educational experiences and opportunities to educators, lawyers, healthcare professionals, and the larger population, co-produced the **Diagnosing Whiteness & Anti-Blackness** ten-part episodic video series to support the book.

His academic disciplines include Afro-Realism; Critical Race Studies; African American Studies; Whiteness Studies; Anti-Blackness; American History; African American Studies; African American History; and how they have shaped American culture and institutions. Dante's continued research interests include examinations of race, racism, and legality throughout colonial and post-colonial America, and their effects on American culture and identity.

Dante is also the author of The 400-Year Holocaust: White America's Legal, Psychopathic, and Sociopathic Black Genocide and the Revolt Against Critical Race Theory. He currently serves as an Adjunct Assistant Professor of Medical Education at the Mayo Clinic College of Medicine and Science. Previously, he was guest faculty at the University of California, San Francisco (UCSF) School of Medicine (2021-2025), where he provided critical education on race, history, and systemic inequities.

In January 2025, Dante **became the target** of a coordinated campaign by right-wing, racist, and anti-Black conservative groups seeking to suppress racial justice education in academic institutions.

Organizations such as **Young America's Foundation**, along with **Campus Reform, The Daily Wire**, and **Fox News**, have actively manipulated his words and misrepresented his scholarship in attempts to discredit his work. As a result of this targeted harassment, Dante has faced **violent threats,** including death threats, underscoring the real dangers faced by scholars and educators committed to truth-telling and racial justice.

Dante officially consults as a legal expert scholar and witness concerning matters regarding race and racism. **Dante was recently instrumental in codifying new law in California (see People v. Finley, 2023).**

Dante has guest lectured at Clark College (Vancouver, Washington), Bellevue College (Bellevue, Washington), Everett College (Everett Washington), Lake Washington Technical College (Lake Washington, Washington), Skyline College (San Bruno, California), and Green River College (Green River, Washington). Dante is a member of the American Association of University Professors (AAUP); National Association for Multicultural Education (NAME); Association for the Study of African American Life and History (ASALH); and the National Association of Diversity Officers in Higher Education (NADOHE).

Dante is a historian, scholar, public motivational speaker, thought-leader, facilitator, and coach. He has worked and consulted for more than 15-years as a human resource management professional **specializing in executive leadership development, coaching, and the implementation of anti-racism organizational development frameworks, strategies, and practices.**

In 2018, Dante partnered with the San Francisco Board of Supervisors to develop and enact the City and County of San Francisco's **Racial Equity Ordinance,** which led to the first-ever citywide Office of Racial Equity (2019).

Dante was previously the Deputy Director for the Department of Public Health Office of Health Equity, in San Francisco, one of the largest public health organizations in the country with more than **8,000 employees.** He led and directed the development and implementation of the department's Racial Equity Action Plan, which focused on improving both workforce and health equity outcomes. He also led the development and implementation of several highly impactful antiracism and racial equity policies and programs (i.e.,

Antiracism Recruitment and Hiring Policy, Healing Time Off, Respect in the Workplace, etc.). One of his most significant accomplishments, while at the SFDPH, was the implementation of the department's first ever Antiracism and Racial Equity Leaders Fellowship, a 12- week cohort which included more than 50 executive and senior leaders.

Prior to assuming this role, Dante was the Director of Race, Equity, and Inclusion at the San Francisco Municipal Transportation Agency (SFMTA), one of the largest municipal transportation agencies in the country, with more than 6,000 employees. He led and directed the design, development, and implementation of the agency's first-ever **Racial Equity Action Plan**, focused on improving workforce outcomes. He also collaborated with his peers on the executive leadership team, which included the Human Resources Director, to develop and enact policies and programs which directly targeted racial disparities and disproportionate organizational outcomes.

While working as a senior Human Resources Manager at the City and County of San Francisco (2016-2019), Dante designed and implemented a citywide anti-racism and bias training, Creating and Inclusive Environment: An Introduction to Implicit Bias. More than 20,000 city employees have received this training to date. Dante also managed and led the team of learning partners and training professionals who delivered the training to all employees and members of the San Francisco Police Department (SFPD). As a part of this project Dante provided consistent feedback and hands-on guidance and direction to the SFPD executive leadership team.

In early 2020, a confidential email written to SFPD Chief Bill Scott, appeared in the San Francisco Examiner. The email to Chief Scott highlighted the depth of anti-Black bias and racism Dante and his team experienced from many members of the SFPD, during the three years they provided training to the department. The feedback Dante provided to Chief Scott, led to Dante presenting his findings to the **San Francisco Police Commission**, as well as systemic programmatic and policy-oriented changes throughout the department.

In addition, Dante King founded the Black Employees Alliance (B.E.A), in 2019. The B.E.A consistently partnered with San Francisco Leadership (Mayor London N. Breed, S.F. Board of Supervisor President Shamann Walton, Hillary Ronen, Matt Haney, and Sandra Fewer), as well as department heads and senior leaders, to highlight and combat racial inequities and disparities. The group's advocacy was in direct response to racial disparities concerning Black employees across all departments, in the areas of recruitment and hiring, pay and promotions, recognition, and discipline and terminations.

Additionally, the Black Employees Alliance was instrumental in compelling and influencing Mayor Breed's appointment of Dr. William Gould IV, whose firm investigated the city's employment practices, issuing a **comprehensive summary of findings and recommendations**. The B.E.A partnered with Mr. Gould and his colleagues to produce information and data that led to many of the findings.

In addition to Dante's Human Resources Management experience, and public service, he has taught courses for Stanford Medical School, Johns Hopkins, UCSF, and the Mayo Clinic. Dante currently **teaches an accredited course through UCSF called, Understanding the Roots of Racism and Bias: Antiblackness and Its Links to Whiteness, White Racism, Privilege, and Power**. As guest faculty at Mayo Clinic College of Medicine and Science, he lectured a two-part course called, The Roots and Lingering Effects of White Supremacy and Anti-Blackness in American Culture and Institutions.

Most recently, Dante developed an additional course called, Developing Antiracism Leadership Competencies to Achieve Inclusive Practices and Health Equity, a collaboration with special guest and co-lecturer, Dr. Robin DiAngelo, author of the books White Fragility and Nice Racism. Dante and

Robin have also partnered to produce the Unlearning Anti-Blackness, White Supremacy, and Racism in American Culture and Institutions Leaders Fellowship, a 16-week virtual fellowship program focused on training, coaching, and mentoring leaders who directly influence and impact change at their organizations.

Dante has consulted and collaborated with organizations in the areas of human resource management, antiracism policy, and program development and implementation. Some organizations Dante has worked with include the UCSF EMBRACE Project, San Francisco Police Department; San Francisco Department of Police Accountability; California State Public Defender's Office; San Francisco Public Defender's Office; Johns Hopkins University; Stanford University School of Medicine; UCSF School of Medicine; Wikimedia Foundation; The Athletic; Oakland Unified School District; UCSF Office of Diversity and Outreach; UCSF California Preterm Birth Initiative; UCSF Alliance Health Project; California Prevention Training Center; San Lorenzo School District Superintendent Office, Evanston Township School District Superintendent Office, and BATS Improv; to name a few.

Dante has keynoted and presented at a multitude of annual conferences. Dante was a featured keynote speaker at the 5th Annual Northwest Region Equity Conference, hosted by Clark College (2024), and the 2nd Annual National Association of African American Parents and Youth (NAAAPY; 2024), and the opening night of Howard County's Champions of Change Conference.

Dante has also presented and keynoted many more conferences including the 23rd Annual Hawaii International Conference on Education, 22nd Annual Hawaii International Conference on Education (HICE), 35th Annual National Conference on Race and Ethnicity in Higher Education, National Education Association's Annual Conference on Race and Social Justice (NEA), American Public Health Association (APHA), Association for the Study of African American Life and History (ASALH; 2023), Eikenberg

Academy for Social Justice Soulwork Annual Conference, Brothers of the Desert Wellness Summit, Race Forward: Facing Race Bi-Annual Conference (2022), American Psychiatric Association's 4th Annual Reverend Dr.Martin Luther King, Jr. program, California Prevention Training Center's Medical Mistrust Conference, Mayo Clinic Annual

Diversity, Equity, Inclusion and Antiracism Annual Enterprise Retreat, NEA Minority and Women's Leadership Conference to Advance Racial and Social Justice, Bemidji State University's 2023 Martin Luther King Jr. Holiday Celebration, Rainier Educators of Color Equity National Conference 2023, 4th Annual Northwest Regional Equity Conference 2023, the 24th Annual White Privilege Conference (2023), 25th Annual White Privilege Conference (2024), Facing Race Conference (2024), Faculty and Staff of Color Conference (2024), Association for the Study of African American Life and History (2024), Facing Race Bi-Annual Conference (2024) and many more.

Dante has been featured in Suite Life Magazine, the San Francisco Sun Reporter's 2022 Special Edition of the Talented 25, and the Grio. He has been featured on The Lurie Daniel Favors Show, The Isiah Factor, The National Desk's Beyond the Podium, Facepalm America, The Todd Allbaugh Show, Legal Lens with Angela Reddock-Wright (KBLA 1580), CAPTC's Coming Together for Sexual Health, BackTable Podcast, The Sisaundra Show, KPFA Radio Interview (B.H. Brilliant Minds Juneteenth Celebration), California Prevention Training Center Podcast, Intentional Conversations with Dr. Nika White, This Week In White Supremacy, The Dawn Stensland Show, recurring guest on Areva Martin In Real Time, The Karen Hunter Show, The Ron Show, The Joan Esposito Radio Show, and KCBS Broadcast News. Dante has also been a featured guest on the What Say U Podcast, hosted by Melannie Cunningham, All About Community with Robert L. Harris, Esq., KMOX The Show, Urban View Mornings with Lamont King and Greg Carr, Word In Black, and a host of other shows and media outlets.

Awards and Future Endeavors

The Bookfest Awards awarded Diagnosing Whiteness & Anti-Blackness first-place awards for 1.) Nonfiction - Politics & Government - Political Psychology, 2.) Nonfiction - Society & Social Sciences - History & Theory, 3.) Nonfiction - Society & Social Sciences - Human Rights & Political Movements, and a second-place award in the area of 4.) Nonfiction - Politics & Government - International & World Politics.

Amongst an array of many awards and recognition, in spring 2024, Dante was awarded the Higher Education Diversity, Equity, and Inclusion Leadership Award, by The National Association of Diversity Officers in Higher Education (NADOHE). In summer of 2022, Dante was **awarded 1st Place, by The Bookfest Awards, in the genre of Non-Fiction History for penning The 400-Year Holocaust. Dante also received the Dr. Huey P. Newton Trailblazer and Legacy Award,** presented by B.H. Brilliant Minds, Inc., for his consistent leadership and advocacy on behalf of Black communities in Oakland and San Francisco, California, and abroad. In fall 2023, Dante was awarded the Carter Godwin Woodson Service Award by the National Association for Multicultural Education (NAME) for a commitment to correcting "deficiencies in American history where African American History and the history of other cultures is misrepresented, distorted, or ignored."

Dante released his second publication, **The 400-Year Holocaust: Toolkit and Workbook,** in April 2023. It focuses on Organizational Change and Development; an introduction to antiracism policy development examples and skills practices, as well as antiracism leadership strategies and frameworks (i.e., Equity in the Center's Awake to Woke to Work, Dismantling Racism's Antiracism Organizational Change, etc.). Dante is also writing his third book publication, Diagnosing Whiteness & Anti-Blackness: White Psychopathology, Collective Psychosis, and Trauma in America.

Education

Dante holds a Bachelor of Arts degree in African American Studies, and a master's degree in Education, from California State University, East Bay. He also possesses a Human Resources Management certification. Dante started doctoral work in Educational Leadership and Social Justice, with principal focuses in challenging White supremacy and anti-blackness, and their cumulative affects on Black people, White people, and all participants in American culture.

In spring 2024, Dante was awarded an honorary doctorate degree in Humanitarianism from the School of the Great Commission (SGC). The School of the Great Commission is accredited by the International Association for Quality Assurance in Pre-Tertiary and Higher Education, American Accrediting Association of Theological Institutions, World-Wide Accreditation of Christian Educational Institutions, and Southeastern Association of Bible Colleges.

Community Outreach and Volunteer Efforts

Dante is the Executive Director of Blackademics: Addressing Anti-Blackness Around the World, INC. Blackademics is an educational and charitable non-profit, focused on educating students and families across race, about the legacy and persistence of White supremacy and Anti-Blackness in America, as well as worldwide. Dante is a board member for the B.H. Brilliant Minds Project, LLC, a local Bay Area, California, non-profit and charitable agency focused on bringing healing to African American people, through community service and outreach. He has served as a board member for the B.H. Brilliant Minds Project, LLC for over 15 years, while also serving the agency through education and book donations.

Previously, Dante served as a board member for the Sexual Minority Alliance of Alameda County (SMAAC) Youth Center. During his tenure as a board member for more than four years, Dante focused SMAAC's mission and goal on serving underserved, unhoused, and unsheltered Black LGBTQ+ youth. In addition, Dante mentored and tutored many youths during his time at SMAAC. Dante has also helped organizations like AMASSI and the AIDS Project of the East Bay with their sexual health outreach efforts.

While in high school, Dante joined the AmeriCorps program created by President Bill Clinton. During his time with AmeriCorps, Dante was employed at the East Lake YMCA in East Oakland, where he worked as a youth outreach worker, mentor, and tutor under Margaret Wimberly's supervision.

Shortly after high school, Dante became involved with a non-profit which was housed at the Allen Temple Church in East Oakland. This opportunity allowed him to tutor at his old elementary school, Daniel Webster. These experiences were crucial in shaping Dante's future as a leader, educator, and public servant.

Dante previously attended the Center of Hope Community Church, where he helped people from the unsheltered and unhoused community. This experience led Dante to collaborate with friends and family in proactively purchasing food, water, and toiletries to deliver directly to people throughout these communities.

In 2016, Dante became involved with The Village, a prison outreach program that catered to helping Black men in prison. Dante began reaching out and connecting with prison inmates. His goal was to provide guidance, aid, and comfort. Dante became deeply involved with these efforts, and has donated, to date, more than $100k in resources to over 15 men. Donations have included loading monies onto JPay and Connect Network accounts to ensure inmates can write letters to, as well as call their families; ordering thousands of dollars of Secure Paks; as well as driving to see and visit inmates in prison both in northern and southern California. Additionally, Dante has written several early release letters to support early prison releases for reformed prison inmates. Dante has been successful in helping two men access early parole releases.

Dante's drive and ambition, which aim to authentically uplift and help others, have fueled his long history of public service, allowing him to attract and sustain many meaningful and long-lasting relationships.

WEBSITES:

www.danteking.com

www.diagnosingwhitenessandantiblackness.com

DEDICATION

Mom — You are my life. None of this—none of me—would exist without you. You are my first home, my forever love, and the center of my being. Every day I live is for you—to honor you, to make you proud, and to bring joy to your heart. Your love, care, and protection are the foundation of all I am. There will never be enough words to thank you for everything you've done to nurture, strengthen, and sustain me.

I dedicate this book—and all of my work—to the sanctity of human life across the world, in enduring hope for our collective survival in a world rooted in peace, love, and the true essence of human and spiritual divinity.

COMMENTS FROM COURSE

Racism is prevalent and intersects with all systems and structures of power, especially capitalism. It's often imperceptible to those in positions of privilege until a person or situation makes it apparent, while being painfully obvious to the oppressed. For me personally I think the materials suggest an ongoing work of shifting frames and perspective to see outside my privilege

1) I have learned how the founding laws of the United States codified dehumanizing black people, rewarded anti-black racism and terror, and punished people who did not comply. I learned to see this history in the present(all around me, in the news and in my own interactions with others), and to see how it has socialized me. 2) As a white person, the understanding that I need a community of accountability, has been profoundly reinforced, so that I have a reflection of the ways I cause harm that I do not see.

The depth and breadth of white psychopathy and anti-blackness woven into the laws, culture and immoral fabric that is America. And the complete absence of acknowledgement of that history and arrogance and promotion of white psychopathy and evolving anti-blackness with complete disregard to any complicity or desire to absolve or redeem themselves. Also, the anti-blackness practiced by blacks and generational seeds of psychopathy ingrained into our behaviors and culture and the continued elevation of all things white and European over our own logic, language and culture.

The historical roots of racism in the USA are deep and broad and codified into pretty much everything that the USA is today. Large portion of the population has not thought about any of this to any great depth so they do not realize just how unequal things are in the present day.

Since coming to this country, white people have acted out of white moral values (psychopathic and sociopathic) and we continue to be trained and reinforced every day as terrorists toward people of color, and Black people especially. I have a lot of work to do to have full access to my empathy for the racial traumas experienced by Black people especially and people of color.

This country has a long standing, purposeful, deviant concept about black people regardless of age, gender, medical condition or socioeconomic status. There is no safe space for black people in this country where white people can not enforce their bias and abuse the power that white supremacy and privilege affords them. Even people of color in authority in these situations enact these powers without second thought. Whiteness gets out of control very easily and other whites do little to nothing to stop it or slow it down.

1) White supremacy and anti-black racism are not devoid of morals, they are a clearly executed set of psychopathic and sociopathic morals backed by the power of every US institution. 2) The amount of time and resources it takes to shift white leaders into a zone of anti-racist learning and practice is insane, and worth it, if it means our Black leaders experience less white inflicted harm, and as a result, gain more life.

The level of legal subjugation and terror of the Black experience in America; the psychopathic nature of Whiteness and how it was passed down generation by generation, so that even as laws changed the psychopathic thoughts and behavior did not

Anti-Blackness is REAL and is the ONLY descriptor needed to explain what white is...by framing what 'White Is NOT,' we/all of us (Black people included) validate and give meaning to Pro-Whiteness and White Supremacy. This is NO ACCIDENT - Full stop. We are fixated on Black because it permits White to be slick.

Psychopaths with authority have jurisdiction over Black bodies, and they continue to rationalize and justify this mistreatment. Society has defined whiteness as an entitlement to safety, privilege and power. It has also defined anti-Blackness into our legal, moral and economic institutions.

"Progressive white people may cause the most daily racial harm" "White fragility is not weakness per se – it is powerful means of everyday white racial control as it leverages historical and institutional power"

I see politics and political decision-making differently. I see that American sociocultural and political institutions quickly adapt to continue to oppress and harm Black (and BIPOC) communities. Even looking at recent legislation and SCOTUS rulings, it's easy to see how nimble these institutions are at doubling-down to do real harm to Black people. As a political science educator, this means that I am better able to teach college students about this history and intentionality. As a campus leader, I am better able to develop professional development opportunities and collaborate on meaningful antiracist policies and procedures.

These are not just learnings. They are a place of deep connection and accountability. For every session I attend, I am fueled with a renewed and empowered commitment to further my anti-racist leadership practice. I'm strategically challenged to soften my edges and approaches in order to build tougher, more sustainable, and steadfast disruptions of my and my people's white racist moves.

I really appreciate the intellectual, emotional, and cognitive load that Robin and Dante have taken on to curate this training. I can see the impact on Dante by the end of each session, and his vulnerability and honesty here has been such an offering. I want to express my gratitude for this immense labor for helping me to know and do better. While these sessions sometimes jump around -- which is hard for my neurodivergent, higher ed-trained brain to follow -- the vast amount of information and the amount of pattern-finding, identification of threads, and constant reflection has been so enriching. Thank you. Sincerely.

The depth at which the racism/anti-blackness is build into every fiber of our country -Details of the impact on people of color today and my contribution/complicity in the harm - we are not a community in this country, there is no mutually beneficial relationships especially for black people that were intentionally written out/blocked out

Anti-blackness has been indoctrinated into US culture, laws, learning, and values. As such, it has become part of all of our identities making it very difficult to remediate and instead it needs to be a constant vigilance to check ourselves and our surroundings and to be an ally to black colleagues, friends, family, and community members.

Systematic and intentional laying down of racial hierarchy and racism in the law and thus in the culture of this country; goes so far back that we don't even see it as having been orchestrated, just as the way things are. 2. White people and non-Black POC have ongoing responsibility to understand this history and the way that it continues to persist in the present and in all of us. We must remain aware, take it into our hearts, and then fight against it actively in our every day lives.

1.anti-black racism has been baked into culture and law since the beginning of this country's history. 2. We need to focus on how we participate in white supremacy now instead of trying to excuse ourselves by thinking the harm was done by our white ancestors.

These learnings have profoundly shaped my leadership approach by deepening my commitment to centering and empowering marginalized voices while shifting my focus away from trying to change those resistant to equity efforts. Two specific examples include: Prioritizing community-centered initiatives: I now invest more energy in creating spaces for healing, empowerment, and growth for Black students and employees. For example, through the Serenity Seekers initiative, I focus on supporting women in recovery by fostering environments where they feel seen and valued, instead of expending energy on convincing others to acknowledge systemic harm. Challenging unjust policies: Recognizing the pervasiveness of anti-Blackness has strengthened my resolve to confront policies that may be legal but unjust. For instance, I advocated for changes to hiring practices that subtly exclude BIPoC candidates by collaborating with leadership to challenge outdated interpretations of I-200 and develop more equitable recruitment processes.

This approach underscores my leadership's focus on dismantling barriers rather than seeking validation or acceptance from resistant stakeholders.

Although I am not necessarily in a leadership role, these learning have given credence, evidence and records as validation and proof beyond what formerly was what I may've consider fringe thinking, paranoia and blanket generalization without exception. I am now armed (and in fact emboldened to share and express in a form of righteous indignation that which I'm confident and believe is based in black and white rooted fact, written into law and thousands of records of performances and acts of commonplace anti-blackness over at least five centuries of our history to speak freely and openly to the ongoing reality of living amongst a society whose majority suffers from malignant diabolical psychopathy.

Knowing that laws have historically been working against Black people, it has opened up the question of why would I think it would be different now? I know one of the ways that shows up today is that "professionalism" in the work-place is based in white supremacy and used to weaponize rules against Black people, but it has brought forth other questions, like what other rules do we have at my organization that enforce white supremacy? I think historically I have tried to "keep the peace" and now I wonder how that has actually been suppression and minimization of Black and Brown experiences. Recently there was an instant where a Black clinician was sharing with me how she felt like she was being questioned clinically by another Black staff member because of the complexion of her skin. My impulse was to be a "peacemaker" but instead I decided to pause that impulse and reflect. I realized in the conversation that the employee who questioned her has never questioned me, a white clinician, and that she was completely right, therefore instead I validated her experience. We then spent time unpacking colorism and how anti-Blackness can show up in all communities, including in the Black community. We also spent time unpacking how white supremacy seeks to divide and explored how she wants to respond and how she wants to move forward. We talked through how she could address this or support I could give her in that.

I am trying to be very conscious of how I show up at work in terms of working to be concise and not separating myself, but implicating myself; I have also apologized to colleagues for behavior without expecting a response. Honestly the rest I am still unpacking and trying to name specific ways I am still upholding white supremacy, looking to implicate myself; question why I need validation; and practice sitting in feeling shitty. I am still doing a lot of reflection and exploring to better see where and how I need to make shifts in my leadership. I have also bought the docu series and have a meeting set-up to talk further about how to use the tool in my Office.

Awareness of my own positionality as an Asian woman and what I am allowed to do with my voice (loudly advocate, going against stereotype of the weakness and silence) and awareness of how my counterpart leader, a Black man, has very different constraints on what he can do with his voice because of stereotypes and racism against him. 2. I feel continued urgency, but also more clarity on how to stand with my Black/AA colleagues in their leadership.

There aren't adequate words to express how outstanding this course is. Everyone should take it- and I am letting those within my personal and professional circles know it. The profound love for Black people and extreme generosity towards white people that Mr. King put into developing and facilitating this course is awe-inspiring, and even more importantly, change-inspiring.

This training helps me understand the roots of the racism and antiblackness. A very effective presenter who was articulate and presented the information clearly & powerfully. The only thing: as an ESL & somewhat hearing impaired person, I wished that the clips were louder and had had captions on and I wound have gotten even more out of this training. Thank you!

Dante, you are an absolute GEM! Thank you, thank you, thank you! Thank you for existing. I continue to rave about the impact your course had on me and how we all should be the impact in how we support and show up for Black folx and fight against anti-Blackness every single day...to be conscious. I could write a book about how much this has impacted me but it wouldn't be enough. I appreciate you and the constant work you put forth EVERY DAY in order to educate folks and uplift the voices and stories of those that have been silenced for far too long. We can never learn enough. I am purchasing your book and look forward to reading it. Again, thank you so much. I appreciate you!

This workshop was one of the best educational experiences I have had and I was a graduate student in psychology and the law for over a decade. I believe the insight I gained and the historical perspective I was given has fundamentally changed me and the ways in which I will move forward personally and professionally. I am very grateful for all the emotional and intellectual labor Professor King invested in us and this experience, as well as the value placed on an interactive approach to learning. Thank you!

My two biggest takeaways are that anti-Blackness is a deeply rooted disease, and I cannot be responsible for "curing" white people. It is both systemic and endemic.

1) Distinction between anti-Blackness and anti-racism - through our conversations, I think I have leaned more into this subtle and significant difference 2) Understanding the legal policies and religious practices that have reinforced anti-Blackness

www.ingramcontent.com/pod-product-compliance
Lightning Source LLC
LaVergne TN
LVHW030332070526
838199LV00067B/6251